THE BIRTH OF A DILEMMA

BY THE SAME AUTHOR

as Philip Mason

Year of Decision:
Rhodesia and Nyasaland in 1960
(Oxford University Press—Institute of Race Relations)

Prospero's Magic:
Some Thoughts on Class and Race
(Oxford University Press—Institute of Race Relations)

(ed.) *Man, Race, and Darwin*
(Oxford University Press—Institute of Race Relations)

(ed.) *India and Ceylon: Unity and Diversity*
(Oxford University Press—Institute of Race Relations)

An Essay in Racial Tension
(Oxford University Press—Chatham House)

Christianity and Race
(Lutterworth Press)

Common Sense about Race
(Gollancz)

as Philip Woodruff
(published by Jonathan Cape)

The Men Who Ruled India
I. *The Founders:* ⎱ history
II. *The Guardians:* ⎰

Colonel of Dragoons: an historical chronicle

Call the Next Witness ⎫
The Wild Sweet Witch ⎬ novels
The Islands of Chamba ⎭

Whatever Dies: stories

The Sword of Northumbria ⎱ adventure
Hernshaw Castle ⎰

Lobengula, King of the Matabele, 1870–93

The Birth of a Dilemma

THE CONQUEST AND SETTLEMENT
OF RHODESIA

PHILIP MASON

Published for the
Institute of Race Relations, London

OXFORD UNIVERSITY PRESS

LONDON NEW YORK TORONTO

Oxford University Press, Ely House, London W.1

GLASGOW NEW YORK TORONTO MELBOURNE WELLINGTON
CAPE TOWN SALISBURY IBADAN NAIROBI LUSAKA ADDIS ABABA
BOMBAY CALCUTTA MADRAS KARACHI LAHORE DACCA
KUALA LUMPUR HONG KONG TOKYO

© Oxford University Press 1958

First published   1958
Reprinted 1962 and 1968

*Reprinted by lithography in Great Britain
by Jarrold & Sons Ltd, Norwich*

PREFACE

Central Africa—by which I mean the two Rhodesias and Nyasa-land—is the meeting place not only of black people and white but of different ideas as to how they should behave towards each other. It is thus the key to Africa; what happens there is likely to decide what becomes of the continent and may make a great difference to what becomes of the world.

That is why the Institute of Race Relations—then a larva within the cocoon of Chatham House—decided that Central Africa was the first and most important area to which its attention should be turned. It was the generosity of the Rockefeller Foundation that made possible travel and a prolonged stay in the Federation, but it is to be emphasized that neither the Rockefeller Foundation nor the Institute of Race Relations is in any way responsible for any opinions expressed in this book, which are those of the writer alone. And it must be added that this book represents the first fruits only of the travel and research financed by the Foundation; development in a later period will be traced by another hand and the present writer also intends to complete his work. A third book is in progress, on the Belgian Congo, so different from the Rhodesias and so much alike, and that too is part of the scheme we owe to the Foundation.

There will be academic objections to this book. Its history is mixed with anthropology and its anthropology with history; both draw help from archaeology and indeed from any source available. To objections of this kind the answer is simple; the situation with which the book deals is confused and complex, no less confused and complex than the life of man, and the life of man is not divided into compartments, nor can any one way of looking at it be final. And, for myself, I would rather present a picture that attempts, however inadequately, to reproduce the

Preface

rich confusion of life than confine reality within the shapes which
are convenient, and indeed appropriate, for the instruction of
youth and for a university syllabus, but which lose their value
in a wider field.

P. M.

CONTENTS

Contents

ILLUSTRATIONS

MAPS

ACKNOWLEDGEMENTS

The author's thanks for permission to reproduce copyright material are due to: The Director, National Archives of Rhodesia and Nyasaland, for 'Lobengula, King of the Matabele, 1870-93', from a sketch by E. A. Maund (1889) worked up by Ralph Peacock (Frontispiece); Rhodesia House, London, for the three photographs of the Zimbabwe Ruins (facing pages 68 and 69); Miss G. Caton-Thompson for the sketch on page 65 and 'Soapstone Birds at Zimbabwe' (facing page 69) from her book *Zimbabwe Culture* (Oxford, 1931); the National Museum of Southern Rhodesia for 'Copje at Salisbury, 1891' and 'Mashona Village' (facing page 164) from *Sketches of Scenes in Mashonaland* by H. Thomassett; *The Illustrated London News* for 'The Laager at Bulawayo, 1896' and 'The Mangwe Post, 1897' (facing page 165), 'False Alarm at Bulawayo, 1896' and 'Relief of Inseza' (facing page 197).

INTRODUCTION

It may be that in the next few years man will make such misuse of what he has learnt that fifty centuries of accumulated knowledge dissolve in radio-active dust. In that case, other conflicts of this century dwindle in scale till they appear neither more nor less important than the love-making of flies. But if this catastrophe can be avoided, then the chief source of bitterness that will remain in the world is likely to lie between the West and the peoples of Asia, Africa, and perhaps South America.

By the West, I mean nineteenth-century Europe and her heirs in America and the Antipodes, in particular the old colonial powers and the United States. And here the fact must be faced that the United States has become in a sense the leading colonial power. Her people hate the name of colonialism and their form of it is not military and administrative so much as cultural, commercial, and industrial, but from the receiving end it appears none the less aggressive for that. Indeed, compared with the old colonialism of the flag, the soldier, and the policeman, it is certainly no less pregnant of violent change in the way people live, and for that reason may at times seem even more aggressive.

Over against the colonial powers stand all those people on whom the weight of the West fell in the nineteenth century with an impact sometimes deadening, more often enlivening, but always a weight, something external. There are two main groups of these people, the old civilizations of Asia, whom the West found stagnant or dormant and stung back into aggrieved and sometimes reluctant life; the young new peoples of Africa whom the West found technically backward, not yet linked together in widespread political organizations. But because their relations with the West have been similar, they are linked by a strong emotional tie.

The people of the West are on the whole fair, the others by comparison dark. That is a point to which some people have attached importance, which others regard as an accidental quality of no significance. Let us leave open for the moment the question of whether fairness and darkness have anything to do with such qualities as energy and intelligence; let us keep in mind the simple physical fact that these differences exist and set it beside certain broad aspects of history. First, in the period from Vasco da Gama to Cecil Rhodes, the expanding energy, the restlessness, the discoveries, were on the fair side. Before that, one cannot be so positive; for a long time civilization, the arts, progress in spiritual perception, in religion, in philosophy, had been elsewhere, at one time in China, at others in India or among the peoples of the Middle East and the Eastern Mediterranean, people noticeably darker than those of Northern and Western Europe; the fair for long displayed mainly barbaric energy. Flashes of something more, it is true, began after a time to appear among the fair—Charlemagne, Alfred, the saints and poets of Ireland—indications that might have warned a heavenly observer that even barbarians had possibilities. Still, from the Prophet's flight from Mecca till the beginning of the Renaissance, the balance both of energy and civilization still lay on the dark side; Europe was on the defensive, notably in Spain and Hungary.

But the Moors were driven out of Spain, the Turks turned back from Buda Pesth, Lepanto was fought and won. The tide had turned and it was now the fair people of North-Western Europe with whom the balance of energy lay; it was they who eagerly explored the heavens and their own bodies, wrenched the world apart to solve its mysteries, ransacked the continents alike for wealth and ideas. In these years after the Renaissance, physical fairness came to be regarded as the badge of a person belonging to the energetic expanding culture; it is still a badge, and an inescapable one, in the new conflict of the twentieth century. Fairness and darkness still stand as symbols of past domination, past subordination; they are badges in the turmoil and conflict which develop day by day, as the civilizations once stagnant come to life, as the new young peoples begin feverishly to absorb all they can of a world becoming in a physical sense yearly more easy to devour. Both the old peoples of Asia and the young of Africa become day by day more determined to assert their right to live their own way and to decide for themselves how much they will take of what the West has to offer. The people of the North-West, younger in a sense than the Asians, older than the Africans, stand between them, eager to sell tractors, universities, thermo-nuclear plants, a way of life; eager to buy alliances, uranium, groundnuts, copper. They are a minority in the world as a whole; it is to their own interest—even if more generous motives are suspect—that the world should not stand in hostile camps, and that, if it must, the division should not be made on the basis of this particular badge. Yet the badge of fairness is still worn as a badge and in some areas its presence still arouses the bitterest rancour and resentment among those who do not wear it, its absence among those who do. And in other areas it has become a matter of indifference.

At the end of the nineteenth century, the West was dominant in every continent of the world. Europe, North America, and Australasia were in white hands; South America was ruled by predominantly white minorities, Africa and large parts of Asia were controlled by European powers, while those parts of Asia that were formally independent came under Western influence in various ways—by imitation, as in Japan; by choice of advisers, as in Siam; by dictated treaties, as in China, or by a combination of these and other methods, as in Persia.

The West was supreme. And to that supremacy reaction came swiftly. It was not an utter rejection of all that the West had brought; far from it, much was eagerly absorbed, both of ideas and of technique, while there was often courtesy, sometimes even affection, between those who, on the whole, brought and those who, on the whole, received. But a reaction began; an eagerness to cast these new ideas into moulds wholly Indian or Japanese, to take no more than was wanted, and at the taker's pace and in the taker's way. Much was taken, and to the direct debt of ideas taken was added another debt, a new vigour that was born in opposition and was nourished by the adversity on which nationalist leaders thrive. Hinduism was forced alike by the aggression and the example of the West to put her house in order and cast out much that was evil; the same kind of process took place in Japan and later in China.

Today the leaders of Asia and Africa find they must express in every public utterance their impatience of any checks on their political independence; yet even as they pronounce the rhetorical phrases, they grow in awareness of their need for technical help and finance, of the inability of any lonely little power to protect itself in a predatory world. The West, meanwhile—on the whole and as a rule—disclaims the idea of clinging to the old form of dominance; lays emphasis instead on a willingness to offer without compulsion or condition the advice, the technicians, the finance, that are needed; stresses the inter-dependence of nations, the close mesh of the defence network; speaks of the free world, of liberty, of opportunity for the individual. The colonial powers are ready—most of them and for most of the time—to abandon the old form of military and administrative colonialism; not yet quite sure that former pupils can do without the other kind; eager to find a way by which it can be made tolerable.

It is not easy for a nation to cast off the heritage of its past, still less for a group of nations. The West has been slow to learn from her pupils. Britain, winner in the colonial race, ruler of the widest empire, had often taught with a high sense of mission; she was the first to learn herself, to realize that her mission included the final step of devolving power. Her first lesson was unwillingly learnt in America, at Ticonderoga and Crown Point; it was never wholly forgotten. The doctrine that sprang from that lesson was triumphantly affirmed in Canada, Australia, and New Zealand. It was stated in relation to India so far back as 1813 and restated again and again in the debates that every twenty years reviewed the work and revised the constitution of the East India Company. It was remembered in India by the greatest servants of England in the East; 'when the improvement of the natives reaches such a pitch,' wrote Mountstuart Elphinstone, Governor of Bombay from 1817 to 1823, 'that it is impossible for a foreign nation to retain the Government', then the English would go, 'and take the glory of the achievements as our sole reward'. That was the authentic note of England's policy; to govern until a foreign government was no longer needed and to govern as a trustee for the people of the country. Towards the end of the century the principle was re-discovered and restated with a difference in regard to Africa in such phrases as 'trustee-ship' and 'the dual mandate'.*

But to that policy, the true policy of England at her best, there was always opposition; it was the opposition sometimes of England at her worst, of rich men greedy for more; sometimes it was merely negative and pusillanimous; there were setbacks and exceptions, even in relation to India, while in Southern Africa there was a wholly different set of circumstances. And the West as a whole cannot yet be said to have accepted that policy even as an ideal; if we in Britain can point to Ghana, Nigeria, and the West Indies as evidence of good faith, there are other parts of the map to which an intelligent and educated African will turn his eyes.

Such a man may concede Britain's readiness to be generous over Ghana and Nigeria, though he will probably see it more as realism than as generosity. He will see it as a recognition that a people cannot be held down by force for ever, that to give freedom is the best chance of keeping friendship and getting a share of trade. But he will go on to speak of South Africa, which he will see as a country where one-fifth of the population are determined to keep all political power in their own hands; he may concede that it would involve some sacrifice if the West were to give up South Africa's strategic advantages, her gold and uranium, in return for the luxury of expressing disapproval of her domestic policy; he might even concede that, South Africa being a sovereign state, it would not be easy to do more than

---

* I have said much of this before. But I think it is true and I cannot hope that every reader of this book will have read what I have written elsewhere.

express disapproval. But he would certainly add that the refusal to make this sacrifice throws doubt on all professions of belief in democracy as a principle. And then, if he were addressing an Englishman, he would come to the heart of his charge and continue on some such lines as these:

'And what are you going to do about Rhodesia and Kenya? Devolve power in such a way that we can all have a share of it? Or give it weakly away to an electorate in which Africans have no real share? We in Africa are more and more conscious of all that we have in common with each other; we have been long enough in bonds and we have a continent with great resources. Some day we shall control it ourselves. To whom shall we look as guides today? Whom shall we then take as friends? You, who have taught us so much? Or the Russians, who promise us an equality over which you hesitate? Or the Asians, who have memories like ours of past humiliation? We shall turn to those who bring us the hope of equality, who offer freedom.

'Please be clear about one thing. We put freedom before gold. You may talk to us for hours about economic advantages, technical assistance, and the need for capital, but not a pulse will beat faster. We expect help of that kind—yes; if your principles are what you say, you ought to help us in that way. But we don't see that you have any moral right to make it dependent on our giving a privileged position to a few Europeans; in your own country you've been gradually breaking down class privilege for fifty years. Why should we enshrine privilege in Kenya and Tanganyika and Rhodesia by devices that make the votes of Europeans count in some special way, so that we, who are so many more, can never outnumber them in Parliament? If you persist in this injustice, we are bound to turn to others who offer equality and freedom and whose fine words have not so far been given the lie by their deeds.'

To this in Kenya, Rhodesia, and South Africa, the descendant of Europeans is apt to plead that he too has a place in the country where he was born; that it was his fathers who brought to Africa the rule of law, the arts of civilization, the very principles of democracy, and the ideals of altruism now invoked; that it is his energy, capital, and experience that maintain the economic life of the country; that because of their special position as an apostolic minority, he and his friends, if they are to go on living their own kind of life and shedding its light on the darkness around them, must preserve some degree of political control for a long time to come.

This debate continues; it is a problem not only for Britain but for the French, who, by their *loi cadre*, have now accepted a form of the policy of India and Ghana for what they call 'black Africa', but not for Algeria. It is the territories where men wearing the badge of fair skins have settled that have become, in the eyes of those with the dark badge, the testing ground for the West's pretensions to a new heart. If a way can here be found of living peacefully together, then the lining up of dark people against fair may cease; the ranks are broken. But if the situation in these countries is to be one of smouldering revolution, flaring occasionally into active rebellion or civil war, as recently in Kenya and at the time of writing in Algeria, it becomes both a reproach to the conscience and a threat to the security of the West. Tempers throughout the world will grow shorter and sympathies become irrevocably committed; the conflict between dark and fair will grow nearer, the badges be fixed more firmly and—in the immediate future—a vast recruiting ground will be opened to our enemies in the cold war.

English* people have not much more formal political responsibility for the Union of South Africa than for Algeria; as between Kenya and Rhodesia, there can be no question that Rhodesia is the more important testing-ground, both because it is a richer

* I often use the term English to include Scots, Welsh, Canadians, or even Americans, indeed all who speak English from birth. This is the French practice today and was followed by the Scots themselves not long ago, before tribal self-consciousness grew so acute. And when I speak of England, I am usually thinking of the idea of England, rather than of some act of the government or Parliament of Great Britain. But I do not pretend to be consistent. For the pedant I justify my use as the figure of rhetoric known as synecdoche. Who would say: 'Great Britain, with all thy faults, I love thee still'?

country industrially and because more Europeans live there. Rhodesia, then, for any Englishman who concerns himself with the future of this conflict between dark and fair, is the key point, the centre of the strategic position.

The test comes on the spot; in the end, the conflict will be decided in Africa. From outside, perhaps the best contribution is understanding; this book is written in the belief that there can be no understanding of the present without an understanding of the past; that it is usually worth pausing and thinking: 'How did we get into this situation?' before going on to consider how to get out of it. It is written also in the light of certain other beliefs or prejudices which it is as well to state and recognize.

First comes a conviction that the relations between any two human beings are always complex. They are not stable from one moment to another; at a given moment they are never simple. Irritation arises between the most loving couples; the most domineering husband sometimes needs comfort and reassurance from the wife he bullies; hatred, between people who actually see each other, is often interrupted by moments of compassion or understanding. Relations between groups of people may in one way be still more complex, because there is the difference between individuals to be taken into account as well as the difference between moods in the same individual. On the other hand, relations between groups may sometimes and in another way be simpler, because they are more easily given a formal expression, as happens in war. And emotions are infectious: while it is easy never to see, in any real sense, someone on the other side, easy to persist in a mental picture—of Germans, of Jews, of Russians, of Negroes—which is consistent only because it is artificial, it is easy to shut out pity for someone felt to be wholly alien and unreal. In the face of the complexity and inconsistency of human beings, a writer should, I suggest, cultivate not only a humility before the facts, but a much deeper humility before the vastness of a subject from which no parts can be conveniently isolated. He must, I suggest, recognize that there can be no finally and exclusively true description or analysis of the relations between people, only a number of views from different angles. No generalization will always be true; new aspects of reality will always be coming to light. To apply the methods of physical science may be helpful up to a point, for a particular purpose and within defined limits, but the results will not necessarily apply outside those limits. To speak of scientific truth—if that implies exclusive universal and final truth—can in this field only be misleading.

No one who has not made his home in a country can understand it: true, but it is also true that no one can understand a country he *has* made his home. Two pictures at least are needed, one to provide understanding from within, the other, from outside, to relate what is seen to the rest of the world. It is in these beliefs that I have tried to put together a view of Central Africa before Europeans took political control, a view admittedly written from outside, by one who had made a number of visits, but has not made his home in the country, a view which must therefore miss much, but which gains something too from detachment.

There is not much that is original about it; it nearly all comes from other people, but, so far as I know, no one else has tried to put side by side the pictures provided by such different people as missionaries, hunters, traders, and anthropologists. The pictures differ sharply; the Barotse, for instance, seen through the eyes of a missionary and of an anthropologist are hardly recognizable as the same people. To believe, as I do, that neither the anthropologist nor the missionary tells the whole truth is not to belittle the work of either. On the contrary, the mind gains a cutting edge from self-imposed limitation or discipline, and within self-imposed limits it is possible to be more dogmatic than in a wider context. But there remains the need for comparison, assembly, and synthesis, and here dogmatism is out of place. Again, the story of Lobengula has been told before, but usually by someone who saw through the eyes of Rhodes or of Jameson or of the Chartered Company or of Lobengula. I have tried to see through different sets of eyes in turn; I have tried to talk to people with views of as wide a variety as possible.

To other prejudices, I must confess briefly. I believe that contact between peoples and the exchange of ideas has been the most potent force in human progress—whether in philosophy or in material comfort—and that in the last century and a half what is commonly called colonialism has increased the pace at which ideas are exchanged and has contributed to human growth and mental development as no other institution could do. I do not believe that economic motives are the sole or even the principal factor in human conduct; all the evidence seems to me against such a view. It was not economic calculation that brought England into the war in 1914 or that brought in America in 1917, that made England forbid the slave trade in 1807, that influenced India's attitude over the Suez crisis in 1956; it was emotion—of sympathy, indignation, anger—not calculation. And I believe that though a man is a creature of the time in which he lives, shaped by the people he has known and the books he has read, he can influence his times as they influence him, responding to a challenge or avoiding it, swimming with the current or climbing out on the bank and even perhaps deflecting it. One Churchill altered the history of Europe by the march to Blenheim, another by rhetoric, emotion, and an obstinate pugnacity after Dunkirk. Yet these last qualities by themselves would not have availed without the calculations on an aeronautical designer's drawing-board. Again, not long after Dunkirk, the Italians showed that tools will not win battles in which people have not put their hearts. Neither tools nor resolution are in fact enough without the other. And, given that the will and the emotions of any one human being are unpredictable, to apply the methods of physical science to history or politics and expect them to produce accurate results is as wise as believing there is a certainty for the Derby. That is not to say that anyone who has made up his mind to bet should not study the form and the breeding.

I use the ordinary accepted English terms for African tribes that are well known, such as the Matabele and the Angoni, rather than forms grammatically and phonetically more correct, such as Ndebele and Ngoni, simply because the latter are confusing to most English readers. And the reason why I have not pursued at any length (as I am told a real historian would do) the threads of policy which lead back from Rhodesia to England is that they seem to me to have very little to do with the subject of my book.

What follows is meant for anyone who takes an intelligent interest in the prospects of conflict between black people and white, but in particular for those who live in Rhodesia and Nyasaland and who have not time to browse themselves among the books I have used as sources. In a sense, this is a record of my own attempt to see in proportion and perspective the results of visits, talks, and reading. It is a by-product of a larger work, the first instalment of others; my visits to Rhodesia and the help I have had in collecting information have been financed by the Rockefeller Foundation, to whom I am deeply grateful. I am also glad to have the opportunity of expressing my thanks to: Mr. H. V. Hiller of the Central African Archives for much help, particularly in the matter of illustrations; to his staff, and particularly Mr. A. R. Taylor, who has been unfailingly and cheerfully more helpful than anyone has a right to expect, and Dr. Lewis Gann, who has supplied me with many ideas; to Dr. Roland Oliver, Professor Margaret Read, and Professor Max Gluckman; to Richard Gray, Margaret Usborne and Janet Evanson.

P. M.

Part One

AFRICA UNTOUCHED

I. First Encounters

In the southern part of Africa, peoples profoundly different in appearance, in temperament, and in background have come together in a prolonged encounter, in which the weapons at first were rifle and assegai, later pay-slip, union ticket and ballot-box, tax-receipt, court-house and newspaper; in which there has been room on one side for fidelity, affection, and respect as well as fear and distrust, on the other for esteem as well as contempt, for benevolent self-sacrifice as well as for brutality and greed. Hostility has alternated with a readiness to learn and a willingness to teach, sullen rejection with eager imitation. The outcome cannot be known and may in the end have results as far-reaching—for both peoples concerned—as any contest yet recorded between men. But heavy with coming strife and tragedy though the first meetings were, they cannot, by a truthful historian, be displayed in colours so sharp and bright as those he might use of the meeting of Cortes with Montezuma.

The first officials of the Netherlands East India Company at the Cape, the peasants from the Low Countries whom they brought from Europe, the Huguenot reinforcements who joined them after the revocation of the Edict of Nantes—these first settlers at the Cape were confronted with no Aztecs or Incas, no kings or priests, but with Hottentots and Bushmen, poor and ill-organized tribes, living very near the lowest level of human comfort, with hardly so much idea of providing for the future as squirrels or beavers—or so at least they must have appeared to the settlers whose fields and cattle they raided. Even when the oxwagons began to roll further and further from the Cape and when contact was made with the Bantu-speaking peoples, the edges of the encounter were blurred by previous knowledge and

15

some idea of what the other would be like was almost always present in the minds of either party. Nor was the meeting pregnant, as in America, with immediate doom for one race; the conflict was to develop slowly and indeed, even today, no one can suppose that the crisis in this dramatic relationship has yet been reached.

But though something was known of the tribes likely to be met, so vast was the area unexplored that it continued to offer a lively challenge to the imagination. From the Limpopo to the Sahara, Africa was unknown a century ago to people of European stock. The Mediterranean North, the tip of the continent which is now the Union of South Africa, the outline of the coast—these were familiar, but the rest was an enigma. The mouths of the rivers were guarded by swamps or by bars swept by heavy surf; once these sentries were passed, the rivers of the East coast came down in cataracts and gorges, while on both coasts 'fever' was a comprehensive term that covered a host of diseases, deadly to the stranger and debilitating to the native.

Since the sixteenth century, the Portuguese had held scattered forts along both coasts but their early attempts to penetrate the interior had died away before the reign of Queen Victoria; long before this story begins, the wind of energy within the bubble of their vast empire had stretched the envelope beyond its strength and had been scattered in the surrounding air. Their forts along the coast of what is now Tanganyika and Kenya they had lost to the Arabs, their inland missionary stations to the jungle. A broken tower, a rusty bell in a tangle of vegetation; nothing beside remained. But for three hundred years and more they had been on the coast, and rumours of their ways and doings had seeped inland, just as rumours of what is now Rhodesia had seeped out.

Some of what seeped out was hearsay, tales told to a Portuguese missionary or officials by Africans who themselves had the stories at second-hand. Some of it was based on brief explorations in the early sixteenth century which were not followed up, some on reports by people whose interest it was to show that the territory would repay some outlay on development. That there is today some archaeological support for these rumours is less important, from the point of view of this book, than that the English, both of the Cape and of England, had heard them and were encouraged by them in that vigorous optimism that drove the Victorians into every corner of the world. The missionaries, the hunters, the prospectors, and the traders who from the middle of the century onwards faced the dangers of this unknown country had all heard of the gold of Ophir and the country of the Queen of Sheba. Diverse though they were in conscious motive, in way of life and in attitude to the Africans they were to meet, they had one thing in common, a robust if romantic belief in 'something lost behind the ranges', a belief that further inland there might well be found a reward impossible in the world they knew. Moffat, Livingstone, Coillard thought of a rich harvest of souls to be saved, Baines and Carl Mauch of gold, Hartley and Selous of ivory; none of them would have been surprised to find in Central Africa a people more highly organized and masters of more complex technical skills than any of the Bantu tribes they had known south of the Limpopo. It was the virile energy native to them that drove them north, but their expectations took the form they did because they had heard, directly or indirectly, vague rumours of the Empire of the Monomotapa, of a country where gold was worked and temples had been built of stone.

Picture a map that is only an outline of the coast, with a little colour and a few names spreading north and east from the Cape, the great central mass white, utterly blank, unscored by lines denoting rivers or mountain ranges. Picture this map, with its blank centre, thrown on a screen by a cinema projector; picture long threads wriggling slowly upwards and inwards, each the journey of some missionary, hunter or explorer. And here a few miles of a river's course, here the bold outlines of a mountain, are sketched in, here an ominous shading indicates a desert from which the explorer had escaped with his life and little more. The columns of the Trekkers made thick tracks northwards into the Transvaal, the thin lines of Livingstone's great journey are traced

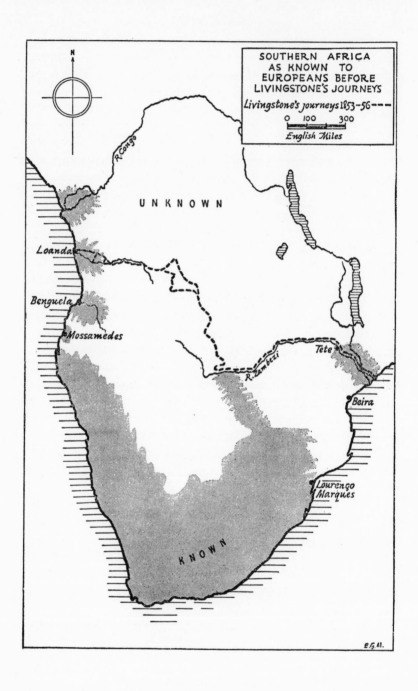

SOUTHERN AFRICA
AS KNOWN TO
EUROPEANS BEFORE
LIVINGSTONE'S JOURNEYS

Livingstone's journeys 1853-56 - - -

0   100   300

English Miles

UNKNOWN

R.Congo

Loanda

Benguela

Mossamedes

Tete

R.Zambezi

Beira

Lourenço Marques

KNOWN

E.G.M.

laboriously across the continent and back again; little by little the map is drawn. And the travellers bring back more than geographical information; they bring confused and contradictory impressions of whole peoples from which it is not easy to disentangle the elements and build up a coherent picture that does not falsify by being over-simple.

This book is an attempt to describe the impact on each other of peoples profoundly different and the results of that impact in the territories now known as the Federation of Rhodesia and Nyasaland. The relationship between the two peoples may be thought of as coming to birth in 1890, when the Pioneer Column marched from Kimberley and hoisted the flag at Fort Salisbury, but pre-natal influences shaped the child and it is worth trying to make first a picture of how these two peoples appeared to each other at their first meeting and what they were really like. To write such words invites criticism; no one can say what they were really like. All one can hope to do is to assemble a series of sketches from different angles, and of these the sketchiest and least convincing must necessarily be the impressions the Bantu tribes first formed of Europeans. One can only guess, piecing something together from the impressions of one traveller, a casual remark dropped by another in passing.

The people of Central Africa must in almost every case have heard of Europeans before they saw them. News travelled among them with some speed and, so far as they understood it, with some accuracy. Livingstone on the lower Zambezi in the sixties heard[1] through Africans what Moffat had said to Mzilikazi 500 miles to the west. Several years earlier, when he came down the Zambezi in 1856, he had found at Zumbo the remains of Portuguese houses, a fort, and a church. The people of the neighbourhood had all heard of the Bazunga, the Portuguese, and knowing of Livingstone's coming had supposed him one of these. But both his appearance and his behaviour seemed to be different. They stared at his hair and his skin and asked him who he was; in his reply he used a word common in Basutoland and Bechuanaland for an Englishman. 'We don't know that tribe,' they replied, and then added: 'Ah! You must be of that tribe that loves the black men.'[2]

On the river itself, then, at least as far as Zumbo, and inland as far from the East Coast as Manicaland, Africans might be met with in the sixties who had seen the Portuguese, or Portuguese and Arab half-breeds. Throughout Mashonaland, there would be men who had heard of the English and of the Afrikaners, who knew enough to recognize that these were people whose ways were different from each other and from the Portuguese. By the mid-seventies, Selous writes that 'a Kafir who is owed money by one Englishman, perhaps the wages for a year's work, will take a letter without a murmur to another Englishman hundreds of miles away if he is told that on delivering the letter he will receive payment'. But he thought there were 'perhaps a few Boer hunters in the interior whose word the Kafirs would trust, but very few'; while 'near Zumbo you cannot get a Native who has been used to dealing with the Portuguese to stir hand or foot unless you pay him in advance'.[3] By 1890, he could write to *The Times*: 'During the last twenty-five years English hunters and travellers have explored every nook and corner of Mashunaland.'*

Whatever the tribesmen had heard, the first glimpse of Europeans must have come with a shock of surprise. Peering from cover at the ox-drawn wagons, wondering at the hairy faces and the lumpy outlines of these strange beings, they were aware, no doubt, of something more than curiosity, of some slight apprehension of coming change in a life that was at least familiar. But not one can have begun to picture the shattering effect this coming was to have, not only on their food, houses, weapons, tools, and clothing, but on their inmost thoughts, their faith in the protection of their ancestors, their songs and dances, even their feelings for their wives and children.

The first reaction was usually not unfriendly. Livingstone on his first great journey across the continent wrote that the chiefs about the headwaters of the Zambezi 'are so proud of the honour of having strangers residing in their villages that it is difficult to

* So he always spelled the word.

effect a departure'.[4] And on his second major expedition to the lower Zambezi, the Shire, and Lake Nyasa, he writes:

but the people came after us with things for sale and invited us to stop and spend the night with them, urging: 'Are we to have it said that white people passed through our country and we did not see them?'[5]

This was as much curiosity as anything else. Coillard, nearly fifteen years later, in what is now Mashonaland, describes a scene familiar from the writings of many others:

That very day in this forest, which has hitherto been so solitary, we caught sight of black figures hiding behind trees, who cast furtive glances at us and disappeared like shadows. Others, growing bolder, approached us little by little, and before evening they brought us flour, peas, groundnuts, rice, etc. . . . From this moment our wagons were besieged by natives from far and near, who escorted us day by day and bivouacked beside us at night, to satisfy their curiosity.[6]

But both Livingstone and Coillard, not to mention a score of others, found that a friendly curiosity was not always the mood. On his first journey, Livingstone, as he drew nearer to the West Coast, found the chiefs much less hospitable; they were inclined to demand presents of substance, the claim often being for 'an ox, a tusk or a man', and they sometimes threatened violence if the claim was rejected. On one occasion, 'at every fresh demand a shout was raised and a rush made around us with brandished weapons. One young man even made a charge at my head from behind but I quickly brought round the muzzle of my gun to his mouth. . . .'[7]

And Coillard in the seventies had the same kind of experience among the Mashona. ' "Masonda does not like the blanket; he wants a canister of powder and a box of caps," came the message. 'I explained that I was not a trader but a messenger of peace . . . but it was so much breath wasted. . . .' And not long afterwards 'troops of men rushed towards us, uttering fierce cries and armed to the teeth with assegais, hatchets, bows and arrows and sharp knives. . . . Masonda, standing on a rock and foaming with fury, disposed his troops so as to surround us, ordered them to take away our oxen, and dictated his terms to us. "So many sacks of powder, so many caps, so many blankets, so many guns and you shall go." '8

There were many such scenes as this. What is perhaps most remarkable about them is that again and again the missionaries were able to extricate themselves without firing a shot or striking a blow. Livingstone believed that the natives were friendly unless they had been corrupted by the slave trade, but this hardly fitted the case of Masonda; there was not much commercial raiding for slaves in Southern Mashonaland, though in a sense every Mashona held his life from the Matabele under a suspended sentence of death—a state of affairs that would stimulate anyone's desire for gun-powder. And Masonda had with him one man at least who had worked in the diamond fields at Kimberley and brought back 'some very undesirable notions'. Perhaps it was true that the first visitors were usually made welcome unless cupidity had been roused by some contact with Europeans or Arabs. And the most frequent kind of contact was a raid by slavers.

But again, a qualification must be made. There is a vivid description—to go back forty years—in *The Life of Daniel Lindley* of the first encounters between the Boer parties trekking North from the Cape in 1838 and Mzilikazi's people in what is now the Transvaal. There was no hesitation here; the people who were later to be known as the Matabele attacked the wagons at once. Lindley saw warriors going through the purification rites that were necessary after battle and when he questioned them learned that the Boers had been taken by surprise in the first encounter and that sixteen had been killed, including women and children, from the party of S. P. Erasmus and P. Bekker.[9] This was perhaps partly because the Afrikaners came with the obvious intention of settling permanently and living in the country, but mainly because the Matabele were a military people, very different from the Mashona tribes and from the Cewa of Nyasaland. This distinction between peoples who had a military tradition and those who had not, between the preyers and the preyed on, will recur as the story develops.

But even where there was no hostility, it must not be supposed that the first curiosity at the sight of Europeans turned easily to admiration. Few travellers have attempted to find out how they might appear to Africans; some have clearly been fed by politenesses. Livingstone, who was entirely alone among them for far longer than most of his contemporaries, wrote: 'We appear to them to be red rather than white and, though light colour is admired among themselves, our clothing renders us uncouth in aspect. Blue eyes appear savage and a red beard hideous.'[10] Others have recorded the Africans' wonder that anyone should conceal an outline so comely and graceful as a human leg in bags of cloth. And later Livingstone writes:

There must be something in the appearance of white men frightfully repulsive to the unsophisticated natives of Africa; for, on entering villages previously unvisited by Europeans, if we met a child coming quietly and unsuspectingly towards us, the moment he raised his eyes and saw the men in 'bags', he would take to his heels in an agony of terror, such as we might feel if we met a live Egyptian mummy at the door of the British Museum.[11]

Much the same feelings would, of course, be aroused even today by the appearance in an English village of a Matabele Induna in his traditional ornaments. In the Nyasaland villages, the first fear disappeared with familiarity and on the European side too something similar took place. 'We soon learned', wrote Livingstone in Nyasaland, 'to forget colour and we frequently saw countenances resembling those of white people we had known in England.'[12] One may guess that Livingstone knew the shock of surprise at seeing his own face in the looking-glass, even, as his eyes fell from the face of the man he was talking to, the colour of his own hand on the butt of his gun, a shock that many of his countrymen have experienced when they came back from a long spell in camp or in a lonely station.

Livingstone obviously wrote with a running pen and expresses at different times sentiments not altogether consistent. He, and all the early travellers, except the Portuguese, came through the Cape Province; if the African tribes they met had heard something of them, they already had an idea of some African peoples. They had lived, if only for a few weeks, in a society which had already settled down into an established form, in which Europeans had already formed mental pictures of the natives of Africa, of the Hottentots and Bushmen, and the Bantu peoples they usually lumped together as Kaffirs. To these pictures the travellers usually supposed it likely that the natives would conform, though there was, as I have said, always the romantic belief that a new and 'better' or 'higher' kind of native might be met with inland. But to such conventional images, the experience will always present exceptions and soon there were many inconsistencies in the generalizations a white South African would make about the natives. Livingstone was not the man to form impressions at second-hand and his opinions are his own, but he too shares the inconsistency common among the white South African of his day and of ours, something of the contrast between condemnation in general terms and a warm and personal affection for individuals.

There are certain themes to which he comes back again and again. His horror of heathendom and of the slave trade is qualified by his Christian conviction that all men have souls to be saved, and by the plain evidence of his senses that people, even people so different as Africans and Europeans, have many wants and emotions in common. And he constantly comes back to the thought that there are resemblances between the poor and helpless of his own country and the poor and helpless of Africa, and that the same behaviour is proper in dealing with either. When answering questions, he tried to imagine the African addressing him as 'a poor uneducated fellow countryman' and he writes that 'the polite respectful way of speaking of what we call a thorough gentleman almost always secures the friendship and goodwill of the African'.[13] But at this point one cannot resist the recollection that with a fellow countryman Livingstone was seldom able to work long without a quarrel.

There is certainly no lack of evidence for his horror of heathendom, a horror he shared with all the missionaries. It was no doubt in that weariness of spirit that sometimes came over the most devoted that Robert Moffat wrote:

> In the natives of South Africa there is nothing naturally engaging; their extreme selfishness, filthiness, obstinate stupidity, and want of sensibility have a tendency to disgust and sometimes cause the mind to shrink from spending the whole life amongst them, far from every tender and endearing circle.[14]

Yet no one can doubt that between Robert Moffat and many of those here so generously condemned a real affection grew:

> I entered, he grasped my hand and drew his mantle over his face. . . . He spoke not, except to pronounce my name, Moshete, again and again. He looked at me again, his hand still holding mine, and he again covered his face. My heart yearned with compassion for his soul.[15]

He is writing of no other than Mzilikazi, chief of the Matabele, so often referred to by the missionaries as a bloodthirsty tyrant; he records the same kind of affection for many others. And Livingstone too knew just the same alternation between a general irritation and a practical personal regard. After his first stay among the Makololo, he wrote:

> They were as kind and attentive to me as possible yet to endure the dancing, roaring and singing, the jesting, anecdotes, grumbling, quarrelling and murdering of these children of nature, seemed more like a severe penance than anything I had met before. I took then a more intense disgust at heathenism than ever before.[16]

Yet he too records again and again his pleasure at some acts of kindness, as for example when Sekeletu, chief of these very Makololo, sleeping in the open on a night which suddenly grew cold, rose quietly and wrapped his own blanket round Livingstone, or when his porters, also Makololo, plunged into a swollen river to save him. And he constantly comes back to the recurring theme of refuting 'the silly assumption that the Negro is this, that, and the other thing, and not, like other men, a curious mixture of good and evil, wisdom and folly, cleverness and stupidity'.[17]

'The Lake tribes', he writes elsewhere, 'are very much like other people; there are decent men among them, while a good many are no better than they should be.'[18]

One other fallacy Livingstone is always eager to combat, that African ideas of right and wrong were basically different from European. 'We knew all this before,' they told him, 'except that we must not have more than one wife. That we did not know to be wrong; but that we should not lie or kill or steal, oh yes, we knew that was wrong. But still we do all these things.' 'The idea', wrote Livingstone, 'of the Father of all being displeased with His children for selling or killing each other at once gains their ready assent. It harmonises so exactly with their own ideas of right and wrong. . . .'[19]

The early missionaries, then—one could go on quoting them to this effect for ever—found Africans in general to be 'not in the least the sweet, simple, affectionate confiding creatures they are represented to be in Europe',[20] but bloodthirsty and callous, careless and dirty, yet they also found in individuals depths of affection and fidelity, sometimes, more rarely, of energy and steadfastness of purpose. And what they disliked they put down to paganism; what won them, they knew, was personal character and shared humanity. 'I feel', wrote Coillard in his journal, 'more and more drawn every day to [Lewanika]. . . . When I said we should know each other better by and by, he looked steadily at me and said: "You speak for yourself, Moruti; but when I once saw you that was enough: I gave myself to you; it is my nature." ' 'A man I pray for every day,' Coillard adds, 'how could I keep from loving him?'[21]

II. The Tribes

Section 1: The Nature of the Evidence

From Livingstone's journey across the continent onwards, the blank spaces on the map beyond the Limpopo are crossed and criss-crossed by a tangle of fine lines, the journeys of European missionaries, hunters, and prospectors. Each of these travellers came back with some picture of the tribes he had met; in almost every case it was related to his own needs and way of life. The hunter would be concerned with the readiness of the people he met to carry his goods, their ability to track animals, their swiftness in following a wounded beast, the courage with which they would stand a charge and hand him his gun. He was not as a rule interested in their own lives and though he might distinguish between the main tribes, he would usually notice only their most obvious characteristics. Selous, for instance, records a chance meeting with a party of Matabele, who 'at length admitted that they had been sent out by Lobengula to murder any strange Bushmen or Kafirs whom they might find hunting in his veldt'. So he said nothing to them of a party of Masaras—Bushmen— for whom he had shot a giraffe, because the Masaras would have had 'a sorry time of it had they chanced to fall into the hands of these ruthless, murdering scoundrels, whose greatest happiness is to stab to death defenceless and unresisting women and children . . .'.[1]

The hunter's pictures then are as a rule drawn in sharp outline and bright primary colours. They are also to some extent contradictory, just as Moffat's and Coillard's are. It would be a dull creature indeed who was wholly consistent and no one should be surprised that travellers so constantly in touch with people so different from themselves should make exceptions to their own generalizations. The hunter or prospector had by tradition a faithful gun-bearer or personal servant for whom he felt real affection, yet he would as a rule condemn in general terms the people from whom his friend came, as individuals and as a society. Both missionaries and hunters started from certain fixed dogmas—religious, moral, and social; they seldom had any doubt, for instance, that it was right to imprison a man for theft and wrong to spear him for witchcraft, while to most African tribes the reverse would have seemed just as plain, imprisonment being seen as heartless and cruel.

However absolute his condemnation in the first place, it did sometimes happen, even to the missionary, that after many years a custom which had seemed wholly immoral was seen in a new light as something useful to society. Daniel Lindley, who came to Africa from North Carolina in 1835, at first believed, like every missionary of his day, that every smallest detail of Western ways that could be taught an African brought him a step along the right road. He records with pride the number of Zulus taught to build square houses instead of round. But by 1869 he had come to understand the social benefits of at least one institution which had at first seemed altogether evil; he shocked the Society to which he belonged by writing in defence of *lobola*.[2]

'*Lobola*' is a word widely used to describe a custom common in various forms among those Bantu-speaking people who herd cattle and inherit from their father's people rather than from their mother's. It means the consideration given by a bride-groom's family when a woman from another group comes to his group as a bride. The first group have lost the reproductive power and the hoeing power of a woman; they gain, say, six head of cattle, but the number will differ from tribe to tribe and place to place and it will be more in a chief's family than in a commoner's. Those cattle will usually be divided, in various proportions, between the bride's father and his near relations. If the bride proves barren or misbehaves or quarrels with her husband, she may, in many tribes, go back to her father's kraal, but in that case his group must either find another woman tᵤ take her place or return the cattle of the *lobola*.

To the first missionaries, this appeared an unhallowed practice, implying the sale of a woman, derogatory in the highest degree to her status as the dwelling of an immortal soul and to the nature of marriage as a binding contract between loving partners. It was only after many years that Lindley perceived that the practice tended to make marriage lasting. The woman's father, and often a brother or an uncle as well, had an interest in seeing that her marriage was a success; they would do all they could to persuade her to settle a quarrel amicably, while the husband knew that whatever his rights might be it would not be easy to get the *lobola* back and that he would need it if he was to get another wife. By forbidding *lobola* to Christian converts, the missionary was knocking away one of the props of marriage as it had existed, and that before a new idea of marriage had had time to become part of their habit of thought. 'Lobola has been,' he writes, 'a great blessing to the people.'[3]

But for one missionary who was ready to learn such a lesson there were a dozen who would not; from the missionaries, if there was no one else to consult, one would obtain a picture of the tribes of Central Africa that was fuller, certainly, than the hunter's, but just as strongly coloured by the beholder's point of view. This is inevitable; the missionary came to teach and to convert. He had an urgent sense of the need to change what he saw and it is exceptional to find a missionary in the nineteenth century who was deeply concerned to record, or even to understand, the heathendom with which he was engaged in combat. It is to a later generation and to men professing a new branch of learning that one must turn to complete the picture.

The anthropologist could hardly differ more completely from the missionary in his approach. He is in no way concerned to teach; it is his intention to observe and to analyse and his chief problem is to identify himself, during the period of observation, as completely as he can with the people in whom he is interested, and yet to detach himself when he comes to the task of analysis.

In this he can never be wholly successful; the more deeply he burrows, as an observer, into the minds and customs of 'his' tribe, the more certainly he establishes a kind of vested interest in all that he has perceived in their present condition or discovered about their past. The anthropologist who has thoroughly dissected a changing society would not be human if he could wholly repress a pang at the disappearance of something to which he alone among his kind holds the key and to which he alone can provide the interpretation. It must become 'his' tribe if he is really to understand it, and therefore, however hard he tries, he cannot be indifferent to it; to some degree he must love or hate it. Yet he can never be one of the tribe; he is the observer, and what he sees are the traits of the observed when in the presence of an observer.[4] And while the anthropologist makes what he can of the tribe, the tribe are all the time making something of the anthropologist; he leaves them a changed man.

From the angle of this book, then, the writings of the anthropologist are evidence, to be set beside the evidence of other people, historians, missionaries, traders, and later native commissioners, expert evidence, given by people who have studied their subject and thought about it, but not for that reason immune from cross-examination. From this evidence, a picture can be drawn of the tribes of Central Africa as they were before 1890, but it is a picture of much complexity and built up from a mass of confusing and often conflicting detail. It is bound to contain generalizations to which there will be exceptions, and it can claim no finality. A picture by another hand of the same subject would doubtless be different.

Section 2: The Backwash from the South

In the first place, all the tribes of what is now the Federation—with the exception of a very few Bushmen—belonged to the great family of Bantu-speaking peoples. There are many Bantu languages, but they have much in common and may be thought of as related in the same kind of way as Spanish and Italian. The peoples who speak these languages come of very mixed stocks;

in the colour of the skin, the formation of the hair and the shape of the features there are striking differences within almost every tribe, and between one tribe and another there are differences: in one it will be the exception to see the very dark skin and the kind of features sometimes seen among the Negroes of the West Coast, in another tribe there will be more people with something of that kind of appearance, fewer with an Arab or Mediterranean look.

Nothing can be said with certainty of the origin of these Bantu-speaking tribes, nor of the stocks from which they are made up. Even about their movements it is impossible to be precise; none of them had the art of writing and their traditions are confusing and sometimes appear to contradict one another. Their history is detective work, in which the historian must piece out the traditions and compare them, check them with archaeology's findings as well as with each other, consider the evidence of language and custom, and in the end put together a case which may or may not convince the court and on which no one can pronounce with complete certainty that this is so.

It is however possible to say that a general movement of the Bantu speakers was taking place throughout the centuries of the Christian era. Of the groups who moved southward and east-ward in the earliest of these movements, it must first be said that they had all taken that one tremendous step in man's mastery of his surroundings, that is the discovery of iron, and as they moved, some groups were beginning to take a second step which seems to be a condition of much progress; they were beginning to till the soil instead of merely driving flocks and herds before them. To adopt agriculture did not necessarily mean that a tribe ceased to wander; some pastoral tribes have for long periods confined their movements to a region within which they follow a cycle of seasonal grazings; most of the agricultural tribes would cultivate a piece of ground for two or three years only before clearing another. But in general to hoe the ground was a practice that slowed the pace of migration.

Nor should one think of any of these groups as though they

were pebbles—unities always contained within one smooth outer crust. They would split and re-form; a travelling group of warriors would defeat a sedentary group and absorb them, settling perhaps on their land as an aristocracy, perhaps adopting their history and traditions, perhaps imposing their own, perhaps in time becoming absorbed themselves. Or they would add to their own number fresh elements from the conquered people and carry them with them on their wanderings; or they would leave a section behind, with some of the memories and customs of the conquerors to become confused with those of the defeated.

No one can say with certainty when this drift southwards began, this process of moving, settling down, breaking up, and moving on again. But it was taking place during the first millennium of the Christian era; it may have been going on before. During that first thousand years, and perhaps nearer the beginning than the end, it seems probable that many of the tribes of Central Africa settled in the country where their descendants were still living when Europeans first came. These were on the whole the tribes who were least organized when the Europeans came, those grouped together under the names Mashona and Batonga, the Ila or the Cewa. But the process continued during what we in Europe would call medieval and renaissance times; there were new tribes pressing on, flowing over, under and round those already settled; fresh waves came on behind them. All this time the drift was still southward and eastward, though with eddies and cross-currents here and there. By the beginning of the nineteenth century a wash-back had begun, which may be thought of as the wash-back of a wave breaking at the foot of a sea-wall. The most tumultuous and massive reflux originated in what is now Zululand, where the chief of a small and previously not very important section of the Nguni group* invented a new technique of hand-to-hand fighting with spear and shield, a new tactical doctrine and a way of cementing his whole people

* The Nguni group include the South African peoples now usually known as Zulus, Swazis, and Xhosas, living in Swaziland, Natal, and the Transkei, the south-eastern fringe of South Africa.

together by a rigid discipline that made them a perfect instrument for war.

Chaka made the Zulus a nation but before he was born there was already a tendency among the small Nguni chiefdoms to coalesce and come together. His personality speeded this movement up and changed the nature of the Zulus—a name which before his time applied only to one small section, but was later assumed, as his prestige grew, by all his allies and dependents. But the creation of his Empire did more than this and much more than merely bring his neighbours under his sway. Zulu armies marched away and set up in the North new kingdoms which followed the Zulu model. Under Zulu pressure, a Basuto horde too broke away from Basutoland and marched north. This washback of returning armies of Bantu-speaking people moving north met in Central Africa tribes who had settled down and others who were still moving south, just as the reflux of a wave meets the next wave and breaks into tumbled surf. In all this Chaka himself was a moulding and determining factor; his strange deprived childhood, his need to impose on others the discipline to which he felt impelled to subject himself, changed the face of southern Africa. And here there is no need to explore the deeper causes that may have lain behind this movement together of people into cohesive masses and their explosion outwards in jagged fragments.

The effect of this wash-back and of the Zulu conquests was profound throughout Southern Africa. Even today, Southern Africans will mention in casual conversation an ancestor lost in 'the troubles', the dispersions. On tribes the result was as devastating as on individuals; the weak and decadent were shattered, the stronger were forced to sharpen their spears and stand on the alert. The Mashona group of tribes had long been settled in what is now Southern Rhodesia; the Zulu hordes drove back through them and over them and in the west settled as conquerors. There were other peoples who were more recent immigrants, or who had perhaps been stiffened and re-organized by a recent wave of immigrants, people more highly organized and themselves predatory on their neighbours; first among these come the Barotse and the Bemba. They stood against the backwash when it met them and again there was a dispersion into cross-currents.

There are four of these northward movements with which we are specially concerned. Three of them are Zulu and one Basuto. In each case a horde rather than an army is the expression to use, because women, cattle, and children were collected and taken with them as they moved. Each cut through the more sedentary tribes, who had paused earlier in the southward march; each pressed on until either contact was made with a powerful and highly organized southward-thrusting tribe who stopped progress, or an area was reached which seemed more fertile than anything ahead. These hordes did not, of course, move in a straight line but zigzagged across the map in search of grain, cattle, and women; the detail of their meanderings may however be disregarded for our purpose and the four thrusts may be shown in four smooth curves as they are on Map II.

Three curves come from Zululand. One, the shortest, under Soshangane, reached the south-eastern corner of Southern Rhodesia and the part of Portuguese East Africa called Gazaland. Soshangane was a younger brother of Zwide, Chaka's greatest rival, and he moved north when Zwide was killed and defeated. The people of this horde will be heard of later; they contributed to the breaking up of the last remnants of the Empire of the Monomotapa and later still, when labour became a problem for the European farm-owners and miners of Rhodesia, they are heard of again under the name of Shangaans.

The second curve follows at first the same route as Soshangane's. Zwangendaba, the leader of this horde, had been a more or less independent chief allied to Zwide; on the defeat of his ally or overlord, he moved north, met Soshangane and his horde, lived beside him for a time, raiding the more peaceful neighbours and maintaining no doubt some amicable understanding as to poaching, but at last quarrelled with Soshangane and moved on, right across Southern Rhodesia, across the Zambezi near Zumbo, northwards into Nyasaland and the north-eastern part of

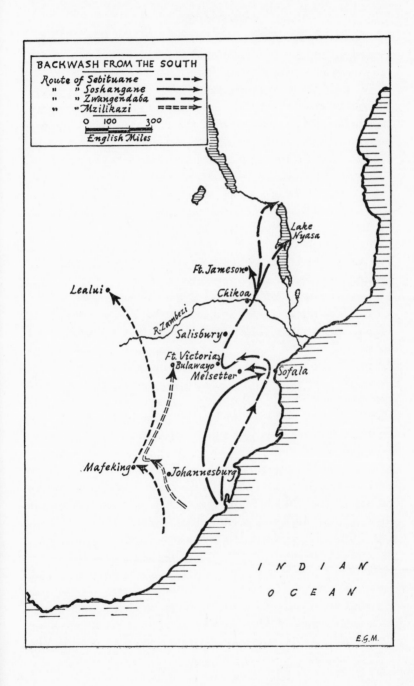

BACKWASH FROM THE SOUTH

Route of Sebituane
  "   " Soshangane
  "   " Zwangendaba
  "   " Mzilikazi

0   100   300
English Miles

Lake Nyasa

Ft. Jameson

Lealui

Chikoa

R. Zambezi

Salisbury

Ft. Victoria
Bulawayo
Melsetter

Sofala

Mafeking

Johannesburg

I N D I A N

O C E A N

E.G.M.

Northern Rhodesia. The horde divided, certain sections staying in Nyasaland and the neighbourhood of Fort Jameson, where they are usually known as Angoni.

The third thrust from Zululand is that of Mzilikazi, a general of Chaka's who turned away from him with his whole army and marched north into what is now the Transvaal. Here he apparently intended to settle—and it was incidentally here that Daniel Lindley intended to set up a mission station. But the wagons of the Great Trek one by one were heaved and tugged across the Vaal river; Mzilikazi's people attacked the Boers and were in their turn attacked and defeated. Mzilikazi and his people moved on across the Limpopo and settled in Matabeleland.

Mzilikazi left Zululand several years after the defeat of Zwide. His people, the Kumalo clan, had joined Chaka early and served under him for some time; they may be thought of as Zulus in the ordinary sense of the word, Nguni people militarized by Chaka. The hordes under Soshangane and Zwangendaba were Nguni neighbours whom Chaka had failed to assimilate; they must be thought of as what the Zulus might have been without Chaka. It might be said however of all these Nguni tribes that they were peoples whose 'external political relations were limited to acts of war'.[5] But there were exceptions to this; after they settled down in the Fort Jameson area, the Angoni seem to have reached some kind of agreement with their closer neighbours, by which they received regular tribute and free passage in return for immunity from raids, and the Matabele are said to have compounded with some of the closer Mashona groups in the same way.[6] But broadly, there can be no question that all these Nguni hordes preyed on their neighbours; all brought back cattle from their raids and absorbed into their own system women, children, and in some cases the more amenable males.

The fourth thrust to the north is Sebituane's from Basutoland. Sebituane was by all accounts a most unusual man; Livingstone describes him as 'of a tall and wiry form, an olive or coffee-and-milk complexion . . . the greatest warrior ever heard of beyond the colony. . . .'[7] He was born in Basutoland, of a chiefly family, though not himself a chief. He and many others went west and north-west from Basutoland in the early twenties into what later became British Bechuanaland; here they were repulsed by the Griquas, half-breed Dutch and Hottentots who lived in a semi-tribal organization, but who were better armed than the Basutos. Sebituane broke away from this defeat with a remnant, of whom he assumed the leadership; he went north, defeating a gathering of Bechuana tribes, suffering, according to Livingstone, 'severely in one of those attacks by white men in which murder is committed and materials laid up in the conscience for a future judgement'. This must have been an attack by the Transvaal Boers, who raided and destroyed Livingstone's own missionary station. Sebituane however survived this attack and several brushes with the Matabele; he went on across the desert, well to the west of Matabeleland, reached the Zambezi, and after various encounters moved into the plateau country between the Zambezi and the Kafue, and here established himself. But he was repeatedly attacked by the Matabele, and, although he always succeeded in driving them off, he decided to move again, being persuaded by a soothsayer to go west into what is now Barotseland.

Here there was an organized kingdom, torn at the time by internal dissension; Sebituane and his Makololo made themselves masters of the Lozi or Barotse,★ but behaved with so wise a tolerance that fifty years later, when Coillard began work there on behalf of the Paris Missionary Society, the Makololo were remembered with nothing but praise. The Lozi adopted their language and many of their forms of polite speech, but after Sebituane's death one of the Lozi princes who had fled to the north returned with an army and restored the Lozi dominion, exterminating the Makololo. But Sebituane is to be remembered;

★ To an English reader, Bantu names appear more confusing than they need because plurals and cases are conveyed by prefixes. The classic example is Baganda, the people, a plural; Buganda, the country where they live; Muganda, a member of the tribe. Ba-, Ma- and Wa- are often plurals; the Nguni use Ama- as a plural as in Ama-Zulu, Ama-Ndebele (which we have turned into Matabele). Si- or Chi- often indicates a language as Si-Ndabele, Chi-Nyanja.

he was a fierce warrior who led his men into battle himself and Livingstone speaks of his feeling the edge of his axe before battle and saying: 'Aha, it is sharp!'; he 'was so fleet of foot that all his people knew there was no escape for the coward', yet he had the rare wisdom of sparing those he had defeated and governing them in accordance with their own institutions and, as far as possible, through their own princes and nobles.

Section 3: The Preyers and the Prey

Thus the backwash of northward-moving hordes went in four thrusts to the four corners of what was to become the Federation —the Shangaans to the south-east, the Angoni to the north-east, the Matabele to the south-west, and the Makololo to the north-west. But of the Makololo nothing survives except their language; their kingdom returned to the Lozi. In the central part of this great land mass, the backwash had set up ripples and disturbances, but the people were still those who had been there hundreds of years before. Here there were many tribes, varied in many ways, yet all with certain Bantu characteristics. They are confusing to study, because they use different names for themselves at different times, while other people have other names for them; they split from time to time into various segments, and yet in a sense the segments may still be grouped together as one people and the relationship to each other of the founders of the various segments is remembered, much as among the tribes of Israel or the Pathans a kind of natural alliance persisted between tribes whose founders were supposed to be the sons of one mother.

It is not to my purpose to list, still less to describe, this multiplicity of peoples, but certain broad outlines must be drawn to illustrate the differences between them and the basic resemblances. First, there is the broad distinction already mentioned between the Conquest States and the rest, between the preyers and the preyed on, as clean as that between lions and antelopes, the eaters of flesh and the eaters of grass. The difference may be based on power rather than on inclination; perhaps all would have preyed if they could. But its existence is clear enough. The Matabele, the Barotse, the Bemba, the Angoni, and the Yao are the chief among the preyers, the lions, the eaters of flesh; the Mashona, the Tonga, the Cewa, are names for loose collections of groups among the antelopes, the preyed-on.★

Next comes a distinction, which at first sight seems almost to coincide with the first, between what has been called a primitive

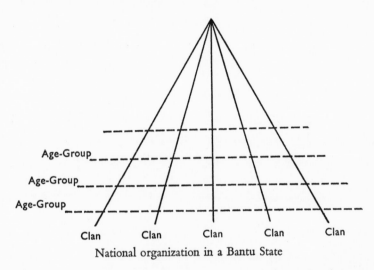

National organization in a Bantu State

state and a stateless society.[8] There is no need to spend many words on definition; there can be no question that the Matabele, the Barotse, the Bemba, and the Angoni were primitive states; they had a paramount chief or king and in each case a complicated organization and system of government in which there is a clear difference between what is national and what is merely sectional. The Matabele, for instance, like the Angoni and all the people of the Nguni group, were organized in such a way that the national organizations cut horizontally across the sectional. Every man had a number of allegiances. Every man, for instance, belonged to a clan, a group based in theory on descent from one ancestor, like the tribes of Israel and the Scottish clans; the clans may be pictured as divided by lines vertical or converging to a

★ See Map III.

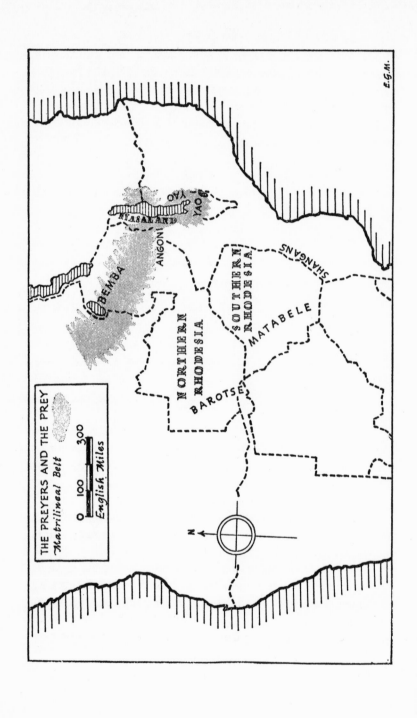

THE PREYERS AND THE PREY
Matrilineal Belt

0   100   300
English Miles

N

NYASALAND
YAO
YAO
ANGONI
BEMBA
NORTHERN RHODESIA
SOUTHERN RHODESIA
SHANGANS
MATABELE
BAROTSE

E.G.M.

point. But he also belonged to a regiment, composed of men of his own age, which cut horizontally across the clan system and might include men of any clan. There were other groupings too, but these are enough to illustrate the point. There were no such horizontal groupings among the tribes loosely known as the Mashona.

Four of the peoples mentioned as the principal preyers have also been mentioned as having a state organization. They were the Conquest States. But the Yao were a stateless people, though emphatically carnivores, their main livelihood coming from the slave-trade. In Livingstone's time, as now, they were to be found round the south end of Lake Nyasa and on the south-east and south-west shores of the lake, having apparently eddied back in this direction from further to the south-east. Mostly Muslims, they acted as collecting agents for the Arabs, who were the wholesalers in the slave trade; the Yao would raid a village, take away all those capable of carrying a tusk of ivory, link them together in long chains, and when a purchaser came along who had cloth, guns, and gunpowder to trade for them, start them on the journey to the coast. These raids were carried out for profit and were thus quite different from the Angoni's, of which the object was to strengthen the state by assimilating captives. The Yao had no paramount chief and no horizontal organizations which cut across the vertical groupings based on descent.

There is a third distinction to be made, between the tribes among whom descent was reckoned through the father and those among whom descent was reckoned through the mother.* As a rule, it was the eastern tribes who reckoned through the mother; a broad band of these people stretches eastwards and southwards from the Katanga area to Lake Nyasa. Into this band, the Angoni thrust in as interlopers from the south and of course count descent through the father. But among the Yao a man's sons hardly belong to him. His heir is his sister's son, the grandson of his mother, and he has a considerable say in the upbringing of his sister's son. Daughters continue to live in their mother's

* See Map III.

village and their husbands usually come to them from outside; a man seems far less at home in his wife's village than in his mother's, where he is with the group to whom he really belongs. The eldest brother is responsible for the protection, good behaviour, and even the health of his sisters, while a wife in case of difficulty or dispute will often turn to her brother rather than her husband and will side with her brother in a dispute against her husband.[9]

Among these people who count descent through the mother, there are many variations of custom; in some tribes the husband must serve a kind of apprenticeship before he is accepted as really belonging to his wife's family and can set up house on his own. In some tribes he can then take a wife to his own home, but in others he normally makes his own principal home in his wife's village, though he will spend a great deal of time in his mother's village looking after his sisters. And there are variations within the tribe; among the Bemba a man related to the royal family can usually keep control of his own children as well as his sister's. In general among the Bemba, the husband seems to have been more successful in asserting and maintaining his rights than among the Yao.[10] Of the five predatory tribes, the Bemba and Yao are matrilineal, while the Lozi count their descent in both lines, male and female, and each have a number of 'homes' with grandparents of either line; children belong to both parents and in the case of divorce, which is frequent, may go to either. But it will make for clarity if one Bantu kingdom is described in greater detail.

III. One Bantu Kingdom

None of these Bantu-speaking peoples had made much advance in those material aspects of life which make it possible to accumulate wealth or to provide for the future. Their architecture was simple and short-lived; they built thatched round huts of poles and mud and could conceive of nothing else. As he drew near the West Coast, Livingstone tried to explain to his Makololo that they would see two-storied houses, but the idea of putting one house on top of another seemed to them absurd. 'Why, the poles from the lower house would stick up through the floor of the top house,' they argued. Their pottery was crude; they had no wheel and did not use the plough. They could work iron and made keen blades for spears; they could weave baskets that would hold water but only here and there were there to be found any who wove cloth. It followed that the standard of comfort of a chief was much the same as the simplest of his subjects. He had plenty to eat; he had plenty of wives; he need not build huts or clear the bush; that was the difference between his life and a commoner's.

This lack of economic development was perhaps partly due to the fact that there was still no shortage of land; agriculture was everywhere of the most primitive order but that did not matter because it was possible to move on when the soil was exhausted. There was no incentive to improve the soil. In Bechuanaland, Moffat wrote:

When they first saw us employ people to convey the contents of our cattle-folds to our gardens . . . they laughed boisterously, supposing it to be one of our foolish customs, to 'charm the ground' . . . their own custom being to chew a certain root and spit on the leaves of a plant to make it more fruitful. . . . It was long before they could be convinced. . . .[1]

It was a wide-spread custom to make 'a garden' by cutting down trees and shrubs and burning them as they lay on the ground, sometimes adding to the pile of boughs from other trees in the neighbourhood. This was the man's work; his wives were responsible for sowing and cutting. Seeds would be thrown into the ashes and the first rain would cause germination. Everyone recognized that after three or four years a garden would get old and the soil weak; then it was time to move on. Either the whole village moved on or the man whose wives had cultivated the garden asked permission to take in a new piece of ground. Because there was plenty of land, this system provided enough for the needs most people felt; the problem to which manure is the answer had as yet hardly arisen.

To an Englishman with the least knowledge of agriculture this will seem almost unbelievably primitive, but in fact where rainfall is low so that crops often fail or where the peace is so precarious that fallow periods are enforced, manuring is hardly needed. In the early days of British rule in Central India, a traveller, William Sleeman, was often told that everyone was delighted to have peace at last, but the crops were getting poorer and poorer. This was put down to impiety, and no one was disposed to agree when Sleeman suggested that when the country had been torn by Pindari and Maratha raids, whole villages were often left deserted for two or three years and thus compelled to lie fallow and renew their fertility. Even today manure is hardly needed in the dry margins of Rajputana because two crops in three fail to germinate.

To this point about agriculture, the Lozi of Barotseland are to some extent an exception; they differ from other Central African peoples in living on a plain which is flooded every year, so that every year they have to leave the plain and stay in villages in the surrounding hills. The villages of the plain are built on mounds and have stood there for many generations, while the cultivated plots have been refreshed and enriched year after year by the floods; the mounds which stand up above the floods have naturally been used as pens for cattle and goats. That is perhaps one reason why the Lozi had a more complex organization than the other kingdoms; perhaps it was because of their fixed self-fertilizing lands that they had, before the Europeans came, specialized slightly more than the others in craftsmanship—though even among them one man could produce little more than he could consume himself, so that here too the King was not much better off as regards comfort than a serf.[2]

It has been said that the measuring of land began in the Nile valley because the floods obliterated field boundaries, which had to be renewed every year; the Lozi are thought to have come into the plain from the north-west, and, since Lewanika, who died in 1916, was distant in the mythology of his people by only nine generations from the Creator of all, they cannot have been there long. Perhaps in another thirty generations they too would have begun to measure land and have evolved a geometry.

The Lozi are the best people to illustrate one broad generalization about the Bantu of Central Africa, not because they are typical but because they display the point more clearly than anyone else. By the time they met the first Europeans, the Bantu-speaking people had not so far shown much initiative or invention in material matters; they had however developed an extremely complicated system of social relationships, and in some cases complicated political and administrative arrangements. To a European of today it may well seem that if only the Lozi had spent less time and thought on the loyalties, the jealousies, the social subtleties of their kingdom, they might have made more progress in material inventions; it may be that this argues a profound difference in their outlook on the world. The Lozi are a good example of the point for a second reason; there is a detailed account of his life among them by a missionary who for thirty years looked at them from the fixed platform of a dogmatic Protestant Christianity, to be contrasted with a brilliant portrait by a modern anthropologist,* from which some reconstruction of their past state is possible.

* In what follows, I am summarizing and interpreting Dr. Max Gluckman unless specific reference is made to someone else; I am also describing, unless

There seems to be a feeling among the Lozi that men and women are complementary to each other in a way that hardly arises among the Zulu groups. Descent is reckoned, as I have said, through both male and female lines and there are duplicate courts, or centres of government, headed by a King and a Lord of the South, who is now usually a woman. Her title is literally Earth of the South; she must always be geographically to the South of the King or Paramount Chief even when she is away from home on a visit; at the gathering to meet King George VI her camp had to be pitched South of the Paramount Chief's. His title is literally 'Great One of the Earth'. There is, however, nothing so simple as a boundary between the two jurisdictions; her villages are interspersed among his. Her court duplicates his; there are the same counsellors and officers, though they all rank after the King's; her court is not subordinate but parallel and below. But in important national decisions, such as making war, the South would follow the North, because the King *is* the land and the nation, and the land and the nation *are* the King.

In each Court, the Council consists of the King and the three Estates of the Realm—the High Office Bearers, the Junior Office Bearers, and the Members of the Royal Family. There are many office bearers with titles which are handed on from one holder to another, a hierarchy in which promotion can be obtained by those who win good opinions. There are Senior and Junior Committees of Council representing the Commons and the Chiefs; there is also a smaller Executive Committee, on each of which each of the three Estates is represented. Any matter might be raised in any of the committees and if need be might be discussed by all three before the full council met. The King makes formal appearances in full council, but it is not his custom to give decisions in open council; the ideal is to let every councillor have his say, starting with the junior, and to reach agreement, not

the contrary is stated, the constitution of the state in its ideal form and therefore use the present tense, although historically much must have been changed by European rule and I am not sure that Professor Gluckman would maintain that there had been one historical moment when it had been exactly as he describes it.

only between individuals but between the three sub-committees, before a report is sent to the King for his concurrence or the reverse. 'All day long,' says Dr. Gluckman, 'streams of messengers go backwards and forwards between the King and his Council' ... 'Kingship is divided between the king and his council'—and within the council power is balanced with the most careful precision between the different elements.

A word should be added about two of the many offices carrying perpetual titles. The Ngambela is the most important of all Lozi offices. The Ngambela is not what the Diwan was to a Mogul Emperor or to a Khalif of Islam, nor what the Chancellor was to a German Emperor; he is not the servant of the King but has a position of his own. He is appointed by the King and is his chief counsellor and judge and the head of his executive; the word is used not only of the great Ngambela, the senior title-holder of the state, but of the chief adviser and representative of every office bearer, down to village headman. Used in this way, it means almost 'deputy'; but the great Ngambela, once appointed, has a chieftainship of his own. He represents the people as against the King and provides a sanctuary from the King's anger. He ought not to be of the royal house. King and Ngambela may not sleep in the same house or travel together, just as in British India the District Judge and the executive head of the district were not allowed to share a house. One prohibition took the form of a taboo and the other of a government order, but the purpose was clearly the same. The second great office is that of Natamoyo, the sanctuary; if a condemned man can reach Natamoyo, he is safe.

These two offices illustrate the balance of power but they are only the beginning of the complexity of the Lozi system. The people are divided into 'sectors', which have little connexion with where they live, but are something between a Scottish clan and the hereditary membership of a political party whose differences as to policy have been forgotten; each man is also an adherent of a 'storehouse', which has nothing to do with his sector and was originally no doubt an economic unit, devised for the payment of tribute and the sharing out of loot after a war, or of game after one of the immense organized hunts of the Lozi. But each storehouse has a member of council as its head, so that every man owes allegiance, to begin with, to the King, to his Prime Minister the Ngambela, to the head of his sector and to the head of his storehouse; in addition, he is likely to be specially associated with at least one member of the royal family and at least one other senior official, not to mention the headman of his village and the four grandparents with whom he has 'homes'.

'Every Lozi,' writes Dr. Gluckman, 'is the centre of a nexus of ties to a whole body of titled councillors, queens, members of the royal family.' These ties change and are partly but not entirely superseded by new ties; all carry obligations, among which the Lozi 'move with consummate skill'. It is no wonder that sixty years earlier Coillard had written: 'These are the most polished people in the world and I think they even outdo the Parisians.' But it may be added that Coillard makes this point about Lozi manners as a contrast to their actions, his pen having just refused to give details 'of the atrocities committed at Sesheke itself on women and little children'.[3]

The Lozi had a saying that other people might have other skills, but theirs was the one special art of ruling.* They were the centre of an Empire; the outlying vassal states or satellites were given considerable freedom to follow their own customs and there was a constant flow inward of young people who were absorbed into the system of the central plain. From the favoured satellites, children were honoured by being chosen by the King; from the outer satellites and beyond, children were seized, by raids in which the grown men were usually killed, but both 'the honoured' and 'the seized' were brought up within the family of those to whom they were allotted and became indistinguishable from Lozi proper.

Law among the Lozi is highly developed, and its ingredients

---

* Others have had the same belief:
        Tu regere imperio populos, Romane, memento;
        Hae tibi erunt artes, pacisque imponere morem,
        Parcere subjectis et debellare superbos.

are not very different from those of the Common Law of Great
Britain and the United States. 'The sources to which the judges
turn', writes Professor Goodhart,[4] 'are in almost all respects the
same: viz. custom, judicial precedent, legislation, equity, morality, public policy, and the laws of physical nature. The chief
distinction is found in the fact that the Lozi precedents have not
been recorded in writing.' And in procedure too there is the
similarity that both parties have the right to be heard and that
there is a distinction between direct evidence and hearsay. There is
too a distinction between law—'a set of rules . . . defining reasonable ways in which people ought to behave . . .'—and the in-
junctions of morality; 'the law', says Professor Gluckman,
'defines right and reasonable ways of acting; the ways of morality
are right and generous'. In some of the cases he quotes the distinction to the Lozi mind (and incidentally to mine) seems to be
between what is proper and may be enforced and what is desirable but cannot be enforced; in The Case of the Ungenerous
Husband, for instance, the judge said: 'We have power to make
you divide the crops, for this is our law, and we will . . . see this
is done. But we have not power to make you behave like an
upright man.' Be that as it may, the distinction between law and
morality is there, for the Lozi at least; with less highly organized
people, it is probably blurred, and the idea of a body of law is
probably less distinct; each case is more likely to be regarded by
itself as an attempt to put things right in accordance with
tradition; the ritual element is much stronger among some
peoples.[5] Among the Lozi, however, the conception of justice
and equity, the idea of the reasonable man and what he may
reasonably be expected to do, the need to hear both sides of a
case and to cross-examine thoroughly, the idea of a body of
precedents among which there is likely to be a parallel for any
given dispute—all these are highly developed and are derived
from their own native institutions.

Here then is Dr. Gluckman's careful drawing of a smoothly
oiled social machine in which political power is checked, divided
out, and controlled, like the thrust of the spring in a well regu-

lated clock; it is a drawing of a society, a drawing from which individuals are on the whole excluded, which is concerned to depict the objects at which the society aims rather than its actual achievement. It is a diagram of the Platonic ideal, not a sketch of sordid life, a loving concept of perfect beauty by Praxiteles rather than a harsh satire by Hogarth.

Turn now to a picture by another hand. François Coillard was a French Protestant, that is a Calvinist, writing and living in Victorian times; his dogmatic platform of values was never shaken by doubt. He was a simple man, a very good man. His faith was such that he laboured for years, losing one companion after another by fever, to win a single soul. He spent thirty of the best years of his life in the Zambezi valley. During much of this time he was either himself teaching in a school for Lozi boys or supervising schools for both boys and girls; he spent hours, when at the capital, in close touch with the King, Lewanika; he spent weeks in laborious travel with Lozis or people of subject tribes as his only companions. He writes with a freshness that is vivid today, describing his hopes and disappointments; he is concerned not with a society but with men and women whose souls he hopes to guide to eternal joy; where he does speak of the society, he is interested in its working in practice rather than in its objects. He is, it must be remembered, writing during the period which came after the extermination of the Makololo, when Lewanika had won the throne by civil war, when he was still far from secure; Dr. Gluckman writes more than forty years after Lewanika came under British protection.

The [Lozi] chiefs [writes Coillard] are always exposed to secret assassination, are naturally suspicious and afraid of each other. . . . When ambassadors come from the capital, no one knows whether, besides the ostensible message they bring, they have not a secret commission to murder someone.[6]

On his return to the capital after a long absence, they said to him: 'You will soon discover that we have yellow hearts (i.e. are jealous of each other) and that our country is a country of blood. The nation is weary; it sighs for peace; it languishes . . . what we seek for is peace.'

Coillard was fluent in the language of the Basutos before he reached the Zambezi and the language left behind by Sebituane was only slightly different; he preached long sermons to Lewanika and his chiefs. They approved when he told them that the King in the sight of God was a servant who had to give an account of his administration, that his subjects were God's creatures and he had no right to put them to death without trial. But they laughed when he spoke to them of theft: 'Everyone steals here,' they said, and it was true. 'In the daytime,' wrote Coillard, 'they come to see us, ask for snuff, talk and are as friendly as possible; and then contrive, before your very eyes, to slip a knife, a hatchet, napkins, or calico, under their armpits.' And again, 'It is hard to recognize our own shirts and stuffs on the greasy backs of chiefs of the second and third degree.'

But he is describing the same people as Gluckman. 'At seven in the morning and three in the afternoon, the king, followed by the drums, the serimbas,* and sometimes his ministers goes in procession' to hear justice. 'Should anyone be accused by the King's order and pursued by a crowd of his emissaries, if he can put his feet inside the court of the Natamoyo, he is saved. Moreover, when the King wishes to assure himself of a man's death, he takes measures to prevent the Natamoyo from knowing anything about it, so that the man may not escape. Alas! In spite of all these precautions, there are few countries more stained in human blood. Sitting in the *lekhotla* (assembly or court) I passed in review these hundreds of men without recognizing one of those whose acquaintance I had made the previous year. "We threw them out," they say, "to the vultures; their bones are bleaching in the sun." ' And again, he writes of the days after Lewanika's succession that the wives of all the chiefs who fled or have been massacred have been divided up among others, 'but the children—those dear little children, some of them so intelligent and so lovable—have all been put to death, to the very last one.

* Serimbas are glockenspiels or xylophones.

They bring us heart-rending details of this horrible tragedy.' And in another place he says: 'The life of a little being, elsewhere cherished, is not of much value—a trifling excuse is sufficient to sacrifice it. It cries, worries its mother, annoys its father, or is perhaps an obstacle to a new marriage. It need not matter! Its mother stuffs its mouth with ashes, digs her nails into its throat and at night the poor little corpse is thrown out on to the dung-hill. . . .'

Coillard's account of his relations with Lewanika brings out by implication the curiosity and the attraction, the exasperation, misunderstanding, affection, and suspicion which each felt for the other. Lewanika took to Coillard from the first, as we have seen, and he was influenced by the example of Khama the Great, Chief of the Bamangwato, who had decided to throw in his lot and that of his tribe unreservedly with the missionaries in religion and with the British in politics. He did not hesitate to proclaim Sunday as a day of rest and order people to listen to Coillard. 'On Sunday morning he came to the *lekhotla* without his drums and collected his people by calling them publicly. There was a fine audience, serious and attentive.' On another occasion, when Coillard had preached on the commandment 'Thou shalt not kill' and had said that kings are the shepherds of the people and servants who will have to give an account of their stewardship, 'The King hung his head and said to the Gambella (the Ngambela) "The words of the missionary have sunk into my heart." . . . He . . . asked me to say them all over again. . . . They made me all sorts of fine promises; no more ordeals by boiling water, no more poison, no more burning at the stake. . . .'

But these good intentions did not last long. Coillard contrasts the care the Basutos took of their cattle with the reckless extravagance of the Lozi, who 'kill and eat, like greedy children, beginning with the best. When the herd has vanished, each man looks at his neighbour and raises the cry: "To the Mashukulumbo"'—that is, to the tribes to the east whom they regarded as their natural prey. Once, when he had determined on such an expedition, Lewanika came to Coillard to excuse himself. '"They ill-treated Dr. Holub, who had just come from me; it is my duty to chastise them. Besides, they are not human beings; they are quite naked. And then," he added hesitatingly, "and then . . . we have no more cattle and we absolutely must have some. But you may be sure it is our very last expedition. On our return, we will . . . all become believers, all Christians . . . all." '

Lewanika had had to fight for his throne; having got it, he pursued his enemies relentlessly and showed no mercy when he caught them. These were the standards of his time and surroundings. But he emerges from every account of him as a man of some nobility, of strong feelings and anxious to do right, a man who would not infringe his own standards of what was fitting. Years later Colin Harding went with him to London and recorded that 'in no single act did Lewanika or his staff commit an offence or even an indiscretion . . .'.[7] And again he writes: 'From an intimate knowledge of King Lewanika covering a period of six years I can . . . say that never did Lewanika lie or deceive me.' For Harding, and for many other Englishmen, Lewanika might pass the standards required for a gentleman; Coillard's standards however were higher. He wrote:

There are great contradictions in this man. He is despotic, vindictive, and as cruel as possible; yet with all that he has good sense, tact, generosity, and amiability. I could easily draw two portraits of him which would have nothing in common.

He listened to Coillard's teaching about slavery and prevented the Mambaris—traders, often with Portuguese blood—from buying his people and taking them away to the West Coast. 'Where do you come from?' was the question Coillard heard addressed to a stranger, 'that you think you can still buy slaves under Lewanika?' But Lewanika could not bring himself to become a Christian, as Khama had; his wives stood in the way; how could he desert them all? And sudden fits of exasperation would overcome him when he thought the missionary had played him false or even refused to help him. 'We are accused of having deceived the king. . . . Bitter little notes and unpleasant echoes brought to my ears the insults the poor man was raining on my head, surrounded by his flatterers and courtiers. . . . What was not our astonishment to learn . . . that Lewanika has in secret sent a young man who attends school . . . here an order to strangle all the workmen who are working here for me!' And on another occasion, Lewanika cried in a fit of anger: 'What good are you all? What do I want with a Gospel that gives neither guns nor powder nor coffee nor tea nor sugar nor workmen to work for me. . . ?' And once again there was a boycott and orders to strangle anyone who worked for the missionaries or sold them anything.

These were passing storms; Lewanika had 'given himself' to Coillard 'to the end' when they first met.[8] And towards the end of their long friendship, one day when he was 'reluctantly taking his leave', Lewanika looked round Coillard's room and said: 'This is my home; I have no other. I have twenty-one wives, but no home!'

IV. Temples and Gold

Section 1: The Empire of the Monomotapa

To these two portraits of the Lozi state might be added half a dozen slighter sketches; Selous on a hunting trip goes to stay with Coillard and pays his respects to Lewanika; the French traveller Bertrand, the missionary Arnot, and later Colin Harding, the son of a Devonshire squire, a police officer under the British South Africa Company—all record impressions more like Coillard's than Gluckman's. The travellers and missionaries noted the imperfections they saw, judging by their own standards, contrasting with their own customs; the anthropologist divests himself of all affection for his own traditions, draws out the intention behind the custom and displays the state as it ought to be, the Platonic ideal. Yet one picture is incomplete without the other.

There is a significant story in one of Selous' books;[1] he was among the Mashukulumbo—the people Lewanika had argued were not really human—at the beginning of an expedition, when he had plenty of powder and bullets, several rifles and trade goods; he was at first received hospitably but was treacherously attacked in the night. The fire blazed up as one of his attackers threw on a handful of dry grass; he rolled away into the darkness and long grass and lay without weapons, unable to intervene, listening to the sounds of a murderous assault. Twelve of the men with him were killed—as he learnt later; for the moment he knew only that he could not find any of them. He was alone in Central Africa, north of the Zambezi, hundreds of miles from any centre where Europeans were known and taken for granted; he was unarmed and had nothing but what he stood up in. He made for the village of the nearest Lozi chief, Sikabenga, a relation of Lewanika's

55

and in arms against him. Selous had not met Sikabenga but knew that he was acquainted with Westbeech, a trader friend of his; he knew that as a Lozi he represented a state, even though he was in rebellion against it; he was in short a point of comparative stability and civilization among the naked and ill-organized Tonga and Mashukulumbo. To Sikabenga then he turned for help, and it does not really affect the point that it was Sika-benga—as Selous learnt long afterwards—who had told the Mashukulumbo to murder him for the sake of his rifles and powder. Nor is this the place to tell how Selous escaped in the end.

There were four states in Central Africa before the Pioneer Column came; as well as the Lozi there were the Matabele, the Angoni, and the Bemba. Of the Matabele and the Angoni we shall hear more later; the Bemba were 'a tall spare muscular people of very mixed type'[2] who moved some two or three centuries ago into what is now Northern Rhodesia from the Congo; their empire roughly covered 'the area between the four big lakes, Nyasa, Tanganyika, Mweru, and Bangweulu'. They were warriors and hunters; even today it is said to be still difficult to interest them in trade or any kind of craft. Their King, who traces his descent back in the female line for twenty-five holders of the title, is emphatically the head of the state; he appoints the members of his family to lieutenant-governorships of outlying provinces and as their seniority increases they are translated to senior appointments nearer home. The worship of the King's ancestors is the state religion, and a man's prestige was formerly reckoned by his relationship to the King, whether a relationship of blood or of service.[3]

One state has been described at some length and must serve as an example that to some extent illustrates the others. Among the disorganized groups, too, one must serve as an example. The Mashona, who are not a tribe but a group of tribes, are important for a number of reasons. It was among them that the Pioneers settled in 1890 and it was rumours from their country that first aroused the cupidity and the romantic curiosity of white men.

Their history has puzzled and intrigued everyone who has thought about it and has usually been interpreted in the light of theories evolved as much from emotion as from experience, based as much on fears for the future as on facts known of the past. Anthropology, history, and archaeology impinge on each other at every turn in Africa; there is no space to deal at equal length with all three, and in so far as that mixture permits, it is with the past of the Mashona, with a mixture of archaeology and history, that this chapter will deal.

It was from the Mashona country that there flowed to the south the rumours of gold and of temples built with stone, all that led men to dream of King Solomon's Mines and the Queen of Sheba's treasure-house. From the earliest period of Portuguese settlement, there had been reports of an Emperor in the interior called Monomotapa—or the Monomotapa, for it was not at first clear whether it was a name or a title—and of a stone temple or fort with writings on the walls. That there was gold was beyond doubt. Quills of gold-dust came down to Sofala in trade and everyone believed that there was a far greater abundance to be had for the digging. The first news of it came from the Portuguese, by the eastern approach; later it was confirmed by British and Afrikaners from the south.

All through the later nineteenth century, hunters brought back news of piles of quartz and shallow gold workings in what is now Southern Rhodesia; in 1867, Henry Hartley and Carl Mauch came back from an expedition into Southern Rhodesia and Mauch described the goldfields he had discovered in the most extravagant terms.[4] Rhodesia was believed to be the Ophir of the Bible and the source of much of antiquity's gold; a rush to the goldfields was expected, but the Tati Goldfield was discovered on the borders of Bechuanaland and Matabeleland, and soon afterwards diamonds were found in the Vaal river. Here were sources of wealth closer at hand than Rhodesia; prospectors put off the day when they would start looking in earnest for the more distant gold in whose existence the soberest believed. But when at last the pioneers came, they found no Monomotapa; indeed, long before 1890 they had learnt that his Empire was no more.

There had been a daring and brilliant exploration as early as 1514, when Antonio Fernandez twice travelled over much of what is now Southern Rhodesia. He went to the Court of the Monomotapa and paid his respects to him at Mbiri, north of Salisbury and near Mount Darwin; he passed near what are now Salisbury and Umtali.[5] Six years later, in 1520, a chronicle gives the first account of the Empire of Monomotapa or Benomotapa.

The chronicler, Damiao de Goes, recalls Herodotus and his tale of a king of Ethiopia who used gold for the fetters of felons in his dungeons; he believes that in the realms of the Monomotapa gold is almost as common. Besides his own central kingdom, which lies inland from Sofala, the Benomotapa is Emperor over many vassals who pay tribute in gold; his rule stretches almost to the Cape of Good Hope.

'In the middle of this country is a fortress built of heavy stones inside and out; it is a very curious and well-constructed building as according to report no lime to join the stones can be seen. An inscription is cut in stone over the entrance, so ancient that no one understands what it means. In other districts . . . there are other fortresses built in the same manner, in all of which the King has captains. . . .'[6] These fortresses and their garrisons are strategically placed by the King to guard the gold mines. The country is abundant in provisions, fruits, and cattle; four or five thousand wild elephants are killed there every year. The inhabitants are black with woolly hair and are called Kaffirs;* they have no idols but worship one God, who is the creator of all things. No crime is punished so severely as witchcraft. The Emperor keeps great state but he and all his people live in huts of wattle and daub. He carries a small ivory hoe to show that agriculture is the basis of his empire and two assegais, symbolic of his double duty to protect and judge his people. Every year he sends people through the land to put out the old fires and light new ones in the King's

---

* *Kafir* is an Arabic word which means one who does not believe, applied by Muslims to Christians as well as pagans. The Portuguese learnt the term from the Arabs; on Christian lips, it must ring ironically on Muslim ears.

name. He has 'as many wives as he can support', but the first is mistress of the rest and her children are the heirs.

This does not sound very different from one of the Bantu states we know of. The Lozi, for instance, still perform a fire-lighting ceremony very like this; so do the Lovedu of the Transvaal, who came from Southern Rhodesia when their ancestor split from the Monomotapa. Thirty years later, another chronicler, de Barros, also writes of the Benomotapa and his dry-stone fortress and others like it, and adds:

> The Natives of the country call all these edifices Symbaoe, which according to their language signifies court, for every place where Benomotapa may be is so called, and they say that being royal property all the king's dwellings have this name.[7]

Not much except the name, Symbaoe or Zimbabwe, is really added by de Barros; he is off the mark when he says the buildings are made of vast stones and far superior to Portuguese work at Sofala in respect of windows and arches. But one of his remarks is worth recording: the kingdom has 'many customs strange to us which appear to be dictated by good policy, according to their barbarous ideas'. That is written in the spirit of the anthropologist.

A century later, Antonio Bocarro, Keeper of the Archives and Chronicler of India from 1631-49, gives a list of the countries tributary to the 'Manomotapa', including the names of some tribes still to be found in Mashonaland, such as Manica and Waungwe, in both of which cases he gives the tribe a chief with the hereditary title used today.[8] He says all the old Monomotapas were buried at a palace held to be 'a great piece of work', but no longer in their dominions. He also says that the central core of the Monomotapa's empire is called Mocaranga. Another chronicler[9] speaks of the 'Reine de Munhay ou de Mocranga'; in the missionaries' and hunters' reminiscences of Victorian times Makalanga is a name widely used for most of the tribes on whom the Matabele preyed, while Coillard always speaks of the Southern Mashona as 'Banyae'—to which 'Munhay' would be the singular.* Of the Wa-Karanga who survive under that name today, we shall hear later.

Bocarro's account of the empire of the Monomotapa is detailed and convincing. There is a regular traffic of light vessels called almadias from the mouths of the Zambezi up the river to Tete and thence goods are taken to Luanza, thirty leagues south of Tete. Here there is a Portuguese official called the Captain of the Gates; he was installed at the request of the Monomotapa and all negotiations with the Monomotapa pass through his hands. Like everyone before and many to come after, Bocarro thinks the country is unbelievably rich in gold; nuggets of natural gold weighing as much as 4,000 cruzados are found lying on the surface of the ground. There is a great mountain called Fura from which Moorish tradition says that the Queen of Sheba took many camel loads of gold. But 'the Kafirs are too lazy to dig for gold unless compelled by the need for food or clothes' and as the country abounds in provisions, this is not often the case.

Zimbabwe, the traditional home and burial place of the King's ancestors is now in the hands of the King of Beza, a powerful vassal: at the Monomotapa's present court he lives inside a high wooden fence, within which are three sections of many dwellings, one for him, one for his queens and one for his servants. There is a list of high officials; they seem to be titles, rather than names, as among the Lozi, and include at least one title, Mangwende, borne by a chief today. The King is served by specially chosen boys, who must be chaste until they are twenty; then they leave the King's domestic service and become officials, rising to be ambassadors and eventually lords of wide lands. The great wife is a 'sister' of the King—which may of course mean a cousin or half-sister; there are nine queens, each the head of a bevy[10] of wives and concubines and each allotted certain royal villages or districts, again as among the Lozi. There must always be nine such queens

---

* Some tribes find the English 'R' difficult to pronounce and some the 'L'; a Mashona servant talking English today is inclined to say 'runch is ready'; one who speaks Sindabele will prefer 'lunch is leady'. Hence the Mashona Maka-ranga became Makalanga to the Matabele. And Wa-Karanga is simply another plural form, alternative to Ma-Karanga.

and if one dies, another woman is promoted to her place.

Some of this can be checked indirectly; three hundred years later, for instance, Selous had, as he says himself, the impertinence to rename Fura, Mount Darwin; he found many old workings for gold and some washable gold still in the river that rises in the mountain but 'not enough to pay Europeans'. The general picture extends and confirms de Goes's portrait of a Bantu state, very like the Lozi state or the Bemba. But the Monomotapa is already far on the downward path; exiled from his ancient capital, he sounds like a ruler living on the prestige of his past, despised as a power but still useful as a symbol.

The viceroys of the Mogul Emperor in the eighteenth century, wrote Macaulay, 'might still acknowledge in words the super-iority of the house of Tamerlane, as a Count of Flanders or a Duke of Burgundy might have acknowledged the superiority of the most helpless driveller among the later Carlovingians. They might occasionally send to their titular sovereign a com-plimentary present or solicit from him a title of honour. In truth however, they were no longer lieutenants removable at pleasure but independent hereditary princes. . . .' Something like this seems to have been happening to the Monomotapa, though his vassals had probably never been 'lieutenants removable at pleasure'; like the later Mogul Emperors, he had been superseded as a source of political and military power, but retained almost magical prestige. The same fate befell the Raja of Satara among the Marathas and one could think of many parallels. Bocarro says that the Emperor's own tribe, the Makaranga nation, were in his day already 'a feeble people', and he describes two occasions when only Portuguese help prevented his defeat by his vassals. After this, in the presence of a number of Portuguese, the Mono-motapa gave the King of Portugal all the mines of gold, copper, iron, and lead, in his dominions, but the silver mines he made a personal present to Diogo Simoës Madeira, who had helped him most. But he was defeated, though not finally, not long after-wards by the 'Baroes' under a chief called Makobe.

All this fits in with another tradition. The Ma-Karanga or

Wa-Karanga today have no memory of former greatness, and are not very pleased to acknowledge their tribal name;[11] the Lovedu of the Transvaal, however, a people whose religion and whole way of life centre round a divine queen who is a supreme rainmaker, say that she is a descendant of the Monomotapa and that they were Wa-Karanga—though they are inclined—it is said—to wonder whether they can really have any connexion with the present Wa-Karanga, who are so far from glorious in their traditions. The Lovedu say they left Southern Rhodesia when a daughter ran away with the Monomotapa's rainmaking medicine; their queens are descended from her and perhaps more is to be learnt of the Monomotapa from them, or from their neighbours the Venda, than from the Wa-Karanga.[12]

The Monomotapa's Empire was, then, already breaking up when Bocarro wrote in the mid-seventeenth century, about the time the Lovedu left. In the early nineteenth century, when the backwash of the Zulu tribes reached Rhodesia, the Mashona tribes were under the leadership of a people called the Rozwi; many Mashona chiefs to this day are not regarded by themselves or their people as properly installed unless a ceremony has been carried out by a representative of the Rozwi. So it looks as though the Rozwi, under their chief the Mambo, somehow took the place of the Monomotapa and his Karanga—but whether by military action alone is not clear. Certainly they seem to have assumed his function as rainmaker with a special magical ascendancy;[13] it has been suggested that even before they were defeated in battle by the Zulus the Rozwi were not so much military as spiritual leaders.

There are traditions that the Rozwi lived in Zimbabwe and the other ruins and there were tales among the Shona of how the Rozwi had tried to move a mountain and of how they had tried to build a tower that would reach to heaven, suggestions that they had undertaken some great work and were supposed to possess some partly divine powers. The Portuguese say nothing of the Rozwi—though in Bocarro's list of powerful officials there is Maguende, and today Mangwende is a Rozwi Chief, of the Wanoe clan, living at Mrewa. It may be that the Ba-Rozwi are the people over whom the Monomotapa ruled, known now by another name. But it seems more likely that they displaced the Wa-Karanga by a palace revolution, though one might have expected that they would have preserved for the Wa-Karanga some magical function, as a Rajput Chief at his accession had to be marked with the blood of a Bhil. And it looks as though by the beginning of the nineteenth century, when the Zulu tribes began to wash back from the south, the Ba-Rozwi had begun that descent from an Empire based on power to an Empire based on prestige, a descent on which so many other imperial peoples have found their feet reluctantly set, a descent on which they themselves had speeded the Wa-Karanga.

Section 2: *The Ruins of Zimbabwe*

Thanks to the Portuguese, the Monomotapa is a less shadowy figure than most of his Bantu contemporaries. But it looks as though the Monomotapa and the Wa-Karanga were supplanted by the Wa-Rozwi, and it may be that the Monomotapa too supplanted someone else; it certainly cannot be assumed that Zimbabwe or the gold workings are necessarily the work of the Monomotapa and his Empire.

Pause a moment, and consider the walls of Zimbabwe. They have excited the imagination of everyone who has seen them; like the Pyramids, they have also excited surmise of the wildest nature and served as a foundation for theories not very defensible in the light of archaeological facts. It is not surprising; the ruins in themselves are impressive, and they are a challenge to any enquiring mind because they are in such marked contrast with the architecture of any people who inhabited the country when the Europeans first came. The name Zimbabwe means Stone Houses or a Great House, and was used, as the Portuguese Chronicler says, not only of the ruins we call by that name but of Dhlo-Dhlo, Khami, and half a dozen other stone forts. A phrase very similar has been heard in modern times used of a court-house or the burial place of a chief.[14]

Much has been written of these remains, particularly of the one called Zimbabwe; which is clearly the Symbaoe of the Portuguese. The walls of the 'Temple' at Zimbabwe are 35 feet high and 15 feet thick, perfectly smooth, built as the Portuguese said, without lime, and of small stones, not vast monolithic blocks. In one section of the outer wall there is a zigzag pattern very clearly worked into the building; this may have been the writing no one could understand which the Portuguese chronicler mentions.

The mortarless walls have stood for centuries. The granite of the neighbourhood lies in flat sheets which can fairly easily be split into blocks of the size used; not much skill was called for in quarrying and dressing the stones, and whereas the visitor to Baalbek, Stonehenge, or Luxor stands in wonder at the quarrying and engineering of the Cyclopean masonry, at Zimbabwe he is astonished rather at the craftsmanship involved in building walls of such a height, to stand so long without mortar, the outer surface so neatly ordered. The place is like nothing one has seen in Europe or Asia. The entrance to an enclosure, for instance, is usually made by rounding off and ending the wall on either side, with no stone gatepost but sometimes with a groove as if it was intended to let a wooden gatepost into the smoothly aligned round surface. But the lowest course of the wall is carried straight across the entrance; the next curves in towards the doorway, just as a contour line curves in towards a mountain pass; the next curves in still further and so the contour lines make a flight of curved shallow steps until the crown of the pass is reached.

At Zimbabwe there are two principal buildings, generally called the Acropolis and the Temple, and the names seem appropriate; to a visitor, the tangled complex of walls among the giant boulders of the Acropolis certainly suggests defence, while it is hard to believe that part at least of the Elliptical Building or Temple was not used for a ritual purpose. There is a long narrow passage, barely a yard wide and sometimes less, between towering walls, which suggests the approach of candidates for initiation; it can have had no possible use for defence and certainly none for domestic comfort. There are no straight lines at Zimbabwe; the ground plan is a very rough oval, segmented and containing smaller ovals or circles, which are sometimes again segmented. There is none of the geometrical precision to be seen in the ground plan of Stonehenge; one could hardly suppose that the builders had any knowledge of mathematics or astronomy; they had never drawn a string tight between two sticks to align their foundations and it did not even occur to them to keep the walls of the passage roughly parallel by using a measuring stick. They do not seem to have known the concept of measurement at all. But they must have had a high degree of political organization and a disciplined body of intelligent workers.

These are points to strike any uninstructed visitor who is unbiased. But the first Europeans to see Zimbabwe were biased; it seemed axiomatic to most late Victorian Englishmen—and in the United States the idea has persisted longer than in England—that 'Progress' in material discoveries went in a smooth curve for ever and

Steps like the contours in a mountain pass

ever upward unless interrupted by the arrival of barbarians or by civil war or some plague or other disaster.* The Mashona tribes throughout Southern Rhodesia in the late nineteenth century were manifestly incapable of united political effort, and a high degree of organization would be needed to assemble the workmen for a building anything like Zimbabwe, still

---

* There had been a theory since the time of Rousseau that all savages were degenerate, but I doubt whether it was ever a popular theory and certainly in the world after Darwin the widely held assumption was that 'progress' was the general rule.

more to feed the workers while they built. It was therefore taken for granted by most of the first explorers that some completely different people must have built Zimbabwe, and it was guessed, remembering Biblical mention of gold from the south, that they might have been Phoenicians, certainly some people of Semitic speech. And it was generally supposed that the date of the building went back far into antiquity. Later, the settlers came up against the exasperating reluctance of the Mashona tribesmen to work for them, to be punctual, to combine effectively in any task for their own—or even for someone else's—benefit, and they became more and more sure that such people could never have united to raise the walls of Zimbabwe.

Today we are more ready to accept it as normal that a people should degenerate. We know much more of the people who built Avebury and Stonehenge; we know more of Egypt, Knossos, and Mycenae. Above all, at this particular site modern archaeology has put an end to much surmise. The human reason can hardly reject the proposition that if beads or fragments of pottery are found undisturbed beneath a wall, the wall was built after the date of the pottery. And beads and pottery can be dated with some certainty. Again, if the method of construction shows that a certain kind of flooring is contemporary with a wall and if beads on the surface of that floor can be dated, it seems reasonable to deduce that the wall is earlier than the beads. In 1928, Miss Gertrude Caton-Thompson carried out, under the auspices of the British Association, a thorough investigation of the ruins, proceeding step by step to collect an impressive body of evidence, which she examined dispassionately. This investigation completed the earlier enquiry by Randall McIver, also for the British Association. Miss Caton-Thompson suffered from the handicap that much digging for treasure had disturbed the ruins; she had on the other hand the benefit of considerable advances in archaeological technique since the earlier investigations, which, except for McIver's, were amateur or at best semi-professional. Her report is set out with no concessions to the general reader; it is devastatingly clear and unbiased; her conclusions as to dates

would, she remarks drily, be, 'within their own limits of uncertainty, considered final in any other country'.

These conclusions are based on the construction of walls and
flooring and the comparison of objects such as beads and pottery
found at different strata. Very briefly, the higher level of flooring
was strewn with objects from China, Persia, and India which can
be dated as not later than the thirteenth century, while below the
lowest level are found many small beads also imported from the
Indian Ocean and dating from the eighth or ninth century A.D.
These may have belonged to earlier occupants of the site but are
more likely to have been dropped during construction. One
must conclude then that the walls were built not earlier than the
eighth or later than the thirteenth century of this era, much
nearer in fact to the Norman Conquest than to the building of
Solomon's temple, and probably a century or so before the
Conquest. There were two main periods of occupation, but one
merged into the other and there was no clear-cut line between
them; the workmanship of the second period is inferior, but not
different in kind. The evidence points to trade with the coast, and
from the coast to India, China, and Arabia, from the eighth or
ninth century onwards.

These dates have been buttressed, since Miss Caton-Thompson's
investigations, by further research which sharpens the certainty
with which the beads can be dated and by the use of a technique
not then discovered. There are drains at the foot of the main wall
of the Temple which would be needed to let out the water that
would otherwise collect inside in heavy rain; in one of these was
found a beam made from the wood of the tree *Spirostachys
Africanus* (the tambootie). This was an integral part of the base of
the wall, supporting the sluice, and it is not reasonable to suppose
it was put in later. A test by the C14 radio-carbon process, which
measures the loss by radiation since the death of the wood, gives
a date between the sixth and ninth centuries A.D. and seems to
point to the earlier part of Miss Caton-Thompson's bracket. But
this tree, which is repugnant to white ants and therefore valuable
for building, has a poisonous bark. The builders of Zimbabwe

would hardly have cut or handled it till it was dead, and how long dead no one can say.

To all this must be added evidence from elsewhere; there are other stone ruins, similar in workmanship and style, which can be dated by the same methods and are much later. Dhlo-Dhlo, for instance, a hill fort of stone with walls decorated like Zimbabwe's and with many reminiscent features, but on the whole poorer workmanship, is to be dated early eighteenth century. There is really no room for doubt about Dhlo-Dhlo; a Dutch glass bottle and a Chinese bowl, which is 'Ming from a provincial factory' are both late seventeenth or early eighteenth century and were found at the lower occupation level. Since Miss Caton-Thompson's time an independent worker has come to a similar conclusion about Khami. And there is further evidence that stone kraals were being built in Southern Rhodesia until the nineteenth century.

The hunter Selous was a careful observer and remarkably free from bias. So long as he stuck to his own observation he did not go wrong, but in his writings he does not question the opinion of those who said the builders of Zimbabwe came from Arabia.* However, he used his eyes and wrote: 'that the builders of Zimbabwe were a very rude people, possessing no written characters and doing all their building by eye and without measurement, was the impression left on my mind . . .'. He thought that the invasion by 'worshippers of Baal' must therefore go back to a very remote antiquity before the Arabians had learnt to measure, but his own observation led him to suppose that there had been no sudden break but a progressive deterioration; he describes a visit to Makoni, Chief of the Wa-Ungwe—the same whose title and tribe are mentioned by Bocarro—and writes: 'So far from there having been an abrupt transition from a people who built the temple of Zimbabwe to a race who never put one

---

* In his writings, Selous does not question the main tenet of the Semitic theory; but apparently in conversation he went much further and he expressed to Miss Blennerhassett views about Zimbabwe which have been upheld by modern archaeology to a remarkable extent.

The Conical Tower at the Elliptical Building at Zimbabwe

The Elliptical Building at Zimbabwe from the air. Note the open gateways unarched and the rounded ends to walls

Soapstone Birds at Zimbabwe (from G. Caton-Thompson: *Zimbabwe Culture*)

Zimbabwe Ruins: entrance to the Acropolis showing the builders' ignorance of the arch

stone upon another, the inhabitants of Makoni's and Mangwende's countries in South-eastern Mashonaland only ceased to
surround their towns with well-built stone walls during the last
generation, when they found that these walls offered but an
inefficient protection against the Zulu hordes. . . . In Makoni's
country, there is clear evidence that there has been a gradual
deterioration from a people who were capable of building walls
which will compare with any part of the great Zimbabwe to the
very inferior hut-building barbarians of the present day. Makoni's
town as it now stands is a monument of filth and uncleanliness
and is undefended by anything but a small fence. His old town,
which I also visited and from which I believe he was driven by
Umtasa, was surrounded by a moat and a loop-holed mud wall;
whilst the town which it is said was built by his ancestor Chipadzi
is surrounded by a well-built loop-holed stone wall.'[15]

To this must be added the evidence of Selous, Baines, and others
that gold-mining, not merely gold-washing, was practised until
at any rate the first half of the nineteenth century; Selous for
instance mentions a shaft 120 feet deep found in 1891 which had
been worked with a rope and bucket of bark which could
obviously be of no great age, while he examined a working of a
quartz vein in which props had been used to support the roof;
these props had been cut with native axes, still had the bark on
them, and had, he supposed, been abandoned about the time of
Mzilikatzi's invasion, or about 1838 to 1840. Manuel Barretto in
1667 describes in detail the digging of a shaft for gold, made like
a well and no wider at the mouth, and worked with a bucket or
basket.[16]

Nor is this all that points in the same direction. The Lovedu of
the Transvaal and their neighbours the Ba-Venda traditionally
came from Southern Rhodesia; both until recently built stone
kraals and use decorations reminiscent of Zimbabwe. At Zimbabwe the foundations for huts normally include a bench made
of a fine cement of powdered granite; the hut circles at Dhlo-
Dhlo show a bench of the same pattern in a poorer cement; a
modern Mashona hut has just such a bench of mud. And the

ground plans of the Maund ruins at Zimbabwe, and of the other Rhodesian ruins—notably Matendere—have only to be compared with the ground plan of Bantu royal kraals as far apart as Uganda and Natal to be seen to bear a family resemblance to each other and to nothing else. Altogether, the evidence is overwhelmingly in favour of what Miss Caton-Thompson calls 'an unbroken though retrogressive continuity of custom down the ages since Zimbabwe was built'.

There are still some people—but among them, I think, no reputable archaeologist—who cannot bring themselves to believe that the Zimbabwe culture was the product of a Bantu people, and who assume that foreign masters compelled the local people to undertake this work. But to believe this, one is driven to suppose that foreign masters—who must surely have been either Arab, Indian or European?—had sufficient political control to set up a state which must have been elaborately organized and then forced the natives to toil at a building for which they used none of their own most elementary techniques. Surely it is inconceivable that in medieval times any people from outside Africa who had the political organization for such a task should have built a passage with walls from 30 to 40 feet high without using a measuring rod to keep them an even distance apart, or that they should not have told their workmen to draw a string tight between two pegs. And again the total effect is quite unlike anything ever built by Saracen, Crusader, or Hindu—and it has characteristics unmistakably Bantu. The cone-like tower—rather like an ice-cream cone elongated and reversed, or a long dunce's cap with a blunt instead of a pointed end—is, it is true, reminiscent of the minarets on some of the old mosques in Arab towns on the African coast of the Indian Ocean, but that, after all, is the kind of thing that a man might see and remember and try to imitate. We know that there was trade with the coast and though most of it was carried out through intermediaries—or both the Portuguese and the men of Zimbabwe would have known more of each other than they did—there were probably some at least who made the whole journey. There are other examples of Bantu people setting up a tower to mark a chief's dwelling; the idea might be native and its form influenced by memories of one of the earliest of these minarets.

That some people still feel a difficulty about accepting the Bantu origin of Zimbabwe is due to the fact that modern Europeans and Americans live in a tradition of growing mastery over a material environment—though not of the human heart. But let them glance at Ireland, a beacon to Europe, until about the time Zimbabwe was built, a centre of learning and of the Christian faith, sending her missionaries and scholars to Rome and Germany, men skilled in goldwork and the illumination of missals. And hear what the English wrote of the descendants of these same Irish when the Portuguese were discovering the Monomotapa:

'their dwellings are rather swine-sties than houses, . . . the chiefest cause of their beastly manner of life and swinish condition. . . .'

'The Irish would rather still retain themselves in their sluttishness, in their uncleanliness, in their rudeness . . . than take any example from the English either in civility, humanity, or any manner of decency. . . .'

'I omit their common repudiation of their wives; their promiscuous generation of children; their neglect of lawful matrimony; their uncleanness in apparel, diet, and lodging; their contempt and scorn of all things necessary for the civil life of man. . . .'

'Surely there was never people that lived in more misery than they do, nor as it should seem of worse minds, for matrimony among them is no more regarded than conjunction between unreasonable beasts. Perjury, robbery, and murder counted allowables. Finally, I cannot find that they make any conscience of sin. . . .'

'And tenants neither build nor repair their houses, make neither gardens, orchards nor meadows, nor use no enclosures, nor in effect do anything else that may be to the bettering of their tenements. . . .'[17]

These are from different English observers of the Irish scene; they were perhaps not more sympathetic observers than their descendants in Rhodesia and perhaps they exaggerated; a substantial body of proved degradation remains in both cases, though no doubt in both cases it was raids from other people—Norse pirates or Matabele—that completed a process already begun.

What this adds up to is that from Norman to Tudor times there was a Bantu people in Southern Rhodesia who did not measure or draw straight lines, but who were able to produce enough food to maintain a great army of workmen and feed a royal court practising an elaborate ritual; who were capable of an art far in advance of anything known among the Shona in Victorian times; there were people who terraced their fields and worked gold when it was fairly near the surface. They ruled a wide Empire, but their energy, their ambition and their workmanship declined and their realms were beginning to disintegrate by the sixteenth century; the Rozwi, who were smashed by the wash-back of the Zulu peoples, were probably their successors as paramount tribe. Their political organization need have been little more advanced than that of Barotseland, where the Lozi kings decided, whenever there was a sufficient surplus of food, to make a canal that would drain the countryside and serve as a means of communication for their descendants. And the history of the Lozi kingdom in the nineteenth century shows how easy it would be for such a kingdom to disintegrate over a disputed succession, or as the result of a palace revolution; once political control broke down, through civil war or the dissension of a powerful vassal, there would be no more Zimbabwes built. Dry-stone building is impressive on such a scale as Zimbabwe; it is well enough for a fort or a temple or a royal kraal, but for domestic purposes it is neither wind-proof nor water-proof; a far better hut can be built from what is called in Rhodesia *dagga*—a mixture of earth and the material from ant-hills, which sets in a hard mud plaster. Only kings would build in dry stone and once the kings stopped building, stone would fall out of use.

Let me summarize. The Zimbabwe Culture reached its peak

between the ninth century and the thirteenth, probably nearer the ninth. The archaeological and historical evidence points to a strong and extensive Bantu State centred on Zimbabwe, producing much better artists and craftsmen than later; the quality of the workmanship steadily and progressively deteriorated.

The Portuguese at the beginning of the sixteenth century met and negotiated with an Emperor called the Monomotapa, his tribe being the Ma-Karanga, Ma-Kalanga or Wa-Karanga, whose power over his vassals was already declining and who, a century later, was defeated, not finally, by Makobe of the 'Baroes', who may perhaps have been the Ba-Rozwi. There is no evidence to show whether the Monomotapa succeeded or supplanted the rulers and builders of Zimbabwe. The Ba-Rozwi were overlords of the Mashona tribes at the beginning of the nineteenth century and are still required to confirm the accession of a chief. They were defeated by the Zulus and the coming of the Matabele demoralized the Mashona tribes still further.

All this has some relevance for today. It is true to say that the Matabele came into the country not long before the Europeans; it is untrue to suggest that the Europeans came into an empty country. They came into a country underpopulated and with stretches fairly recently made empty, largely by the Zulu incursions. The previous inhabitants could not defend it against them and thus lacked the most widely accepted of all title-deeds. They were disorganized and demoralized when the Europeans came, but it is not true that they were hereditarily incapable of progress or combination. They had taken the step forward into the Iron Age, they had organized a highly centralized state; then something had gone wrong and they fell back. No one can be dogmatic as to why, but, like the Neolithic people who built Stonehenge, like the Irish who led North-West Europe in civilization, like the Romans, like a score of other peoples, they fell back. Such a recession is due to many complex causes; there is no reason to suppose it is final; what men have done once they can do again, and sometimes they do it better.[18]

V. The Bantu Achievement

Section 1: The Kings and their People

It is time to look back, to sum up this attempt to picture the peoples of Rhodesia and Nyasaland as they were in Victorian times, to consider what hints it may provide of the likelihood of strife or agreement in the future. Three Zulu peoples are established at three of the corners—the Matabele to the south-west and the Shangaans to the south-east, the Angoni to the north-east; in the north is the warrior state of the Bemba; in the north-west is the most highly developed political state, the Kingdom of the Lozi or Barotse; round the south end of Lake Nyasa are the Yao chiefs, disparate groups, hunting-dogs for the Arab slave traders. In between these predatory, expanding peoples lie many smaller ill-organized tribes, bound together in much smaller groups, some of them often lumped together under the name Ba-Tonga, those who are judged.

In Southern Rhodesia, the tribes now called Ma-Shona have no common name for themselves, though they speak dialects of what is basically one language, and the only name to describe them jointly is one Europeans have borrowed from the Matabele. They have forgotten that they were once united by allegiance to an Emperor, the rumour of whose power had reached to Europe and had been confused with uncertain traditions of Prester John, with a vague belief that there had been ancient African kingdoms in the time of Solomon. Because they have forgotten so much, it is not clear whether it was this Emperor, the Monomotapa, who built the forts that lie here and there in their country or a predecessor of whom nothing is known; all they do remember is that the Rozwi were once rulers among them, but the Rozwi were defeated by the Shangaans, and from Livingstone to Dr.

Jameson, Europeans who come into the country speak of the Mashona tribes as 'abject, broken people', 'a timid and broken-spirited race', incapable of uniting among themselves and at the mercy of the Matabele raids. There can be no serious doubt that defeats by the hordes of the Zulu backwash were the final blows to a people who had already degenerated and lost much of the skill and all the ambition of their ancestors.

There were wide differences between the tribes of Central Africa; the better organized felt for the worse a complete contempt. There was, for instance, a great range of difference between them in the respect paid to a chief. But in spite of these real differences, it is possible to generalize. There is an element common to the chiefship even of the Bemba king and of the kraal head among the Mashona. There are aspects of society which all share, Rulers or Judged Ones, Preyers or Preyed On. They show little desire to improve their comfort or physical well-being but a concern for personal relationships and an ability to conduct themselves through a maze of tangled political allegiances which is most marked among the Lozi but seems almost as true of the Zulu peoples and the Bemba. And there is a quality in their ideas of kingship and chieftainship which all to some extent display, a quality that comes unexpectedly to anyone whose experience has been among Asian ideas of kingship.

The point is seen most clearly, of course, among the tribes who have managed to coalesce into a state, but the same kind of relationship exists in embryo in the smallest political unit possible, the unit from which the tribes are built up. This, among the people who reckon through the father, is the kraal or hamlet or homestead in which a man lives with his wives, married sons and sons' children. Among the people who reckon through the mother, the corresponding unit would be a man with his sisters and their daughters and daughters' children, but among them there will rather more often, it seems, be others attached who are not related by kinship, something nearer the European idea of a village. In either case, there is a village headman who is probably related to most of this little group. When he dies, the group will

often split and new groups be formed with new heads, traditionally going away to new village sites.

These little groups, kraals or hamlets or 'extended families',
will usually be in some way grouped together into some wider
formation, either locally, in a sort of Rural District or ward, or
perhaps by descent or supposed descent into a sub-clan, and here
again there will be a head or sub-chief. The nearer the tribe has
come to being a state or a nation, the more likely it is that this
grouping together of smaller units will be based on an area rather
than on descent. And so the larger organism is built up, though
there will often also be horizontal cross-sections organized in a
different way, such as groups initiated at the same time into the
duties of manhood. In all these groupings, the head—the headman, the district sub-chief, the chief, or king—is in a relationship
to his people which involves him in duties and responsibilities at
least as much as privileges, while his power is balanced against
their interests in various ways, partly by the widespread knowledge of what is the customary line of conduct in a certain kind of
case, and partly because he is almost always required to consult
a council of some kind before acting.

This reciprocal relationship is most clearly seen in the case of a
king—even among the most apparently autocratic—but it is
there too among the headmen.* First, the chief is identified with
the people and they with him. He *is* the land and the people as a
whole; he represents the dead ancestors who are the guardians
of the people, the people and all they have belong to him, he is
their father, his health and strength ripen the crops, he can make
rain, he feeds the people by his bounty and when he assumes the
chieftainship he loses the right to his own comfort. Among the
Zulus, the King's son may not call him father, for is he not
equally the father of all the people?[1] A Bemba headman must
fertilize the ground, before a new village is occupied, by a ritual

* A distinction is made, I know, between the tribes who have divine kings,
an institution supposed to be derived from Meroë and Egypt, and those who
have not; to me, as an amateur whose reading has been far from wide, this
seems a difference of emphasis that has sometimes been given too much
importance.

act of intercourse with his wife; all chiefs among the Bemba are said to 'work the land' and to 'spit blessings over the land'.[2] The Shona regard the chief as 'the same life-essence as the ancient begetter of the clan' and whoever injures the health or manpower of the clan injures the chief.[3] 'When the King dies,' say the Lozi, 'the nation falls into a coma.'[4] The Lovedu still speak with horror and fear of the years following the death of a Queen in 1894 when drought, rinderpest, and locusts produced a famine that may have destroyed a third of the population—but it was only to be expected, for the Queen's death dislocates the order of nature.[5] The king is the ritual guardian of the land, but, the Lozi say, 'chieftainship is slavery' and in his speech of accession a Lozi King is remembered by many to have said: 'You have chosen me, you have killed me.'[6]

The king, then, *is* the land and the people and with the power of chieftainship goes the burden of responsibility. Such an identification, strongly felt on both sides, may in itself act as a balance against the unscrupulous use of power; a man does not injure himself. But stronger are the compulsion of customary law and the need for consultation. Gluckman has a story that the Zulu King Mpande, a brother of the great Chaka, heard a dispute between a favourite of his and a plaintiff in which customary law was clearly on the side of the plaintiff. Mpande had to give his decision in accordance with the law, but escaped its consequence by executive action, sending men to wipe out the plaintiff and his family so that the judgement could not be executed.[7] Chaka had strengthened out of all recognition the autocratic power of the chief in the executive field, but even he and his brothers dared not cut directly across customary law. The law, even here and throughout the Bantu world, is felt to be above the king.

Consultation varies very much in the form it takes but in every tribe of which I have heard there are circumstances in which the chief must consult others. Even among the Bemba—whose King among all these peoples came the nearest to absolute power— there are hereditary councillors, who cannot be removed at the King's will and who exercise a considerable influence, no doubt as a rule by informal advice but in the last resort by refusing to perform ritual acts essential to the King—refusing, so to speak, to vote spiritual supplies.[8] The elaborate balances of power among the Lozi have been mentioned already; the Shona display in a form rudimentary—or perhaps debased, for it may have been far more elaborate in the days of the Monomotapa—something not unlike the Lozi system of Estates of the Realm; a chief some-times has two sets of councillors, one consisting of the heads of wards or villages and the others chosen by himself, so that different interests are represented.[9] There is wide admiration for a man who will speak his mind to a chief and for a chief who will listen to advice; 'a chief does not decide for himself, he speaks the mind of his people, he is their voice,' an old Yao chief told me. The custom is wide-spread of the junior councillor speaking first, so that he may say freely what he thinks; what is felt to be right is that when he has heard everyone speak the chief should express the general view, in which thereafter all are united.

The chief danger to an organized Bantu society, one of the states, was civil war, usually due to a disputed succession. There were rules of succession, but they were not strictly kept; in fact the word should be principles, rather than rules, for in almost all tribes a man obviously unsuitable would be passed over, while an exceptionally able man would often get the succession over his seniors' heads. It was thus possible to avoid, as a rule, the succession of a weak king, but only by introducing an element of uncertainty that left the door open to dispute. There was also the danger of an element of the tribe splitting off in revolt against a tyrant; Zulu and Matabele history shows this happening constantly and though the danger of such a split might operate as a check on the power of the king, it was also a potent bar to progress.

The Shona avoided this particular hazard, but by a custom which may have contributed to the decline of energy and ambi-tion among them; brothers succeed each other as chief until a whole generation is used up, and there was thus apt to be a succession of elderly chiefs who reigned for a few years only. But it may be that in the time of the Monomotapa the difficulty was avoided by consultation in a sort of inner council; the decision today has always to be given by a tribal spirit (the Mhondoro) and when chieftainship meant leading an army, the spirit may have exercised a more rigorous selection and cared less for seniority.[10]

Disputed succession wrecked the Lozi kingdom in the mid-nineteenth century, and until the Europeans came civil war must be reckoned, for the Bantu states, as a danger at least as serious as attack by another state. Even the Zulu regiments could not make much headway against an organized state; Chaka's armies could not subdue the Basutos, nor could Mzilikazi or his son Lobengula the Lozi; the Angoni hordes seem to have split when Zwangendaba died and never seriously to have attacked the Bemba. The smaller tribes were of course powerless against external attack by one of the organized states, and for a group of uncoordinated tribes such as the Shona or the Tonga to unite became an almost impossible feat, once a powerful neighbour like the Matabele had them with their heads down as a subject people. And there were few tribes who could reckon themselves exempt, either from Matabele or Lozi raids in the west or slave traffic further east. For the great states civil war; for the lesser people, raids—these were dangers as serious as drought or plague.

That chief and people are one and the law the expression of the joint will—not only of the present chief and people but of their ancestors in the past—this deep-rooted feeling is important in what is to come. A people with such traditions are unlikely to take kindly to a law imposed from outside, strange to their ideas, made by another people, beyond their power to influence. They are not likely to co-operate willingly in executive action for which there has been no preparation by consultation; they may obey but in their hearts they will not accept. And surely this concept of kingship and people will affect the Bantu in their approach to the modern world, their organization of trade unions and churches, their working of democratic institutions. It strikes one as far more adaptable to democratic processes than those of India, Persia, or China before the nineteenth century. Lewanika

as a king is more like Edward I than like Louis XIV or Aurang-
zebe. It is true that he leads a life nastier and more barbarous than
these monarchs, because even among the Lozi there has been so
little storing of surplus energy in provision for the future. But he
is one with his people, not in the sense that they must conform to
his whims, but in that his skill consists in guiding and moulding—
and to some extent being guided by—both barons and commons,
while he is always subject to a law he cannot override.

He is one with his people and they one with him. And here is a
danger. While, in theory at least, every man should speak his
opinion before the king, it is generally felt that there must be no
more dissension once the will of the people has been pronounced
by the king. There is no conception of good-humoured opposition; a minority, the unsuccessful party in a rebellion, is ruthlessly
exterminated.

Another point emerges that will affect the future. Here are
people much concerned about personal relationships, not interested in providing for physical needs. They are to come in
contact with people who by insurance, trusts, wills, and every
legal device they can create wish to provide material wealth for
their descendants.* And the representatives of Victorian Europe
who come to Africa have left their families in order to seek their
fortunes; they are less concerned with personal relationships and
more with wealth even than their fellow countrymen.

Section 2: The People and their Life

In general, the Bantu people made little attempt to provide
against famine or drought. To store grain of course is not easy
in a country where there are such wide variations in temperature
and where white ants will eat anything but steel or rock. Irrigation is the best provision against a dry year and it is hard to
understand how a people who learnt to work in iron should have

* Galsworthy has fallen from favour as a novelist but is not to be despised
as a social historian; Timothy Forsyte's will was a peculiarly Victorian idea,
aimed at amassing the maximum wealth in the far future, with no concern for
contemporaries. And think of that strange Victorian device, the Tontine,
described in *The Wrong Box*.

failed to think of bringing water to their crops. But they neither stored water by dams nor lifted it by any of the methods common in the Middle East or India, nor even used simple irrigation by gravity. In the eastern parts of Mashonaland there are old terraces which probably belong to the time of the Monomotapa or before, and that is the nearest they came to storing water.

The newcomers to this country, the settlers from the Cape and from England, were to make much of the insecurity of Bantu life, subject to raids and the fear of death or slavery, to drought and hunger, to fear of witchcraft and magic, and to the danger of a horrible death if accused of witchcraft by others. That all these dangers were very real is perfectly true; Livingstone writes of travelling through the 'extensive highlands' of the country north of the Zambezi and east of the Victoria Falls, where 'only a few years since . . . numerous herds of cattle furnished abundance of milk and the rich soil amply repaid the labour of the husbandmen', while on this second visit he was 'constantly passing through the ruined sites of utterly deserted villages'. 'From Monday morning till late on Saturday morning, we did not fall in with a single person. The Ba Toka were driven out of their noble country by the invasions of Mzilikazi and Sebituane.'[11] Of the same people, a modern anthropologist writes that they were 'smashed by the raids' of the Lozi and the Matabele, made usually 'for slaves and cattle and the pleasure of raiding'; 'by 1890, they were a broken and a beaten people'.[12] Again and again, travellers and missionaries speak of going through the sites of villages where the huts are charred circles of ashes, where they are sickened by the stench of dead bodies. Selous was confident that it was as a result of raids by Zulu peoples, Shangaans or Matabele, that 'the high plateau of Mashunaland, which at no very distant date must have supported a large native population, once more became an almost uninhabited wilderness . . . .'.

For a modern European to make a true picture of what life can have been like for one of the Tonga or the Mashona 100 years ago is almost as difficult as to imagine the emotions of an antelope or a giraffe in their capacity as the natural prey of lions.

Perhaps it is still harder for the educated African of today, driven as he is by an emotion that urges him either to forget or to glorify the past. One may, however, be fairly confident that the giraffe would rather risk the lions than live in a cage. And there is evidence[13] that the Mashona at any rate preferred the risk of an occasional raid by the Matabele to peace and the continued presence of Europeans—or at least, that they very soon came to think so. One may surmise that most of the time they were able to disregard a danger that seemed remote until it occurred, a danger that was visualized, if at all, as something that happened to other people.

It is still more difficult to form any idea of how pervasive was the fear of witchcraft; it is there today but few are ready to talk about it truthfully. Intense fear, obviously, would be produced in a person smelt out as a witch or in anyone who supposed he was himself bewitched. But again one may guess that the Bantu tribesman was not as a rule more concerned about the dangers of witchcraft than a grazing eland with lions or a London pedestrian with traffic. After a stay of eighteen months in the Southern Sudan with the Azande, a people in whose lives witchcraft appeared to play an immense part, Evans-Prichard[14] came to the conclusion that no member of the tribe was quite sure that he was not himself a witch; he hoped he was not, he certainly feared the machinations of others, but—and again this is surmise—perhaps no more than a modern American fears cancer.

On the opposite side of the account, one must assume a certain sense of security within the tribe, a confidence in known remedies to deal with known evils. This too is something of which no one can be certain; it is difficult not to suggest the answer one expects and no questioner is either free from bias or able to conceal his bias from the person questioned. And among the questioned there is almost certainly a sentimental nostalgia for a past that has been forgotten. Still, it is possible to form an impression—and it cannot today be more than an impression—from the memories of missionaries and native commissioners who were in close and constant touch with those who remembered the old tribal days.

It is an impression of a life that, with intermittent misery and fear, did as a rule provide satisfaction. A man knew where he was; he knew his place in tribal society and his place on the ladder between his ancestors and his descendants. For almost any misfortune, there was a magical reason and he knew where to go for advice as to the source of the evil; he knew where to turn for means to combat his affliction and take his revenge. There were known remedies for known evils. Again, life was not dull; there were times of periodical excitement when grain was cut or sown, when boys were initiated or girls married. Wide-spread among the Bantu peoples is a delight in artistic improvisation, particularly in speech, in dancing and in music. A man who can argue a case eloquently is universally admired; he enjoys his own eloquence and others enjoy listening to him. This, among the Nyakyusa, for instance, is traditionally the hall-mark of education.[15] And no one can have spent even a very short time among Bantu or Negro people today without noticing their love of eloquence and their spontaneity in music. Their music indeed has spread all over the world in the syncopated rhythms of jazz, in its spasms of individual creation. And surely it is partly the same impulse that brings the speaker to his feet in prayer or testimony in the religious ceremonies of separatist sects. Both in Africa and the Caribbean, the impression is of a people whose interest in life centres on conversation with friends, on parties, on ceremonial speeches, on dancing, on music, not prepared or learnt but created from the feeling of the moment, not in the least on building up possessions. And surely much of this must have been present in tribal life; surely, so long as no alternative was presented, tribal life did provide a deep if intermittent satisfaction.

Indeed, it may well be that what was wrong with this life was that it was too satisfying, and that is why it did not produce the divine discontent, the enquiring mind, the thirst for knowledge and mastery that drives men to discover new worlds, to write poems or study the heavens. A readiness to take the world as it is found rather than try to better it was certainly a characteristic of these people; to guess why this should be is to explore the outermost wilds of conjecture. Yet suggestions have been made.

That life was too easy,[16] that they could always move on to fresh land, that the challenge presented by nature was not sufficiently severe—these variations on a single argument to me seem unconvincing. They are in the first place based on the assumption that material betterment is man's main object—and that is a European assumption which does not always hold good even in Europe, much less in Asia or Africa. In the second, they do not fit the climate; winter nights in Rhodesia are quite cold enough to make one take an interest in clothing and housing; the soil is not fertile and generally compares poorly with India or Europe; there was, it is true, plenty of game but by themselves the Africans do not seem to have been particularly successful in securing it; Selous—and indeed every hunter—gives the impression that not only his own porters but the people of village after village were starving for meat. The settlers who were to come found no lack of challenge. And in the third place, it is a theory that does not fit the Bantu character. The first settlers spoke of idleness, apathy, lack of interest, but it was an impression that all who have known them well have come increasingly to contradict. Capable of long, passive endurance in the face of suffering, they have—many of them, the best of them—a joyous resilience, and a zest for what is new, that is far indeed from apathy. But this must remain a matter of personal impression.

Or was it perhaps that the system of bringing up children produced a profound content, an easy belief that the heavens would always provide something, just as that bountiful breast had always produced milk?[17] This argument has been used and is still sometimes quoted. It is true that Bantu children are both weaned and house-trained much later than modern European children, that they are never denied the breast when they cry, that they are generally spoilt in their infancy; that when they are at last weaned the process is extremely abrupt. It is argued on the one hand that the lateness of weaning and the long contact with the mother give the child a warm sense of security that prevents competitive action; on the other, and not very consistently, that the late and

Lobengula's Kraal at Old Bulawayo (from a sketch by A. A. Anderson, author of *Twenty-five Years in a Wagon*, 1887)

War dance of the Matabele as witnessed by Sir Andrew Smith at Marico, 1835 (from a drawing by C. D. Bell)

Young Matabele Warrior (from an original sketch by Thomas Baines in the British Museum)

abrupt weaning splits the child's world and brings him so sharply into contact with harsh surroundings that his personality never becomes wholly integrated. To give a verdict on such questions as these would require a separate volume; most people today would probably agree that treatment in infancy may profoundly affect the personality, but would preserve a sceptical caution to any theory that relates every aspect of later life to what happened in infancy, still more to any attempt to reduce all human motives to one, whether that one is sexual lust, lust for power or fear. The one requirement of any theory is that it should fit the facts, and most unbiased observers, surely, would be suspicious of any generalization that does not take account of Chaka, Khama, and Moshesh of the Basuto, great men by any standards and in different ways, while others again would say that integration is just what the anxious bustling European seems most to need, what the best of the Bantu seem to possess. And if suckling and weaning play so decisive a part in making character, why did the Zulus, with no change in these habits, suddenly become the scourge of Africa, exploding across the continent and eating up the peoples like locusts? Why does the same system in infancy produce the fierce Matabele and the peaceful Mashona?

Again the general level of health must affect a people's achievement and their outlook on the world. Today the African from Lake Nyasa who is 'recruited' for work in the Union of South Africa, the copper mines of the north or the farms of Southern Rhodesia is usually suffering from malnutrition and much more often than not from internal parasites; germs of bilharzia and malaria are almost always present in his body, though in a concentration over which friendly forces can keep the upper hand except in times of stress or extreme exposure. Whether and how far this was true 100 years ago no one can be sure; bilharzia is believed by many people in Rhodesia to be a recent importation but there is evidence that it occurred along the Zambezi in Livingstone's time;[18] there can be no doubt that malaria was endemic. As to nutrition, the hunters and missionaries speak again and again of the people's desire for animal fat, and of the

shortage of salt. Coillard himself speaks of the pleasure of crunch-
ing up salt by itself and eating it like sugar; Livingstone constantly
returns to the theme of salt and how much easier it is to do without it when living on meat. The missionaries and hunters of
course were accustomed to the free use of salt and were more
conscious of being without it than their porters, but there can
hardly be a reasonable doubt that most of the Bantu were
desperately short of salt as well as of fat and animal protein, and
there is no very obvious reason for thinking that there were fewer
parasites in their bodies 100 years ago than today. Altogether, one
must assume that among most tribes there was a majority who
can never have felt the energy of being really well. That would not
apply to the Matabele warriors, who lived on captured beef and
were credited with being able to run immense distances without
rest, nor to the central core of aristocrats among the other predatory peoples.

In some other parts of Africa there are indications that the
aristocrat who was released from the necessity of continuous toil
began to form some concept of the proper life for a gentleman,
as it was conceived by the Attic or Dorian conquerors in Greece:
the Batutsi of Ruanda are described as having 'leisure to cultivate
eloquence, poetry, refined manners, and the subtle art of being
witty when talking and drinking with friends'.[19] But there is
little sign of this in Central Africa; there was indeed no aristocracy
really comparable to the Batutsi, even among the Lozi. The
Matabele, by living on their neighbours, could have found time
for a fruitful leisure but their state was founded on an outlook
Spartan rather than Athenian. Indeed, in Victorian times, there is
little to show that any of the people of this region had much
admiration for visual art or any skill at it; certainly there is
nothing comparable with the products of the Congo or the
Western Sudan.

Still more surprising is the shortness of memory. The bards of
Rajput princes could recite the unwritten chronicles of their
masters for 1,500 years. That the Mashona within three centuries
should have lost all traditions of the Monomotapa, that even

chiefs whose ancestral titles are mentioned by Bocarro among his vassals or courtiers should have forgotten him, suggests that his supplanters were successful in imposing some taboo on the mention of his name; if not, one must postulate a depth of degenerate barbarism and a disruption by the Nguni hordes so complete that it is hard to imagine.

Section 3: The Seeds of Strife

The missionaries condemned the whole congeries of Bantu tribes unhesitatingly on moral grounds. Scholars of a later generation judge praise or blame alike to be out of place. But mankind in general does pronounce judgement and in the political debate which today is continuous, all parties alike are inclined to appeal for evidence to a past which each judges, interprets, and even constructs in his own interest. Generalizations abound; it is worth trying, surely, to make a dispassionate appraisal of how far they are true and how far they were likely to affect future relations with Europeans.

It was said that the Bantu were blood-thirsty and without pity. Certainly they were callous about human life and suffering, but it is not yet two centuries since an Englishman mentioned quite casually in a report to London that it was the custom of the English at Calcutta to flog men to death for any of the petty offences punishable in England by hanging. Nor did the Bantu take such trouble to inflict extreme pain as Europeans in the Middle Ages, or the Chinese at least until the nineteenth century. Matabele raids were of course ruthless; each of their warriors at an annual feast danced a pas-seul of self-glorification and boasted in mime of how many he had killed, a child in arms counting the same as an adult; scores of up to twenty are mentioned. But the devastation the Matabele left behind them was perhaps no more complete than that achieved a century before by Pindari freebooters in Central India or—to go back one more century—by the troopers of Wallenstein or Gustavus Adolphus in Europe, or Cromwell in Ireland. And accounts by those who followed Renaud's advance on Cawnpore in 1857 describe a countryside as devastated as any Livingstone saw. Central Africa in mid-Victorian times was what today is called a power vacuum; that is to say, there was no one with both the strength and the will to enforce peace. And in a power vacuum these things do happen.

Pity is a nursling of recent growth and is delicate even today. It grows most easily in a soil of leisure and comfort, which did not exist in Central Africa. What is more, mere existence involves callousness and it is to some extent a matter of convention what it is that a man hardens his heart to and what it is that he is tender about. The convention is easily shattered; callosities grow quickly. English ladies who were hardly moved by the bomb at Hiroshima excite themselves about a trapped rabbit or the sale of a pony from the New Forest to a butcher; Hindus who did not shrink from slaughtering Muslims in 1947 think with horror of the death of a cow; I know of a Bechuana tribesman who after a stay on an English farm shook his head at the cruelty of people who would take a calf from its mother and make it drink from a bucket. One may conclude that the Bantu sixty years ago had little experience of pity and did not show much to other people; that does not mean they are a people lacking in pity today. Indeed, the reverse seems to be true; from many sources one hears that the Bantu regard the Europeans as cold, hard, cruel, and take it for granted that they themselves feel pity for each other.

There is a rider to this; in so wide a subject every generalization suggests an exception. The point is stated by Paul Bohannan of the Tiv, a semi-Bantu people of Nigeria, but it is of wide application in Africa. 'The moral attitude to homicide . . .', he writes, 'is on a scale of values determined by the social distance between the people involved.' It is nothing, in other words, to kill a stranger; to kill a brother is an act of horror. That surely is true, with modification of emphasis, of most African tribes and perhaps no less of the Highland Clans before 1745.

It is said that the Bantu are suspicious. Certainly suspicion is in the air one breathes when talking to the educated Bantu of today and among the villagers too; an agricultural officer coming to a village in the Northern Province of Nyasaland with young citrus trees for free distribution was recently pelted with stones because the inhabitants believed that once they had watered the trees and grown them to maturity, the Government would say the trees were theirs and take the land from them. There are many other stories of the same kind. Is this a result of their treatment at the hands of Europeans? Or does it derive from their own past? Both, I suggest. They surely have good reason to suspect that Europeans may take the land of Africa. And surely suspicion of anyone outside their group must be strong in any society of small units with no law between the units but the strength of the strong; the Homeric heroes are as suspicious as the Bantu, and Odysseus, chief of a small island, is praised for his caution because he never speaks to a stranger without assuming some feigned part.

After cruelty, the second main count in the missionaries' indictment would probably concern women. It is true that the Bantu had not thought of marriage as a loving partnership between equals who took pleasure in each other's company; in every tribe it seems to have been rather a contract between groups, in which as a matter of convenience certain services and rights were transferred. But for pleasure in companionship, men turned to men and women to women. Lewanika's words to Coillard— 'This is my home'—show the ultimate barrenness of the Bantu kind of marriage and it is hard to see how a more fruitful human relationship could have developed without the destructive enlivening force of a wholly new set of ideas.

Here perhaps lay one of the most fruitful causes of misunderstanding in the future. Marriage to the Bantu was a part of the tribal system and the natural order; the woman was expected to work for her husband in the fields, to bear him children, to cook him food. Her influence might be considerable but her formal place in the household was emphatically second. The Bantu picture of marriage—in spite of very wide differences between tribes—was generally such that marriage in the Old Testament, when the missionaries came to explain it, was easily intelligible;

Jacob working for Rachel, Sarah urging Abraham to take Hagar her handmaid, the relations between senior and junior wives— there was no difficulty in understanding such stories as these. But, except to Chaka, the penalty of stoning to death for adultery would seem to the Bantu excessive and in general the act of sex seems to have been regarded as a natural function which ought to be performed with some artistry, in which instruction was given to both sexes at the time of initiation. It was part of nature, to be taken naturally, inter-acting like all parts of nature with super-natural forces, so that among some people there would be ritual acts of intercourse to fertilize a new field or bless the setting up of a new homestead, in another there would be abstention between man and wife before a hunt or a ceremony, an abstention of a ritual or even magic nature. Among the Zulu, marriage was delayed for military reasons and conception before marriage was a disgrace, but though it might provide a magical benefit one does not get the impression that any Zulu except Chaka thought of sexual restraint as having any virtue in itself.

The act of sex then was something natural and a part of nature, but marriage was a social contract and the rules forbidding or permitting marriage and regulating sexual contact outside marriage were everywhere an essential part of the whole network of society; they were part of the society, and marriage, being between groups, linked society together. Marriage might be relatively stable among the Zulus, more liable to dissolve among the Lozi; there might be a dozen gradations of difference between a dozen tribes. But in each case the system had grown slowly and naturally and a balance had been built up to which all the institutions of each tribe had contributed. Thus at this tribal stage the breakdown of one institution was likely to be fatal to the whole system of marriage and sex relationships. And in the new world that was to come with the coming of the Europeans, marriage, initiation, the whole complex of institutions, in the form they had once taken, were to suffer many shocks.

Nor was this all. Among the people the Bantu were to meet a long period of development had produced an utterly different set of ideas about sex and marriage, a difference that was to embitter relations and permeate the thought of each race about the other. European beliefs about marriage had grown from a very complex religious and psychological background. Old Testament tribalism, not so different from that of the Bantu, had developed on two lines. Tribal rules and taboos had been codified into a strict ritual observance, while there had been a parallel advance in the Wisdom literature of the Apocrypha towards a system of morality derived not from magical compulsion nor from external authority but from an inner integrity. In the first century of the Christian era, this system of morality was refreshed and transformed into a new stream by the Christian revelation; at the same time Jews and Christians alike were confronted by a pagan world which had lost faith in magical taboos regarding sex and among whom few had found an inner moral integrity arising from philosophical convictions; the result was a despairing and rather gloomy practice of sexual excesses of great variety. Christianity reacted strongly against these excesses and divagations, preaching a Way of the Spirit in which sexual restraint played an important part, a Way that would lead to spiritual joy in this world and the next. This was coupled with teaching of the supreme value of the individual soul, whether housed in a male or female body.

This teaching—which in the context of this book it is of course important to remember is not European in origin—flowed Westward. Made the official religion of the Roman Empire, Christianity was again and again in danger of eclipse in the Dark Ages; it suffered from strange heresies and fanatical extremes. But for 2,000 years certain constant values remained, common to all the main streams of thought and revelation and to most heresies, to the troubadours of Provence as to the most rigorous of medieval ascetics and the most austere of Calvinists. All agreed on the value of the individual soul, whether male or female—and here is the difference from the other Asiatic religions: all —though in varying degrees—believed that restraint in sex has a spiritual value of its own; all, though often unconsciously, made some attempt at the sublimation of sex, at directing the purely biological urge into such channels as mystical devotion to the Virgin, romantic devotion to a mistress perhaps glimpsed only for a moment, or, more remotely, to the lifelong study of philology or the perfection of a spinning-jenny. And here the Christian tradition is sharply differentiated from animistic religions, magical practices, and all those systems for which the only common name is paganism.

The first representatives of the Christian tradition who came to Southern Africa were missionaries who believed consciously in these ideals and tried to follow them. Later came many of whom this could hardly be said, but all had been brought up in a society in which they were the official currency. The invaders might themselves in practice disregard, but in the nineteenth century they would seldom in theory disown, a respect for womanhood as an ideal, a belief that sex was a part of man's make-up that linked him with the beast and that he had also another link with some exterior spiritual force, a belief that in marriage there should be companionship, respect, and similarity of interest.

In all this there is implicit a dualism, a concept—which the humblest Pioneer would have understood—that in every man there was something of the beast and also something opposed to the beast, which he might have called either spiritual or rational. It is a dualism which in the life and teachings of the founder of Christianity has been resolved into a unity of purpose and integrity of person but which is heavily stressed and not finally resolved in the writings of St. Paul; it is far more apparent among the Northern Europeans who were to invade Africa than among the Southerners. But among all to some extent is to be found an unresolved dualism, the feeling that whenever the act of sex is performed a concession is made to the beast. It is not peculiar to Christianity; it is the theme of Euripides' play *Hippolytus*, in which an image of the Goddess of Chastity stands on one side of the stage, of the Goddess of Love on the other, and in which the whole action is concerned with the conflict between the two ideals of conduct. It is, surely, implied in a rudimentary form, in the ritual abstentions from intercourse before a hunt or after breaking the ground for cultivation among the Lele and others.[20] But it had become much stronger among Christian Europeans than in any other cultures. Strong already in the Middle Ages, the feeling came up into consciousness among the Victorian English when Darwin put natural selection before them as the method of evolution and faced them with the horrifying fact of their common ancestry with the beast. Their response was prudery about the mention of sex, a chivalrous exaltation of woman—or at least of the Victorian lady—as fragile, pure, and apart; and as an ideal of manhood, Kipling's Brushwood Boy, the youngest Major in the Army, gallant in action, devoted to his work, unkissed at thirty by any woman but his mother, known in the Mess as Galahad.

It was to this period and this tradition that the Pioneers belonged, to a society in which at its best sex was sublimated and idealized, at its worst unhappily repressed or indulged in with a conviction of wrongdoing. To men from such a society, people who looked on sex as the Bantu did must seem shameless and immoral; to some, an active temptation, to others a target on which to project their own repressed desires. Wherever the Victorian English met women who did not wear stays and petticoats, this conflict arose; in the Pacific they were perhaps more apt to yield to temptation, in Africa, to attribute lewdness to those in whom they tried to repress their interest. In a later generation the roles were sometimes to be reversed; Africans brought up in the Mission School were to be shocked by Europeans who had learnt from Freud the importance of avoiding repressions and had forgotten the Christian teaching of the dangers of an empty house, swept and garnished.

I have been trying to consider the Bantu as they were before the coming of Europeans and how far their institutions and ways of thought might be expected to fuse with those of the new-comers. And in such an attempt what is known of tribal life today helps to interpret the past; the anthropologist comes to the rescue of the historian, just as the historian may set the anthropologist's work in perspective. There are two aspects of African tribal society, described by other writers too, but put with admirable clarity by Paul Bohannan, writing of the Tiv:[21] they illuminate the difficulties of every African king and perhaps of every leader who is not a military dictator. The Tiv, says Bohannan, are confronted with two dilemmas, individual and social. He writes: 'First the individual dilemma. It is dangerous for any man to become prominent; he is immediately the target of . . . malice. . . . A prominent man is considered dangerous; no one has any real confidence that he will not use for his own personal advantage every bit of power he can get. On the other hand . . . every Tiv wants a prominent man to protect him against others and at the same time fears that man as he may act against himself.'

Nothing could be clearer than this. The second or social dilemma arises as a result of the first. A man may find himself a leader of a village A as against another village B; he may also be a leader of A and B as against some other grouping of villages. 'Depending on his character and the frequency with which he has appeared as a leader in the wider grouping, he may have considerable influence in B, even as opposed to A, but that influence is regarded with suspicion and jealousy by all members of B, who are convinced that he is bound to favour A at their expense. Equally, in affairs between A and B, A will regard as wholly unjustifiable any favouring of B at their expense.' If he should favour B too much, he will lose influence at once in A and will then automatically cease to be of importance in B. If on the other hand, he shows no favour to B, his position will be jeopardized as leader in the wider grouping. 'The effective juggling of these factors is the practical art of Tiv politics,' writes Bohannan —a sentence from which one might well omit the word 'Tiv'.

Section 4: A People in Waiting

Returning to the Bantu tribes as they were before the Europeans came, one is conscious of a lack of any ferment that would bring new growth to life. There can be no doubt that among many tribes much of the traditional teaching was meant to discourage as an impertinence originality and all desire on a young man's part to better himself at the expense of his fellows. The virtues most extolled by the Bantu are held in esteem in the West too, but with a different emphasis, and the Bantu emphasis is unlikely to make for invention, discovery, or long painful toil. Among the Lovedu, for instance, 'conduct that promotes smooth relationships is good';[22] courtesy and respect due to age are of greater importance than truth. Moderation, compromise, humility, are rated higher among these descendants of the Monomotapa's tribe than courage; laws and institutions are not ends in themselves but exist for people, and if one party seems dissatisfied by a court's decision—why, the court will usually re-open the case and hear the parties again and try to find a decision which both can accept; agreement is prized far more highly than any form of compulsion or resort to rules. There is little idea of an abstract or absolute justice nor of that less respectable idea, an outraged moral system that has to be appeased. To get somewhere by the appointed moment seems a strange ambition and they cannot understand how Europeans tolerate the loss of human life involved in the use of motor traffic.

This is the ethical teaching of one tribe—as recorded, one must add, by one observer. But though these counsels of prudence, restraint, and moderation do not accord with the Zulu praise songs and public boasting, the teaching of the Lovedu does echo thoughts and ways of looking at life that are common to many tribes, that may almost be spoken of as characteristic of the Bantu, that link up with their view of the cosmos. Their world is almost always one that was created by the acts of a Creator, thought of in a shadowy way as now remote from the affairs of men, certainly not as sustaining the world by a continuous act of creation, but as having, so to speak, wound it up and set it going, just as some eighteenth-century deists believed in Europe. But of course their thoughts, even in one tribe, even in one person, are not consistent; thoughts on such a subject seldom are consistent; perhaps never, unless reduced to writing. And in most tribes, in varying proportions, some elements of three distinct sets of ideas are to be traced. In one, a remote and slightly absent-minded Creator may be induced by constant reminders to use his influence to keep natural phenomena on the normal course and avoid disasters such as drought or locusts; in the second, this kind of power, or some of it, has been delegated to a rainmaking king or a group of ancestors who by the use of charms or words can coax certain reactions from what we should call natural forces; and in the third, which is magical not religious, the charms compel the reactions. These three ideas are not usually felt to be inconsistent and often exist side by side in the same person. In all, what is desired is to preserve the customary course of things, to make sure that creation does not get off the rails.

The Bantu universe, as it was before the impact of European ideas, was everywhere one in which some of the forces of nature could be guided by religion or compelled by magic; those that were evil and disruptive were usually no part of the original creation and might be deflected without question of offending the Creator. Everywhere the dead were able to affect the health and well-being of the living. Everywhere the abnormal was feared. A custom recorded of the Baluyia of Kavirondo is[23] surely typical of Bantu thought: they offer prayers to God to 'let things take their normal course', 'to let the sun rise and shine as usual'. Indeed, all the magical and religious practices of this people seem designed to prevent anything unusual or, when the prodigy has occurred, to quarantine it off and prevent the contagion spreading. Birth and death are felt to be abnormal, but in a much higher degree the birth of twins or the appearance of a child's upper teeth before its lower. Wide-spread among all the tribes is this suspicion that anything out of the ordinary is harmful and that the universe is likely to do one a wrong and always waiting to pounce. All this makes a discouraging world for any child that is more than usually intelligent or inventive, and it will be seen that it is not easy to translate into a Bantu language such words as 'adventure' or 'romance', ideas that played a big part in the minds of the hunters and settlers of Victorian times.

One more characteristic must be noted. Among a people who

had no idea of money, there was usually also little idea of equating a favour given with a favour received. It is said of the Lovedu[24] that 'there is complete disregard of equivalence between what is contributed by a partner and what he is entitled to'. Among the same people, when beer is provided for a working-party in the fields, gate-crashers who have done no work 'drink calabash for calabash with the workers'. This attitude, enjoined on Christians in the parable of the workers in the vineyard, does not come easily to Europeans or Asians, corrupted by many generations of commerce, but is natural, surely, to most of the Bantu; it is a difference as likely as almost anything could be to produce friction between master and servant or buyer and seller.

And when the missionaries came, it must be remembered that they brought with them two sharply contrasted sets of ideas on this subject. To the Africans they appeared to be people with possessions; they had blankets, guns, powder, wagons. Even the most frugal sat on chairs, ate off table-cloths, hung pictures on their walls and varied their diet; they used strange and complicated tools, bought land to live on and in short stood for a world based on legal ownership by individuals. They brought with them a religion which had matured and reached its fulfilment thousands of years after the beginnings of individual ownership on the Tigris and the Nile, hundreds of years after Isaiah had preached against joining field to field, at a time when landlords already had unjust stewards and tenants who would not pay their rent. It was a religion which took property for granted as a social institution and preached that giving it too much importance was a spiritual encumbrance. Every act of the missionaries argued a belief in property; out of church they would scold their converts for being improvident, yet in their sermons they told their hearers to consider the lilies and the ravens and pay no heed to material needs or to the future—advice they seemed most markedly not to take themselves. It is not surprising that the Bantu have sometimes found honesty a rather confusing virtue.

Many amiable characteristics the missionaries would usually concede that the Bantu possessed—patience and cheerfulness perhaps coming highest among their virtues. But even their virtues, in the new world that was to come, would be of little help to them. They were to meet a people who had come to admire energy and efficiency, success in a material world and the achievement of comfort, who to get these things for a few years in their old age, were prepared not only to risk death but to work without relief or apparent pleasure for the greater part of their lives. These tendencies in the European were only a part of his heritage, but when he came into contact with the Bantu, in whom they were so markedly lacking, he developed and exaggerated them.

The counterpart of this exaggeration of typically European behaviour was that for the Bantu all that was most African, all that was most characteristic of his nature, worked against him in the new environment. His delight in improvisation would seldom be of use in contact with a people who liked to reduce the element of the unforeseen and work by exact time-tables; his belief in magic made him attribute the results of his own inexperience or clumsiness to the malevolence of enemies or spirits; his training in politeness made him untruthful; his interest in personal relationships made him neglect the serious business of money-making for gossip.

Thus the seeds of strife and misunderstanding were present from a time before the Europeans came. The newcomers found people who had made little progress towards any provision for a material future more distant than the next crop, who in Victorian times had no visual art worth the name, while their music was impermanent because unrecorded. Nor is there any evidence that their religion provided, as the religions of the East do, a personal inner life of devotion; they had neither saints nor sadhus. But many states had come into being that were as well organized politically as Mercia or Wessex before the reign of Alfred; the Bemba, Barotse, and Matabele were better organized than Alfred's Wessex; the idea of law among the Barotse was far more highly developed. And the Bantu system did produce, in Khama and Moshesh, if not quite in Lewanika or Mzilikazi, royal statesmen who can be spoken of in the same breath with Alfred. It was the misfortune of the Bantu that it was at so late a stage that they came into contact with the complex system of law, religion, and literature that had grown up in Western Europe. The gap was too wide for an easy fusion.

If Wessex had not produced an Alfred at the right moment and England had been overrun by the Danes, darkness and heathendom would have covered the land and England might have fallen back as far as Ireland did; in that case a true fusion with the Normans would have been delayed for centuries. As it was, the set-backs in European history were never final; there were always ashes still alight somewhere from which to re-kindle the fires. Ireland and Northumbria sent monks to Germany, Alfred called scholars from Rome, the Normans brought back to Britain something of what had been lost since Alfred's day. From the time the Romans left Britain till well into the Middle Ages, degeneration, darkness, and relapse were never far away, were constantly getting the upper hand, but were driven back again and again by fresh reinforcements from another part of the battlefield.

What was saved—again and again by so narrow a margin— was a liquor that had been blended by centuries of history; it had been strained, distilled, mixed, held up to the light and judged, strained, and blended again. The heritage of Babylon, Assyria, and the valley of the Indus—all the accumulated learning and speculation of great cities and empires—had passed both to Egypt and to the Jews and by each had been transformed; what resulted was blended again. Contrast for instance the divinity of the Tower of Babel, a story which belongs to the earliest layer of the Pentateuch, with the teaching of the Book of Wisdom, written perhaps 600 years later, after the captivity of Babylon. And while spiritual wisdom developed among the Jews, drawing strength from across the eastern desert, knowledge of letters and numbers, art, clothes, religion, passed from Egypt to Crete and Mycenae, from Argos to Athens and then back to Alexandria. The rich vintage of Judaism, already fortified with juices from Babylon and Assyria, came to its maturity in a moment of time, was blended with Greek philosophy and again was mixed with the younger wines in the great vats of Rome. It was this draught—the progressive revelation of some 3,000 years—that Charlemagne and Alfred fought to preserve for their descendants.

In Europe there was this great advantage: the cross-fertilization that was constantly taking place was between stocks not too widely different. The Normans were a little ahead of the Saxons in armour and offensive weapons, in building and feudal organization, but not much; their ideas and institutions could fuse naturally and easily within a few generations. Yet I live in a village that is called Sherfield English because in 1303 it was held by one Roger L'anglois, Roger the Englishman. Two hundred and fifty years after the Conquest it was still so unusual for an Englishman to hold a village that it took its name from the fact.

But the Bantu had tasted no sip of the imperial liquor brewed by Babylon, Egypt, Palestine, Greece, Rome, France, Italy, and England, until it was brought them—not always by the worthiest purveyors—across a gulf much wider than 2,000 years. It was 5,000 years since geometry had begun as the floods subsided on the Nile and the Tigris. Some expiring flaw of wind had brought them with its last puff the faintest trace of a scent of Egypt; from Egypt through Meroë on the Upper Nile perhaps had come their knowledge of iron and pottery, of domestic animals, something of their ideas of kingship. But not writing or numbers or the idea of measuring, not even the wagon-wheels that brought conviction to Jacob, not even the plough.

They were a people who moved on from place to place, whether they were agriculturalists who moved slowly or pastoralists who moved more often. They did not own land as individuals; it had not occurred to them that land was something that could be owned as a spear was owned; it was something of which a man might have the use if the king agreed, but the right to use it was not something that could be exchanged for something else. It was the king's duty to see his people were fed and so he gave them land; it was his duty to make the rain; but land was hardly more subject to ownership than rain. And not much progress is made until men start to improve land for their successors. It is not surprising that degeneration and darkness should have gained the upper hand over the builders of Zimbabwe, just as they have gained the upper hand in Europe again and again; what is difficult is to find a reason for the sudden spurt of progress that Zimbabwe represents. Indeed, what needs explanation throughout history is not the long periods of stagnation, but the short bursts of energy when the wind of the spirit blows and the mind is adventurous and enquiring and new discoveries are made, when a spark in that strong wind will put an end to the rubbish of old growth.

That breath, that spark, was lacking. A people capable of controlling and organizing complicated political systems and of arguing subtle legal points, were hopelessly divided among themselves, isolated from the great streams of human thought, for the moment stagnant, bereft of inventiveness and the fire of enthusiasm. They were a people in waiting; waiting for a force that would unite them, that would revive them with fresh ideas, that would bring both the wind and the spark to grass eager for the flame.

Part Two

CONQUEST AND SETTLEMENT

I. The Chameleon and the Fly

Section 1: The Road to the North

'Did you ever see a chameleon catch a fly?' Lobengula, King of the Matabele, asked of the missionary Helm. 'The chameleon gets behind the fly and remains motionless for some time, then he advances very slowly and gently, first putting forward one leg and then another. At last, when well within reach, he darts his tongue and the fly disappears. England is the chameleon and I am that fly.'[1]

It is a saying that describes admirably the essence of what was happening in the five years from 1888 to 1893, but of course it makes things seem much simpler than they were; 'England' was not one creature, stalking closer and closer with predatory eyes on the fly, but a complex bundle of men and motives. Nor was Lobengula the unsuspecting fly but a more tragic figure; he perceived his doom, he saw again and again the only course that might avoid disaster, but by the nature of his kingdom and the people who surrounded him, by the nature of the threat, he was prevented again and again from doing what he knew to be best and was forced to play such cards as he had in a way he knew must lead to disaster.

He is a figure picturesque as well as tragic; 'a grand old savage',[2] wrote one of the pioneers who came to his kraal, naked 'save for a thin roll of blue cloth round his waist' and a sporran of monkey-skins, a 'fine coppery-bronze in colour', 'scrupulously clean in his person', weighing about twenty stone, but 'not unwieldy in his stoutness', 'tall, well-built, and every inch a king'.[3] 'Lo Bengula walks quite erect, with his head thrown back and his broad chest expanded and as he marches along at a slow pace with his long staff in his right hand while all the men around

shout his praises, he looks his part to perfection,'⁴ wrote Sir
Sydney Shippard. And another said: 'I have seen many European
and native potentates, and with the exception of the Tsar Alexander, never have I seen a ruler of men of more imposing appearance.'⁵

He received visitors in 'the buck kraal', and of the many
Europeans who came to see him, mostly begging for favours,
almost all found they had to wait some time in the hot sun, in the
acrid smell of dung and drying skins, before he would emerge
from the covered wagon he used as a bedroom. An uncomfortable
sojourn in barbarous surroundings, and only too often it was to
find the King evasive and reluctant to give an answer. He saw
the pit that was digged for him; he would turn away if he could.

This evasiveness had been there to reckon with thirty years
earlier, in the time of his father Mzilikazi, even in the case of the
first Robert Moffat, whom Mzilikazi as a rule loved and admired.
Promises would be made; yes, a piece of land would be allotted
for a mission station, men would be sent to build a house. But in
fact nothing would happen; weeks would pass and then a sudden
and inexplicable hostility would appear, only to be replaced by a
friendliness just as hard to understand. 'A hostile feeling against
Mr. Moffat was growing. On the morning of October 21st, the
white men awoke to a great uproar . . . the whole town was on
the move. The king's wagons led the way. . . . Moffat jumped on
his horse and rode after the king to try and find out the meaning
of it all. He was not allowed to approach the king, however, and
had to return to camp. This rebuff was soon followed by greater
insults. Messengers came to accuse the white men of being
spies. . . . They had only to give the sign'—so the rumour ran—
'and troops would rush in, kill the king and his soldiers and
capture the women, the herds, and the flocks. A wagonload of
goods was demanded. . . . They must no longer fish. . . . They
must do no shooting. . . . They must not move from the spot
where they were camped. They were not even allowed to buy
milk or food.'⁶ But not long afterwards, Mzilikazi received the
party kindly 'as if nothing had happened'.

This alternation of kindly feeling with suspicion was not really surprising. South Africa had a history that was not unknown to Mzilikazi; he knew the long story of Kaffir wars and quiet infiltration; he had heard how first the missionaries had come and then the traders and last the soldiers, how one chief after another had ended in despair or exile or had lived on as a vassal with his power reduced. And there was much in Mzilikazi's kingdom and Lobengula's which Europeans were bound to dislike and the king was well aware of it; they were too far apart in time-scales of development to understand each other wholly; a certain amused liking was often there, sometimes a warmer feeling, but it was always liable to be interrupted by different standards of conduct, above all by suspicion arising from the realities of the political situation.

It was cruelty to which the European visitors took most exception and which on the conscious level was most often put forward as a barrier. Two men, 'Matabele' Thompson and J. Cooper-Chadwick, have described what is probably one incident. Some way from the royal kraal a man had stopped a girl who was bringing beer for the King; he took the beer from her and drank it. He was perhaps drunk already but he knew his offence was serious and fled; he was captured after some days' search.

'His ears have not listened to the king's words. Cut off his ears.'

That was the first order, carried out on the spot. Then came the second.

'He has tasted the king's beer. Cut off his tongue.'

'His nose has smelt the king's beer. Cut off his nose.'

'His eyes have seen the king's beer. Cover his eyes.' This last order was performed by 'peeling down the skin of his forehead till it lapped over the wretched man's eyes'.

Cooper-Chadwick saw this sentence carried out; Matabele Thompson arrived afterwards and saw 'the most awful spectacle I have seen in my life . . . crawling on his hands and knees, a native... with great lumps of flesh hanging from his face, his nose over his mouth. . . . It was awful to see how the king enjoyed the spectacle. He was a savage in the fullest sense of the word.'[7] And

Coillard writes of a little herdboy, questioned about some trifling offence, who began to prevaricate. 'Lobengula ordered him to come and crouch before him. After a long pause, he sprang up and said: "That lying mouth must be punished." He ordered four men to hold him down and seizing a glowing brand himself knelt on his chest and applied it to his lips . . . the poor little fellow's lips were quite burnt away.'[8]

Yet not long after the first of these incidents, all the white men in the country 'being assembled to celebrate St. Patrick's day', Cooper-Chadwick suggested 'we should all there and then adjourn to the king and ask him to join us in drinking St. Patrick's health'. They found 'the old buster' in a very good humour; he asked very amusing and shrewd questions, and eventually drank off three small bottles of champagne 'without a wink, graciously bending his head and mentioning St. Patrick's name before each'. This was on 17 March 1890, when feeling in Bulawayo ran high against the Europeans. And there was still another mood in which Europeans came before Lobengula. Sir Sydney Shippard wrote: 'I was careful to have seats carried in by my servants, as I found that all Europeans here without exception are accustomed to sit on the ground before Lobengula, exactly as the natives do, some of the old white inhabitants, and even some of the new concession seekers, actually grovelling before the Amandebele Chief with their hands on their knees and thus sidling up to their places in the circle in the crouching attitude of the natives who are fawning on him for boiled beef and Kaffir beer.'[9]

To explain the political realities which formed the background to this alternation of horror with amused tolerance, of scorn with obsequious fawning, it is necessary to go back a few years and also to look at the map. Matabeleland blocked the road from the Cape Colony to the north. That was the cardinal fact. And in the nineteenth century the Cape Colony and its people looked to the north as naturally as the older of the United States looked to the west. It was the road of expansion and progress but it did not, as in America, lie across vast prairies but through a narrow

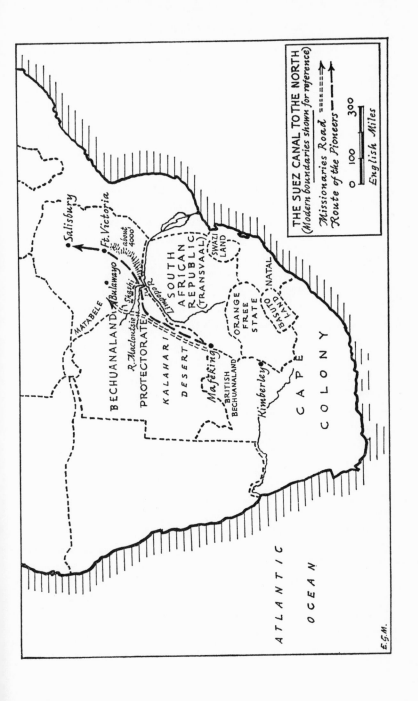

THE SUEZ CANAL TO THE NORTH
(Modern boundaries shown for reference)

Missionaries Road ========>
Route of the Pioneers ----->

0   100   300
English Miles

Salisbury

Ft. Victoria

about 4000'

Sigati

Bulawayo

MATABELE

BECHUANALAND

R. Macloutsie

PROTECTORATE

KALAHARI   DESERT

Limpopo

SOUTH AFRICAN REPUBLIC (TRANSVAAL)

SWAZI LAND

ORANGE FREE STATE

BASUTO LAND

NATAL

Mafeking

BRITISH BECHUANALAND

Kimberley

CAPE   COLONY

ATLANTIC

OCEAN

E.G.M.

defile. The Kalahari desert forced every road to bend eastwards, while the great block of the Transvaal—Kruger's South African Republic—stopped the way if one went too far to the east. To go west was to risk dying of thirst; to go east might well mean being stopped, turned back, or even imprisoned. Only a narrow road was left between these dangers, and that road naturally debouched in Matabeleland.

The Transvaal had once been annexed to the British crown and for a short time it had seemed as though the party among the burghers who were prepared to acquiesce in this annexation might prevail. That hope had died; Majuba had been fought and a British force defeated; Gladstone's Ministry had restored the Transvaal's independence, subject only to restrictions on expanding northwards and to dealing with foreign powers. It had fallen to John Moffat to announce the retrocession after Majuba to the African chiefs of the Transvaal. 'A few spoke but for the most part there was the silence of despair. One gentle old man, Mokhatle, a man of great influence, used the language of resignation. "When I was a child, the Matabele came, they swept over us like the wind and we bowed before them like the long white grass on the plains. They left us and we stood upright again. The Boers came and we bowed ourselves under them in like manner. The British came and we rose upright, our hearts lived within us and we said: Now we are the children of the Great Lady. And now that is past and we must lie flat again under the wind—who knows what are the ways of God?" The others took a different tone. All protested, some in plaintive tones, others in the language of fierce defiance. . . .'

But within a few years those chiefs were forgotten; 'their bones', writes Moffat, 'lay bleaching round the mountain fastnesses to which they had trusted in vain.'[10] At the time with which we are concerned, the years from 1887-93, when the sands were running out for the Matabele, that strife was an old tale and the main conflict in the Transvaal was between the burghers—the survivors, sons and grandsons of the original trekkers—and the Uitlanders, that is the immigrants, mostly British, but with a strong element from the European continent and many Jews.

On the one side stood a people of peasant origin, speaking the dialect called the 'taal', which was to become the Afrikaans language, determined to stick to a pastoral way of life, their faith the Calvinism of the seventeenth century, a people reading only the Bible, of which they believed every word to be divinely dictated, a people bitterly opposed to any change; a people of the saddle, the rifle, and the open air, with a high belief in their God, a high sense of hospitality, honour and the moral law, strict in observance of their code, rigid and unbending. Facing them was the shifting, greedy, kaleidoscopic world of the mining camp, of men out to make their fortunes quickly, men with no God but gold, men of a new world which had lived through the Age of Reason, heard the worship of the Goddess of Reason, had seen the coming of machines. The Uitlanders were hampered at every turn by restrictions that were usually obsolete and often corrupt, denied any say in the government, not only of the Republic but even of the city of their creation, a city growing swiftly into a roaring cosmopolis, a city of gold mines, banks, saloons, gambling-dens, yet a city that was still treated by its rulers as a *dorp* in the veld in which certain undesirable aliens had come to live. 'An unequalled climate', wrote Lord Randolph Churchill, 'a soil of exuberant fertility, mines of gold, silver, coal, and iron, all of great richness: the Boers in their stubborn and mulish ignorance have resolved that so far as in them lies none of this great wealth shall be taken advantage of and developed.' 'In a country where . . . the rapid construction of railways is essential . . . the same stubborn ignorance, the same mulish folly, has successfully delayed any such construction.'[11]

It was the 'perverse simplicity' and the injustice—as it seemed to the English—of the rulers of the Transvaal that made it an impenetrable obstacle to any plans of expansion northwards. The burghers had turned back and even imprisoned the first missionaries sent by the Paris Missionary Society to teach the heathen further north; they had attacked and destroyed the station laboriously built up by Livingstone. They had disliked missions because they did not want the natives educated and strengthened by new knowledge; this attitude to the preaching of the gospel—their own gospel—had relaxed since those early days and by now they were themselves engaged in mission work. But they were certainly not the people to permit a new state to come into being beyond them, a state sure to be founded on principles of conduct and belief which they detested; if they could control the life-line to the south of such a state they would squeeze it till death resulted.

There could then be no doubt in the mind of anyone with his eyes on the north; anything more ambitious than a shooting-party must go by the 'missionaries' road', the narrow strip that lay west of Kruger's boundary, in country where there were still water-holes, before the desert became impassable for oxen. This strip was what Rhodes called 'the Suez Canal' to the north; it led through Khama's country to Matabeleland. A small party prepared to face danger could leave it and go still further west through the desert to Lake Ngami, as, at the risk of his life, Livingstone had once done, but this could never be a regular route. Further north it would be possible to turn east, curving along the northern bank of the Limpopo, a route that would avoid Kruger and also Matabeleland proper but would bring the traveller among the Mashona, over whom Lobengula claimed sovereignty. Neither missionary, trader, nor hunter would make much headway there unless Lobengula had 'given him the road'. It became then the custom to go north by the missionaries' road to Lobengula's court and there wait his favour before going on.

At first, the white visitors to the court of Mzilikazi had been missionaries, seeking leave to set up stations and attempt to convert either the Matabele themselves or the Mashona tribes to the east on whom they preyed. Livingstone, Moffat, Coillard, had come with petitions of this kind; Coillard was refused permission to go to the Banyai (that is, the Mashona) but allowed to go on to the Barotse. Moffat was in the end permitted to set up a station but neither he nor anyone else had any success in converting the Matabele; the missionaries in Matabeleland, wrote

John Moffat, the son of Robert, 'do not exercise the slightest
influence on those around them'. These first petitioners had no
selfish objects; of those who followed soon after them—men
such as Selous—some sought to make their living by hunting or
trading, but they had no objects inconsistent with the Matabele
way of life. 'Most of them were hunters and travellers, men of
respectable characters, gentlemen in fact; in whose conduct and
deportment the natives saw nothing to conflict with the teaching
of the missionaries', wrote Moffat, of Bechuanaland but it was
as true of Matabeleland. 'Later on there came visitors of a different type. . . .' And by 1890 there was quite a settlement of
Europeans at Bulawayo, among whom were certainly some 'of
a different type', traders or adventurers living a life of idleness
while they hoped for a rich prize to come, concession-seekers,
feasting where they hoped to be masters, like Penelope's suitors
in the Odyssey.

The first concession was made in 1869 to Sir John Swinburne
as representative of the London and Limpopo Company; he was
granted mining rights in the Tati area, to the extreme south-west
of Matabeleland, in country to which Khama and the Bamangwato might have entered a claim if they had thought it worth the
risk. Several companies besides Swinburne's were formed to work
gold in this area, though with little success till the railway came,
but Lobengula must have found the Tati settlement a trial and in
1887 he issued a commission to the manager of Sir John Swinburne's company, Sam Edwards, the son of one of Moffat's
colleagues, a man Lobengula had long known and trusted. 'As
the laws of my country are not suitable for the government of
Europeans . . . I, Lobengula, . . . hereby authorize you . . . with
power . . . to make by proclamation all such laws and regulations
as you may consider expedient and necessary for the peace, order,
and good government of the Tati district . . . and to represent
me in all matters occurring in the said district. . . .'[12]

It was not to be expected that Lobengula should have heard
of the Mogul Emperors, rulers of more millions than he of
thousands, monarchs whose wealth was famous throughout the

world. Two centuries earlier those Emperors had given, though
with less formality, just such concessions to certain countrymen
of Sam Edwards, permitting them to exercise a jurisdiction not
very clearly defined, but real enough, at Madras, Bombay, and
Calcutta. In both cases, the concession was made necessary by the
contrast between the standards of a loose local administration and
the expectations of a foreign people used to something quite
different, to a stricter protection against crime and a more formal
adjudication in disputes. In both cases the result was loss of
sovereignty. For Lobengula, the chameleon had come a step
closer. All the same, to grant the Tati concession was probably
the wisest thing he could have done—and in that judgement the
tragedy of his situation is implicit.

The road to the north debouched, then, in Matabeleland and
all who came by the narrow strip between the Transvaal and the
desert came to Lobengula's court. And in the eighties the pace
was quickening. The European powers were casting greedy eyes
on Africa and so were individual adventurers. Many people
believed that in Matabeleland and Mashonaland there was gold
as rich as on the Rand; many pressed that way, determined to
make their fortunes. One man, who had already made a fortune
for himself, was determined to ensure that in this new territory
the flag that would fly should not be the tricolour of the South
African Republic, not the flag of Germany or Portugal, but the
Union Jack.

Section 2: The Treaty

Men have written of Rhodes as though there were something
unusual about his dreams of grandeur. But many young men have
pictured themselves leading armies across the world and disposing
of continents; the odd thing about Rhodes was that he had the
knack of making these boyish dreams come true and that,
perhaps for that reason, he never grew out of them. Nor was
there anything unusual about his sincere belief that the Victorian
Englishman was the fine flower of creation, that the most fortunate destiny that could befall anyone was to be a British

subject; in this he represented most of his countrymen—though few would have wakened a friend in the middle of the night to remind him how grateful he ought to be. ' "Wake up, Grey, wake up!" "Eh, what's the matter? Is the tent on fire?" sleepily murmured Grey. "No, no, but I just wanted to ask you, have you ever thought how lucky you are to be born an Englishman when there are so many millions who were not. . . ." '[13] Grey and every other Englishman of his day agreed; what was unusual was that Rhodes acted on his beliefs; he thought of his money primarily as something to be used to bring people under the flag.

Rhodes came to regard his own ends as so important that they justified means sometimes far from honourable. But he was aware, in a way his countrymen often were not, of the value, and sometimes even of the feelings, of other people. He came nearer than anyone has ever done to reconciling Afrikaners of the Cape Colony to British rule; towards the end of the South African war, to an audience in a mood of vainglorious triumph, he could begin: 'You think you have beaten the Dutch, but you have not . . . let there be no vaunting words, no vulgar triumph; [you must] make them feel that the bitterness is past . . . teach your children to remember . . . that the Dutch children are as much part of South Africa as they are. . . .'[14] If he was self-centred, he was also magnanimous; if he could be petty about winning at whist,[15] he thought habitually in terms of continents rather than counties and could look both backwards and forwards in time; if his ideals were not so high as those of his critics thirty years later,[16] he did at least take active steps to make them real. It is easy to see the faults—the vanity, the eagerness for power, the cynical phrases, the occasional brutal indifference to whoever stood in his way; harder, over the lapse of years and to a modern mind, to convey the warmth, the generosity, the power of inspiring others with his own courage, above all his practical readiness to negotiate and compromise. It was possible, in his own time, to dislike the high voice, the trick of repeating a phrase over and over again while he rubbed his hands, the untidy clothes —possible, but not for many; the effect he had on most people may be judged from Miss Rose Blennerhassett's account of his arrival at Umtali in 1891. Miss Blennerhassett, a nurse, had been persuaded by Bishop Knight Bruce to come to Mashonaland and was making a start with a hospital at Umtali; she herself was obviously a woman of remarkable courage and determination, great cheerfulness, and a sense of the practical. But there was gloom in Umtali; drunkenness and fever were both sporadic and endemic; and there was 'that terrible African depression, which sweeps over a community as mist descends from the mountain tops'. Then Rhodes arrived; 'he was besieged with petitions of all sorts. Malcontents and chronic grumblers went to his hut and came away in a few moments cheerful and satisfied . . . the man's mere personal magnetism wrought the change . . . everything about the man is big—faults, virtues, projects. . . . He is the darling of Fortune . . . who does not often select her favourites from the Sunday school.'[17]

Rhodes looked north and saw that he must have the 'missionaries' road'. He or de Beers or the Crown or the Colony, or perhaps a body yet to be formed; the detail was sometimes a little blurred. That road, the Suez Canal to the north, was secured when the southern part of Bechuanaland* was annexed as a Crown Colony and the northern part proclaimed a British Protectorate, on 30 September 1885. Politically, the route was now safe through Palapye as far as Tati, which from 1887 was ruled by Sam Edwards on behalf of Lobengula. From Tati the road ran on to Bulawayo and Lobengula's court. If the missionaries' road was the Suez Canal to the north, Matabeleland was the Red Sea. And of Matabeleland proper, the area from Tati to the Victoria Falls and eastward from Bulawayo, say, for 100 miles or more, there could be no question that sovereignty rested at present with Lobengula. There was less certainty as you went eastward into Mashonaland.

Portugal held the coast to the east and professed to be sovereign of the 'hinterland'—but in the course of the scramble for Africa no general agreement emerged as to what this might mean.

* It is really Ba-Tswana-land; the 'ch' is therefore soft.

Was the 'hinterland' the whole area from which trade drained down to a given stretch of coast? Or should a line be drawn on the map perpendicular to the general trend of the coast? The doctrine was never generally accepted and therefore never defined; 'effective occupation' on the other hand was regarded by every power as constituting a claim and this, too, Portugal pleaded.

It was true that in the early sixteenth century Portuguese travellers and officials had gone far into what is now Southern Rhodesia, that they had obtained from the Monomotapa a concession for mining gold, and indeed all metals but silver.* But it was not much use claiming authority from a potentate whose name had been forgotten even among his own clan; of effective occupation in any ordinarily accepted sense the Portuguese had nothing except along the coast and at Tete. As the eighties drew to a close, they once more began to send out parties, with a view to establishing 'effective occupation'—persuading a chief to accept a flag, trading with him, sometimes building a mud fort. But they were really too late; by this time, English influence was stronger than theirs in Mashonaland.[18] Meanwhile, on the West Coast, the German imperial flag had been hoisted at Angra Pequena on 1 May 1883; on the 'hinterland' doctrine, either the Germans or the Portuguese might be presumed to be casting eyes towards what is now Rhodesia; on 24 April 1884, Bismarck took a step in this direction when he announced a protectorate over Damaraland and Namaqualand.

Here, then, in the centre of the continent lay in the eighties a great area believed to be rich in gold, as yet not occupied by any European power, but the subject of shadowy claims from Portugal, eyed speculatively by Bismarck, Kruger, and Rhodes. European powers might be sometimes a trifle cavalier in their attitudes to the sovereignty of African kings but there could be no question of the sovereignty of Lobengula over Matabeleland proper. What was doubtful was how far to the east his pretensions had any validity. His claim was that beyond the territory where the Matabele themselves lived he was king as far as his *impis* had

* See Part I, Chapter IV.

raided, that is, certainly as far, and sometimes beyond, the present road from Salisbury to Fort Victoria. As to his subjects, they maintained that their only boundary was the sea.

In the last days of 1887, Ralph Williams, the British agent at Pretoria, capital of the South African Republic, sent Rhodes privately a piece of news which he at once carried to the High Commissioner for South Africa and Governor of the Cape Colony, Sir Hercules Robinson. President Kruger had accredited to Lobengula's court a Consul, Piet Grobler, and was on the point of despatching him. This was a step in execution of 'a treaty' which Grobler had obtained from Lobengula in the summer of that same year. The treaty was afterwards said to 'bear the stamp of imposture from beginning to end',[19] but there can be no reasonable doubt that Lobengula had put his mark to it. Indeed, he said he had; what he later denied was that he had understood it.

Lobengula once said that there is a fence round the word of a king, and he lived up to that saying when his promises concerned things the Matabele understood and when all the implications and results of the agreement had been stated. But he did—as will be seen—often go back on an agreement that was unpopular with his people and which led to results that they had not expected and he had only feared; in such a case he would say that he had not understood the paper he had signed and he had never agreed to it. Complete reliance cannot therefore be placed on his denial of the Grobler Treaty, but the document itself is suspect on the face of it.

The usual procedure was to sign an agreement with Lobengula in the presence of two independent witnesses who could read it, one of whom was usually a missionary, and to add a certificate by the interpreter that it had been fully explained. The Grobler Treaty bore the marks of Lobengula and four others said to be his *indunas,* * but of no one who could read it except Piet Grobler

---

* Hole says the names of the *indunas* bear no resemblance to any Matabele names and are entirely fictitious. But Moffat spoke to one of the four *indunas* and says that the others were at a distance; their names, however, had been strangely corrupted, as Moffat's Nungu becomes Nowcho in the treaty and his Emganweni becomes Omchaunien. This is partly due to the Afrikaans values of gutturals and vowels being very different from a Scot's.

and his brother Frederick. And it would be hard to convince any impartial court that an unwitnessed document which only one of the parties could read was binding on the other. 'I have no reason to doubt', wrote John Moffat, after careful enquiries, a year later, 'that when he put pen to paper at Emganweni in July 1887 [Lobengula] thought he was simply renewing the old treaty of Umsiligaas [Mzilikazi] and Potgieter, a treaty of general friendship, of which he had been informed that the copy had been lost.'

The Grobler Treaty affirmed perpetual peace between the Matabele and the Republic and acknowledged Lobengula as an independent ally. This much he may have understood, but it went much further. It bound him to help the Republic with troops whenever asked, to extradite offenders, to accept a resident Consul, and, most serious of all, to allow anyone with a pass from the President of the Republic to hunt or trade in his country. As Lobengula said to Moffat, how could he have agreed to give away his country like this? Had he not just refused one of the Grobler brothers, who asked him for an *impi* to fight Khama? Had he not just refused the other permission to live in his country? How could he have signed a treaty that bound him to do what he had just said he would not do?

Apart from all this, the Grobler Treaty was in contravention of the agreement to which the Transvaal owed its independence; the Republic's relations with native chiefs beyond the Limpopo were strictly limited. The Grobler Treaty is not therefore of much importance except as an example of the kind of difficulty with which Lobengula had to contend and because it served as the trigger to the events which followed. The news that Grobler was on the point of setting out to take up his appointment as Consul and Resident brought Rhodes to Sir Hercules Robinson, who was persuaded to send instructions to John Moffat to sign a treaty of another kind.

Robert Moffat, the first of his name, had made Bechuanaland his life's work, but had paid several visits to the Matabele and had founded the mission station at Inyati where Sykes and

Thomas worked. Mzilikatze had loved him and trusted him as far as he could trust any European. His son John had eventually become Assistant Commissioner at Palapye, the agent of the High Commissioner, with a not very clearly defined diplomatic responsibility for relations with the Matabele; he was a diplomatic agent and the servant of the Government but in a sense he was always a missionary at heart, never hesitating to report what his superiors might find unpalatable, forming his opinion always on grounds wider than those of purely national advantage. His personal integrity and his father's name gave him a special position at Bulawayo; he came as near to being trusted as was possible, perhaps for any European after his father, certainly for any official.

His new orders reached Moffat towards the end of January 1888 through Sir Sydney Shippard, who was Deputy to Sir Hercules for Bechuanaland. On 30th January, Lobengula told Moffat he had no agreement with the Transvaal which would permit them to send him a Consul, the text of the Grobler Treaty not then being available to any British authority. On 11 February, Lobengula signed what came to be known as the Moffat Treaty. This was a simpler and shorter treaty than Grobler's, providing in the first article for peace and amity between Her Majesty and the Matabele, and in the second that Lobengula would 'refrain from entering into any correspondence or treaty with any foreign state or Power to sell, alienate or cede . . . the whole or any part of the . . . country under his chieftainship without the previous knowledge and sanction of Her Majesty's High Commissioner for South Africa'.[20]

Thus foreign powers were warned off. Sir Hercules Robinson, in a telegram received in the Colonial Office on 2 April 1888, reported: 'Transvaal has been trying to persuade Lo Bengula to accept their protection and a Resident but he refused. They will not of course like our success but I do not apprehend complications with them; agreement is simply promise by Lo Bengula not to give away his country over our heads and does not commit Her Majesty's Government to defence of Lo Bengula in case of attack. Lo Bengula is being urged on many sides to make alliances and grant concessions and it will be a help to him to be able to point to agreement.'[21] And a few months later the Marquess of Salisbury from the Foreign Office explained the position to Portugal in terms that left no room for misunderstanding. . . . 'Her Majesty's Government have satisfied themselves that Lo Bengula, with whom they have concluded a treaty, is the undisputed ruler over Matabeleland and Mashonaland and that he would tolerate no doubt of his rule over both territories. His authority over Mashonaland is so complete that no person of any nationality can enter it without his permission. . . .'[22]

From now on there was, then, in a national sense, one chameleon and one fly. Germans, Portuguese, and Afrikaners had been told to keep away. But a true picture demands a change of metaphor; both chameleon and fly were composed of many individuals. Moffat wrote on 31 August 1888: 'There is quite a crowd of Europeans here at present and the Chief does not know which way to turn.'[23] The realities of the position are admirably expressed in a letter to the High Commissioner from Sir Sydney Shippard written on 29 October 1888. He had come to Matabeleland to reassure Lobengula and reinforce Moffat; he had stressed, in a previous letter, 'the insatiable vanity and almost incredible conceit of the Matabele Matjaha', the young unmarried warriors, who believe themselves to be invincible and whom Lo Bengula finds it more and more difficult to control. 'A Matjaha rebellion, attempted revolution, and civil war appear to me not unlikely.'[24] And a week later he continues:

My impression is that Lo Bengula and some of his most intimate advisers among the great Indunas . . . are delighted, literally overjoyed at the prospect of an English alliance, now that they find that we are not going to make any exorbitant demand as the price of it. . . . Lo Bengula's present position is most difficult and precarious. He has to consult all the great indunas on all public questions affecting the whole country and the dominant Matabele race; he has to consider the feelings and wishes of the indodhas (the married warriors entitled to wear the Zulu head ring) who form the second line of defence; he has to stave off by all possible means the threatened rebellion of the Matjaha . . .; he has to deal with a steadily increasing influx of European concession hunters who are becoming a source of serious anxiety to him and whom he can now scarcely protect from the bloodthirsty Matjaha . . .; and lastly he has a perpetual dread of an inroad of Boers from the Zoutpansberg. . . . He knows all about Majuba and the retrocession of the Transvaal . . . he knows how England, after the fairest promises, handed over 750,000 unwilling natives to the Boers whom they dread and detest. . . . He is sharp enough and farsighted enough to understand that the English alliance might be his best card if only he could trust the English, but there's the rub. England has a bad name in South Africa for breaking faith with natives. . . .

And Sir Sydney goes on with the words about the chameleon and the fly with which this chapter began.

It would really be nearer the truth to speak of Rhodes as the chameleon, not England. He alone—or perhaps only he and Lobengula of all the actors—saw each step clearly. The first step forward had been the Moffat Treaty, which dealt with the danger from foreign powers. Next came the Rudd Concession, which put individual concession-seekers out of court and gave Rhodes a foothold within Lobengula's dominions, a foothold that was essential for the third step still to come, the formation of the Chartered Company. The fourth step was the march of the Pioneers and the occupation of Mashonaland.

Section 3: The Concession

The emissaries from Rhodes who negotiated the Rudd concession were C. D. Rudd, Rochfort Maguire, and F. R. Thompson, generally known as Matabele Thompson. Rudd had been Rhodes' partner in the diamond mines and in the Consolidated Goldfields of South Africa; Rochfort Maguire, a fellow of All Souls, had been called to the Bar, had been secretary to the Governor of Hong Kong, had at last answered a summons from Rhodes to join him; Thompson, who had lived all his life in South Africa and had helped Rhodes over the diamond compounds, was included mainly for his knowledge of Sindabele and of 'native' custom. They found others before them at Bulawayo who were not to be despised; besides many individual adventurers there were other parties with financial backing in Europe. There were the missionaries, Helm and Mackenzie; there were the old traders, Sam Edwards of Tati, Usher, and Fairbairn, who had custody of Lobengula's elephant seal, without which no document was complete; the syndicate of Wood, Francis, and Chapman; Boggie, Chadwick, and Wilson; Renny-Tailyour, Boyle, and Riley, later concerned in another concession to the German financier Lippert; and Mr. E. A. Maund, acting for Mr. George Cawston and the Exploiting and Exploring Company. A mixed crowd of suitors; it was no wonder that Lobengula was puzzled and there is something to be said for Rhodes' convenient view that chaos would come again unless a monopoly was given to one firm only; perhaps, too, for the corollary, not expressed to Lobengula at this stage, that that firm should be prepared to take a place in politics and administration in something like the way the East India Company had done, as the East Africa Company and the Royal Niger Company were doing elsewhere in Africa at about this time.

At first Rudd's party made little progress; Maguire was dragged before the King for bewitching the river, making it run red with scarlet dentifrice; there were long, hot, smelly waits in the buck kraal; much beef was eaten, much beer drunk. Bulawayo was in a ferment with rumours in the late summer of 1888. The Matjaha were begging the King to let them kill every white man in the place—as a warning to prevent any more coming in; Shippard, they said, was approaching with an *impi*—no less than sixteen full-grown troopers of the Bechuanaland Border Police; he must, surely, be the spearhead of a far greater *impi*, which was only waiting to pounce and take Matabeleland for ever. So great was the suspicion that Shippard was more than once kept waiting on the way for several days at a time, while argument went on at the capital as to whether he should be allowed to advance and while the Matjaha begged to be allowed to go and eat him up; Matabele mothers came to Mr. Helm the missionary to ask him

up to what age the English slaughtered children and to beg him to
intervene with the English, when they came, for the lives of
theirs. Lobengula won, with the help of his wise councillor
Lotje—known to the English in South Africa as the Beaconsfield of Matabeleland. Shippard was allowed to come and
succeeded in allaying some of the chief's anxieties; he persuaded
Lobengula of the advantages of dealing with one reputable
firm instead of a great many, of whom some might not be
reputable.

At any rate, Rudd's affairs went much more smoothly after
Shippard's visit and on 30 October 1888, after two days' discussion, Lobengula agreed to the concession. It was witnessed by
Helm the missionary, who signed an interpreter's certificate 'that
the accompanying document has been fully interpreted and
explained by me to the Chief Lobengula and his full council of
Indunas and that all the constitutional usages of the Matabele
nation have been complied with prior to his executing the same'.[25]
The discussion lasted two days and Helm answered many questions; there can really be no serious doubt that Lobengula and his
councillors did at the time agree to the concession as the best
way out of their difficulties. It provides for the payment to
Lobengula and his heirs and successors of £100 a month for an
unspecified period, 1,000 breech-loading rifles, and an armed
steamboat on the Zambezi, in consideration for which 'I, Lo
Bengula, King of Matabeleland and Mashonaland and other
adjoining territories, in the exercise of my sovereign powers and in
the presence and with the consent of my Council of Indunas do
hereby grant and assign ... complete and exclusive charge over all
metals and minerals situated and contained in my kingdoms
principalities and dominions, together with full power, to do all
things they may deem necessary to win and procure the same ...
and whereas I have been much molested of late by divers persons
seeking ... to obtain grants and concessions of land and mining
rights. ... I do hereby authorize the said grantees ... to take all
necessary and lawful steps to exclude from my kingdoms ... all
persons seeking land metals and minerals ... and I undertake to

grant no concessions of land or mining rights . . . without their concurrence. . . .'

It will be seen that on the positive side this gives the grantees mining rights only—though there is that indefinite phrase: 'all things they may deem necessary to win and procure the same'; the negative part is more comprehensive and no one else is to have either land or mining rights. There is no mention at all of jurisdiction. So far Rhodes had gone nothing like so far as the Grobler Treaty, but the chameleon had moved one step nearer and it was this, deep in his heart, that Lobengula knew and feared.

Here let it be repeated that greed for money as money was not part of Rhodes' nature; greed for power, yes, but a greed for power that was indistinguishable from his belief in what Lugard and Goldie were later to call the dual mandate, the positive duty of developing the wealth of a continent and contributing to the 'progress' of its people. The most disinterested minds of his day thought as Rhodes did, not as to means, but as to the end; Shippard quotes with approval Selous's opinion that: 'the industrious and persecuted Mashonas would welcome with delight the advent of British protectors, under whom they would cheerfully labour to develop the untold mineral wealth of their magnificent and healthy country, only too happy to know that their own lives and the products of their hard toil would be secured and above all that their wives and little ones would no longer be liable at any moment to be either slaughtered or tortured or driven into hopeless slavery.'[26]

Wrung by that liking for individuals and dislike of what they stood for that was to divide so many hearts in Rhodesia, John Moffat wrote from the Shashane River on 2 November 1888, a day or two after the concession was signed: 'As a military power it will be a blessing to the world when they are broken up. When I say this, do not mistake me. I would not do anything to bring about such a result or to break such faith as there may be between us and them, but I am sure that their days are numbered.'[27] And, nine months later, he added: 'The Matabele are a miserable people and have made myriads of other people miserable too.

One daughter of the Chief hung herself last week; this makes three of his children who have committed suicide. Another also tried to do so last week but was prevented in time. One of the old wives of Mzilikazi cut her throat a month ago. The Induna of a kraal near Hope Fountain died lately and two of the wives are daily expecting to be murdered on the charge of having bewitched him. . . .'[28]

Section 4: The Charter

The old system had to go; it was Rhodes' conviction that its place could best be taken by the English and that the dual mandate could be exercised far more effectively and more mercifully by Englishmen than by Germans or Portuguese. He believed that 'progress' would come more quickly if Europeans occupied the country, and he did not question the desirability of 'progress'; it was a view that in 1890 no European would have questioned. And if 'progress' meant no more than economic development, there can be no doubt that the nineties were right as to how it could best be achieved. No one however foresaw all the implications of 'progress', or considered how far the inhabitants of the country were to share in it.

It was in this conviction that Rhodes took the next step, the formation of the Chartered Company. It is no part of the purpose of this book to dwell on the forces with which he had to contend in London, but they must be mentioned. Opinions are not always held consistently and there are many shades of colour among them and between them; as in a rainbow, between any two bands of clear colour there will be an area in which the two colours are mixed. In this matter of Africa, there was the broad division between those who were hostile to an increase or even a continuance of British responsibility and those who were not; each of these broad divisions was again divided into two bands of clear colour with a broader belt of mixed colours between.

First came the radical Little Englanders, Exeter Hall, the Aborigines Protection Society—all who jealously scrutinized imperialism for the stain of greed and exploitation and believed that if power was to be exercised in South Africa it must be closely controlled from London; next in the spectrum to this active radicalism came the purely passive forces of timidity, which feared that expansion in Africa would cost money or lead to trouble with foreign powers, aspects of public opinion strongly represented in the Treasury and the Foreign Office. Between these two clear narrow arcs of colour came a broader band of opinion held by those who shared the two motives in varying degrees. On the other side of the rainbow, from which Rhodes might hope for support, were again two narrow bands of colour with a broader one between. There were those who saw an imperial responsibility which it was a duty to discharge, others who looked only at dividends; between the two, a far greater number to whom, as Rhodes said, 'philanthropy plus five per cent' held some appeal. Those who combined a theoretical altruism with a practical business instinct were probably the most numerous, the radicals the most vocal. The outcome of the struggle, not its detail, concerns us; Rhodes' generalship and his power of winning friends succeeded and the Charter was granted.

The formal petition asking for the Charter set out as the objects of the Company the extension of the railway and the telegraph line northwards, the encouragement of emigration and colonization, the promotion of trade and commerce, the development of mining. But in the Charter itself, to further these objects, the British South Africa Company was given power for twenty-five years—provided that certain native rights were respected, of which more later—to make treaties, promulgate laws, preserve the peace, maintain a police force, and much more besides. The reason for this is clear: colonization could not take place without power to provide the essentials of government; immigrants to Rhodesia from Britain would expect some protection by the police, some arrangement for dealing with criminals. Lord Salisbury, the Prime Minister, would have preferred this protection to be given by a government, a colonial government with a Governor responsible to Parliament. But he knew that Parliament would not yet vote the money for developing a colony and

Sir Hercules from Cape Town had just sent the Colonial Office a vivid picture of Bechuanaland as a Crown Colony run on a shoestring. Lord Salisbury was a master of the ironic under-statement and of the indirect approach; one may suppose that he was aware of a certain satisfaction at getting the reality of British control without the odium and the expense of annexation.

The Charter was granted on 29 October 1899. Its 'principal field of operations' was the area 'north of the Cape Colony and the Transvaal, and west of the Portuguese territories in East Africa'. No boundaries were assigned to the north. In this vast area, the Chartered Company was authorized, with certain reservations, to make treaties and promulgate laws as well as to maintain a police force and undertake public works. Yet on 15 January of the same year, Lord Salisbury from the Foreign Office had asserted to Portugal Lobengula's sovereignty in the most unequivocal terms. How, one might well ask, could a Royal Charter from the British Crown give anyone power to maintain police forces, levy taxes, or try a man for his life in Lobengula's territory?

But the Charter did not in fact profess to grant such powers; it did not assume that the Queen held authority within the area it so sketchily defined. What the Charter did assume was that among the various groups brought together to form the British South Africa Company there were men who already held con-cessions from native chiefs; it did assume that these concessions gave them authority to exercise some sovereign powers and that they would acquire new concessions that would empower them to exercise others. What the Charter gave was permission to certain British subjects, and those only, to exercise any rights that native chiefs might concede.

The Charter could hardly have been granted if there had been no such concessions at all. It depended on the existence of con-cessions as a paper currency depends on bullion somewhere. And its principal backing was the Rudd concession, which said nothing about making laws or colonizing a country with white men, but spoke only of mining—and all that was necessary for mining.

There were other interests concerned, with all of which Rhodes had come to a settlement, but their rights were either still more shadowy than his or were strictly limited in area. They included various companies and syndicates[29] which had been formed to explore and prospect in Rhodesia and Bechuanaland; the African Lakes Corporation, concerned with what is now Nyasaland; and the owners of the Tati concession, where Sam Edwards exercised on Lobengula's behalf just the kind of sovereign powers which the Charter authorized British subjects to acquire and use. The Tati area was a very small part of the Charter's field of operations, but it was the only area in which there was any concession of sovereign rights; the Rudd concession covered a much wider area and with the others constituted a foot in the door; its main value was that it made possible the Charter.

It was therefore essential to hold Lobengula to the Concession, and with this intention Maguire and Thompson had stayed behind when Rudd hurried away with the precious paper, losing his way, incidentally, and stuffing it into an ant-bear hole to hide it just before he fainted from thirst and exhaustion—but that is another story. There must not be a vacuum at Bulawayo—nature abhors a vacuum—that was a phrase that Rhodes repeated over and over again in that high-pitched voice, rubbing his hands against each other. But there was really little chance of anything so negative as a vacuum; there were still the suitors, the hordes of adventurers living on Lobengula's beef and beer and ready to bring all the pressure they could to bear against the monopoly which would end their hopes.

Their first step was to publish in *The Bechuanaland News and Malmani Chronicle* the following notice:

Notice:
I hear it is published in the newspapers that I have granted a concession in all my country to Charles Dunell Rudd, Rochford* Maguire, and Francis Robert Thompson. As there is a great misunderstanding about this, all action in respect of the said concession is

* *Sic:* a spelling mistake.

hereby suspended, pending an investigation to be made by me in my country.

(signed) LOBENGULA

Royal Kraal,
  Matabeleland
    18th January 1889

The original of this notice is signed by three of the suitors, Phillips, Reilly, and Usher, and marked with the elephant seal, which was in the keeping of the trader Fairbairn, but it is not marked with a cross by Lobengula nor witnessed by Helm, the only disinterested person then at Bulawayo;[30] no one seems to have taken very much notice of what probably represented no more than some irritated expression by Lobengula of his deep uneasiness and misgiving.

Another step, and a much more cunning one, was taken by Maund, representing the Exploration Company. Maund, whose company was one of the most formidable rivals of the Rhodes group, was silenced by the time the Charter was granted because his principals had been made parties to it, brought in by the Great Amalgamator, but before that amalgamation took place Maund had persuaded Lobengula to send him to the Queen with two of his indunas and a letter. The Queen replied in a style very similar to his own; language that was dignified but had a touch of the nursery about it was felt to be appropriate for correspondence between the Great White Queen and a barbarian chief, both by the traders who drafted his letters and the civil servants who drafted hers. 'The Queen has heard the words of Lo Bengula. She was glad to receive these messengers. . . . They say that Lo Bengula is much troubled by white men who come into his country and ask to dig gold and that he begs for advice and help. Lo Bengula is the ruler of his country and the Queen does not interfere with the government of that country but as Lo Bengula desires her advice . . . the Queen wishes Lo Bengula to understand that Englishmen who have gone out to Matabeleland to ask leave to dig for stones have not gone with the Queen's authority. . . . The Queen advises Lo Bengula not to grant hastily concessions of land or leave to dig. . . . A King gives a stranger an ox not his whole herd of cattle. . . .' This letter was dated 26 March 1889 and the Rudd concession had been signed and sealed on 30 October 1888, five months earlier; Lord Knutsford, the Colonial Secretary who sent this letter, had not at this stage accepted the idea of the Charter and the phrase about the ox could only be read as advising against Charter or Concession alike. Encouraged by this message, constrained by the mounting tension among his people, and of course egged on by the suitors, Lobengula replied on 10 August: 'The white people are troubling me much about gold. If the Queen hears that I have given away the whole country, it is not so. I have no one in my country who knows how to write; I do not understand what the dispute is about. . . . I thank the Queen for the word which my messengers gave me by mouth, that the Queen says I am not to let anyone dig for gold in my country except to dig for me as my servants. . . .'

This was a genuine letter actually dictated by Lobengula to Moffat. Before this, however, another letter had been addressed to the Queen, this being drafted by Fairbairn on the basis of instructions from Lobengula, and signed by Fairbairn, Usher, and two others of the suitors. This letter, dated 23 April, not being countersigned by Moffat or a missionary, is suspect from the start; it specifically refers to Rudd and his friends and alleges that Lobengula had no intention of signing the concession, but believed he was signing a paper recording no more than a readiness to do business: 'I told them to bring what they would give and I would then show them what I would give. . . . A document was written . . . I was told that in it, were my words. . . .'[31] This is of course an unlikely tale on the face of it; Lobengula could hardly have supposed anyone would go to the trouble of getting his signature to so vague a statement. But an element of truth was no doubt contained in the words: 'I have since had a meeting with my Indunas and they will not recognize the paper.' Be that as it may, this letter did not make any difference to what happened; by the time it reached London, the grant of the Charter had been agreed on and it was in its final stages; it did not in fact influence events any more than the letter of 10 August, which had still not been received on 15 November when Lord Knutsford followed up his March message from the Queen—the letter about the one ox—with a second.

This however conveyed a very different sense. 'The Queen has kept in mind the letter sent by Lo Bengula . . . and has now desired Mr. Moffat, whom she trusts . . . to tell him what she has done for him and what she advises him to do. . . . Wherever gold is, or wherever it is reported to be, it is impossible for him to exclude white men and therefore the wisest and safest course for him . . . is to agree, not with one or two white men separately but with one approved body . . . if he does not agree with one set of people, there will be endless disputes among the white men and he will have all his time taken up in deciding their quarrels.

'The Queen therefore approves of the concession made by Lo Bengula . . . to some white men, . . . who were represented by Messrs Rudd, Maguire, and Thompson. The Queen has caused enquiry to be made respecting these persons and is satisfied that they are men who will fulfil their undertakings. . . . The Queen thinks Lo Bengula is acting wisely in carrying out his agreement. . . . The Queen understands that Lo Bengula does not like deciding disputes among white men. . . . This is very wise as these disputes would take up much time and Lo Bengula . . . cannot understand the laws and customs of white people . . . the Queen thinks it would be wise to entrust to that body of white men of whom Mr. Jameson is now the principal representative in Matabeleland the duty of deciding disputes and keeping the peace among white people in his country. . . . Of course this must be as Lo Bengula likes as he is King of the country. . . . The Queen understands that Lo Bengula wishes to have someone from her residing with him. The Queen has therefore directed her trusted servant Mr. Moffat to stay with the Chief as long as he wishes. . . .'

There is no mention now of giving away one ox at a time and it must have been clear to Lobengula that the chameleon had come another step closer. A year ago with British support he had indignantly repudiated the Grobler Treaty; now the Queen's letter gently took for granted two clauses of that treaty, the presence of a consul and consular authority over European offenders; it was much more tactfully done and with Moffat instead of Grobler, but the substance was the same and he must have wondered how long it would be before the remaining clauses, too, were absent-mindedly hung round his neck.

In all this correspondence there is a time-lag which must have been confusing to those concerned and which makes the story confusing to a reader. Decisions are taken in London on factors long out of date in Matabeleland and the reverse. And it is made doubly confusing by the fact that one can never be certain that any of Lobengula's letters or documents represent his actual words. Still, an impression can be based on the evidence. One must picture Lobengula, knowing nothing of London or the Queen, but seeing the whole situation in the vivid terms of his picture of the chameleon; beset by the Matjaha, the young warriors, clamouring for the blood of Europeans; beset by the suitors, greedy men, clamouring for their own advantage; beset most wearingly of all by his own uneasy, unformulated fears, his knowledge that he could not win in a war with the British, his certainty that the closer they came the harder it would be to hold back the Matjaha, the more inevitable a war would become.

He did sign the Moffat Treaty; he did sign the Rudd Concession; he did understand them and he did at the time believe them to be the best way out of his difficulties; he did at those two stages carry his chiefs and people with him. But he signed doubtfully and suspiciously; his people were still more doubtful. It would really have been better—he must have felt—to have kept all white people at a distance; after he had signed, his own fears, the anger and arrogance of his people, the machinations of the suitors, all combined in a mounting pressure to make him repent of what he had done. Knutsford's letter in the Queen's name with that phrase about the ox increased his feeling that he had given away too much; by September he was sure of it and as a sign to his people that he was now on the other side he allowed Lotje to be smelt out for witchcraft.

That is a simple and condensed way of expressing what happened; Lotje—'the Beaconsfield of Matabeleland'—had been the most steadfast and outspoken adherent of the policy of the concession and the Charter, of making friends with one strong party and thus getting control of the suitors and avoiding war with a more powerful people. There came one council meeting at which the whole trend of the discussion and the King's attitude to him were such that Lotje told Helm when he came out that he was a dead man. A few days later it was true; the diviners had scented death and smelt him out; a detachment of the Mbesu Regiment was sent to wipe out Lotje and all who were his.

To Thompson, the only man left in Bulawayo of the trium-virate who had signed the Concession, it seemed that this brought his own death warrant near. As a boy he had seen his cousin captured and his father surrounded by Zulus and 'several shots fired into him at close range'. For a year he had been in Bulawayo in an atmosphere of continual intrigue, in which the one constant factor was the demand of the Matjaha to be allowed to massacre all Europeans. He heard the news of Lotje's death, saw three armed Matabele near his house and, without even waiting to saddle his horse, fled to Tati as fast as he could ride. This was at the beginning of September 1889; the Charter was to be signed in London at the end of October, and it was signed on the basis of a Concession which in Bulawayo had been repudiated—in the eyes of the Matabele people by Lotje's death, in Lobengula's own eyes by his letter to Queen Victoria. There was no one at Bulawayo to put Rhodes' case; the vacuum had occurred which both he and Nature abhorred and it was at this stage that Rhodes played the best card he had, sending Dr. Jameson to Matabeleland with the double object of reinstating the Concession and preparing for the next step.

II. The Dart of the Tongue

Lobengula had in the eyes of his people repudiated the Concession in September of 1889; the Charter, which proceeded from the Concession, was signed in October as the result of a set of forces and personalities operating in London with little knowledge of what was happening in Bulawayo. On the general situation, Moffat, anxious and divided, again provides the commentary; he had written a year earlier: 'The Matabele . . . have the notion that they are the people and that they can fight the Boers or even the English. The Chief knows better but he is hampered by the ignorance of his people. It is a problem which occupies my thoughts night and day, how we are to avoid the impending collision. . . . To me the only solution of the difficulty is the breaking up of this tribe, but I should be sorry to be the intermediary, for sooner or later I should have to be the herald of war and not of peace. . . . There is some talk of the whole tribe migrating to the north side of the Zambezi; I hope not, for that simply means carrying thither the same murderous system which they have carried out here—the ruthless harrying of tribe after tribe till there is nothing left but a succession of vast solitudes, which the Matabele neither occupy themselves nor allow others to occupy.'[1]

That is the essence of the situation from the Matabele angle. To it may be added on the other side a letter written in March of 1890 by the Secretary of the British South Africa Company to the Imperial Secretary, that is, to the High Commissioner at Cape Town. 'Mr. Rhodes', he wrote on 18 March, 'has for some time felt that to assure the position of the Chartered Company it is necessary to obtain effective possession of Mashonaland in the coming winter [that is, April–September 1890]. He is very strongly of the opinion that this object could not be considered to be obtained merely by sending in one or two prospecting parties and that it is of the utmost importance to form, at as early a date as possible, a substantial nucleus of white population in the country. For this purpose, he does not consider 150 at all an excessive number.'² This is the background to all that followed.

The news of the Charter did not reach Matabeleland till the end of January; meanwhile, into the mounting anger and fear of Bulawayo came Dr. Jameson. He was a man whose gaiety and ready tongue gave him a charm that can be felt across the years; quick in decision, gallant in action, his personality must have cured his patients as often as his technical skill; even in the posed daguerreotypes of the times, his face is at once sensitive and impulsive, yet his actions show him free from doubts, resolute in the course he was committed to. Lack of patience and over-confidence were later his undoing, but at this stage he was patient in negotiation. Jameson was in Bulawayo by 17 October, before the Charter was actually signed, bringing back with him Thompson and also Sam Edwards, for whom Lobengula had a particular regard. He put the original concession into Lobengula's hands and once again explained it to him clause by clause. The chief now took the line that he had not meant to give a general concession, but only 'one hole to dig in'; the only general part of the agreement was that no one else should have a hole to dig in at all, while Rhodes must ask for each hole, one at a time. During the weeks that followed, it seems to have been Jameson's policy to maintain the Concession but not to insist on it; he would resist any attempt to substitute a less sweeping agreement, but in practice would rather slur over its general provisions and concentrate for the moment on getting permission to 'dig in one hole', and thus to implement it in the eyes of English lawyers.

Into this pool, already turbulent enough, fell one more stone, the news that the Portuguese were trying to extend their influence along the Zambezi by building forts and giving flags to chiefs in Mashonaland. Lobengula dictated a protest: 'I send three messengers with this letter to ask you by what authority you are doing this in a country which belongs to me.' Then, remembering the Moffat Treaty, he sent on 22 December a quite inconsistent message to Cape Town: 'Lo Bengula is not in direct communication with the Portuguese Government; he therefore requests Your Excellency to move Her Majesty's Government and bring to an end these infringements of the territory of a friendly chief.'³ This incursion increased the general atmosphere of suspicion that was directed against all Europeans, but must on the whole have helped Jameson to persuade Lobengula that he had to make a choice between evils and that the Company was the least of these. At any rate, he obtained permission to start prospecting to the south of Bulawayo. And a few days later Renny-Tailyour and others who asked for permission to dig were referred to Jameson; the rifles which were part of the payment were put into a store on Lobengula's account; he did not protest and Cooper-Chadwick was appointed to look after them. The Concession was thus, by implication and somewhat half-heartedly, reinstated during December.

By the end of January, the news that the Charter had been signed reached Matabeleland, together with Lord Knutsford's letter of 15 November containing the Queen's advice to Lobengula to deal with the Chartered Company only. The letter was brought by a Captain and a Surgeon-Major of the Royal Horse Guards, with the Corporal-Major of the Regiment and a trooper. The stature, uniform, and accoutrements of this escort were perhaps intended to distract attention from the contents of the letter and in this to some extent they succeeded. Lobengula was interested and impressed; 'he took off and handled one of the cuirasses, asked them to go through the sword exercise, and, in inviting them to attend the "Great Dance" . . . made a point of their appearing in full panoply'.⁴ The atmosphere created was favourable; Jameson asked for another indaba a few days later, told Lobengula that the hole he had dug in the south showed no payable gold and said he did not want to extend his digging towards Bulawayo for fear of disturbing Matabele villages. 'Then you had better go somewhere else,' said the chief. Jameson asked if he might go east. The chief agreed; he was shown a map on which had been drawn a route planned by Selous, skirting Matabeleland and leading into the Mazoe country in Central Mashonaland. Might Selous have some of Lobengula's men to cut a road for the wagons? Yes, he might. But, went on Lobengula, making a last dart from the shadow of the landing-net like an exhausted fish, 'go and find out where you want to make your road and then come to me and I will give you the men to make it'.[5]

This was enough. Jameson left on 14 February and by 20 February, Sir Henry Loch (who had succeeded Sir Hercules at Cape Town) passed on to Lord Knutsford a telegram that he had received from Rhodes: 'Lo Bengula has sanctioned our occupation of Mashonaland. . . .' This was, quite simply, not true; he had sanctioned the Company's digging in Mashonaland for gold. Sir Henry, however, naturally took the telegram at its face value; he referred to a rumour of an incursion from the South African Republic into Mashonaland; he had already been instructed to warn President Kruger that this would be regarded as an infringement of the Queen's Protectorate. He continued to Lord Knutsford: 'I consider it will be impossible to prevent a rush to Mashonaland goldfield unless British South Africa Company are allowed to anticipate such a movement. . . . I earnestly trust that the time and responsibility for giving sanction may be left to me.' Lord Knutsford consulted Lord Salisbury at the Foreign Office. The Foreign Office replied on 7 March 1890: 'His Lordship considers that it would be dangerous to withhold much longer from the High Commissioner authority to sanction the advance of the Company's armed police force into Mashonaland.'[6] And on 10 March, Lord Knutsford gave the High Commissioner the authority he sought.

Thus a concession which gave Rudd and his colleagues permission to mine had been used to obtain a Charter which authorized them to exercise any sovereign rights which might be conceded to them. None had been conceded except at Tati; Moffat's right to try British subjects had so far been assumed without discussion. Permission to dig in Mashonaland had been reported as permission to occupy, and on that report the Secretary of State had empowered the High Commissioner to slip the leash when he judged the moment had come.

Sir Henry Loch, the High Commissioner, was not however immediately satisfied. Preparations for the march of the Pioneers and the occupation of Mashonaland had begun as far back as October of 1889, but Sir Henry understood the legal situation very clearly and had written to the Company: 'it will of course be very important, before introducing such a force into Matabeleland . . . to ascertain clearly that its presence there will be acceptable to Lo Bengula. . . . The Company no doubt understands that the Concession above referred to does not confer such powers of government or administration as are mentioned in clauses 3 and 4 of the Charter. Those powers will have to be obtained whenever a proper and favourable time for approaching Lo Bengula on the subject arrives.'[7] That time had come and in February 1890 it had been reported that the chief had sanctioned the occupation of Mashonaland, but both the High Commissioner and the Company were aware that it had been a somewhat grudging sanction. This was the more dangerous because the High Commissioner had been misled as to what had been sanctioned. 'It was feared', writes Mr. Hole, 'that he [Lobengula] might upset the contemplated expedition by sending objections to the High Commissioner.' So Jameson went back to Bulawayo in April.

He now explained the scope of the expedition. There would be 100 wagonloads of provisions and mining-tools; there would be a detachment of police—to Lobengula indistinguishable from soldiers—to protect the Pioneers. There can be no doubt that Lobengula saw what this meant; he raised every objection he could think of, but to all Jameson found an answer. 'Against whom,' Lobengula asked, 'are these workers to be protected?' 'Against the Boers', was the doctor's reply, 'against the Portuguese, against anyone else who might molest them.'[8] A much less intelligent man than Lobengula could guess who that 'anyone else' was expected to be; nor could he believe the precaution unreasonable. At last Jameson felt he had no hope of getting further; he announced that he was going and on the last morning, his horses saddled, went to say good-bye to the King.

There was a respect, indeed a guarded liking, between these two men. Lobengula had responded to Jameson's doctoring of his gout and to his gaiety and frankness; he showed again and again that he distinguished between such a man as this and those thinking only of their pockets. On Jameson's side, there lay, beneath the bantering good-humoured firmness that it was proper to display towards a native potentate, a genuine understanding of the King's dilemma, he had too a share of the feeling, wide-spread among Europeans, that it was a pity Rhodes could not get his way without causing so much embarrassment to Lobengula, 'who wouldn't be so bad an old buffer if it weren't for the Matjaha'. There was no doubt of his embarrassment today: 'The door of the Chief's hut was in two portions, an upper and a lower, and leaning over the lower half he had his last and final interview. The old King was stark naked, somewhat agitated—an unwieldly mass of dark copper-coloured flesh moving restlessly up and down within the dim, uncertain light of the hut.

' "Well, King," said Jameson, "as you will not confirm your promise and grant me the road, I shall bring my white *impi* and if necessary we shall fight."

'Lobengula replied: "I never refused the road to you and to your *impi*."

' "Very well," said Jameson, "then you acknowledge that you have promised to grant me the road and unless you refuse now, your promise holds good." Then as the King remained diplomatically silent, Jameson said: "Good-bye, Chief, you have given your promise about the road and on the strength of that promise I shall bring in my *impi* to Mashonaland"—and he left.'[9]

So it was done; an unwilling half-consent from a King who knew that his people were against him, but who realized better than they the consequences of refusal, who believed Jameson's clear statement that his *impi* would come with or without consent

and fight if need be. 'I know very well', Moffat had written just
a year before, 'that nothing is further from the thoughts of either
Chiefs or people than the introduction into any part of their
country of a colonizing population. However desirable such a
result might appear to us, to the natives it means only one thing,
which they have seen . . . over and over . . . further south; it
means that the white man having once got one foot planted
firmly on their land will soon have both feet on it . . . till he
becomes the owner of all the land and the native has become a
squatter on sufferance in his own country.'[10]

That this was indeed Lobengula's view is clear from what
followed when the Pioneer column began to collect on the
Macloutsie River. He wrote to Loch a letter for the Queen:
'When we joined together, why do you send your *impi*? Rhodes
. . . paid me money for which I gave him a piece of ground. . . .
If you have heard that I have given my whole country to Rhodes,
it is not my words. I have not done so. Rhodes wants to take
my country by strength. . . . Your words were, I was to send to
you when I was troubled by white men. I am now in trouble. . . .'[11]
Loch replied on 4 August: 'The Queen assures Lo Bengula that
the men assembled by the British South Africa Company were
not assembled for the purpose of attacking him, but on the
contrary were assembled for a peaceful object, namely searching
for gold. . . . They were ordered to travel at a distance from the
Matabele kraals and always to recollect that Lo Bengula is the
friend of the Queen and that the Queen wishes to maintain peace
and friendship with Lo Bengula.'

The march of the pioneers is a story for another chapter. Here
it is necessary to complete this account of the chameleon's step-
by-step advance with emphasis on the legal aspect; the realities
beneath the formal moves are another matter. On 6 June 1890,
the Imperial Secretary wrote to the Secretary of the British South
Africa Company: 'Having carefully considered the political
position the Governor and High Commissioner considers the
time has arrived to give his consent to the entry of the Company's
forces into Mashonaland by the route already agreed upon—that

is to say, by a route that will skirt Matabeleland proper and leave all Matabele kraals to the north and west of the expeditionary force. . . . The object to be attained is the peaceful occupation of Mashonaland, and it is desirable that all officers should be instructed to be most careful and prudent in the treatment of the natives . . . and to respect their prejudices and susceptibilities. . . .'[12] On 27 June, the Pioneers crossed the Macloutsie River and on the 30th were met by a party of Matabele with a letter from Lobengula:

'Has the King killed any white men that an *impi* is collecting on his border? Or have the white men lost anything they are looking for?'

To this Jameson replied that this was a working-party, protected by soldiers, who were 'going to Mashonaland along the road already arranged with the King'. The column waited some days for stores, then forded the Shashi on 11 July and the advance proper began. On 6 August another protest was received from Lobengula—alleging that Jameson had agreed to dig only in specified places, that the only place authorized had been near Tati, and that Jameson had misunderstood him when he said good-bye in April. To this the inept reply—sent not by Jameson but by Pennefather, commanding the police—was that the column must march on in accordance with the Queen's orders. Colenbrander, who brought this letter, was Lobengula's agent, but he felt more at home with the Pioneer column than with the indunas who had been his companions; he talked freely to the Pioneers and gave them his opinion that Lobengula had sent his letter as a move in internal politics, to gain time with the warriors, and did not expect it to have any effect on the movements of the column. The answer, however, abandoned the legal fiction of Lobengula's willing consent and brought in the Crown directly. The Pioneers, it will be seen, had no use for legal fictions. On 12 September, at Fort Salisbury, the Union Jack was hoisted, a salute fired, and 'possession taken of Mashonaland in the name of the Queen'.

The Pioneers had come to occupy Mashonaland. They had

each been promised fifteen gold claims and a 3,000-acre farm; the notion that the expedition was intended only to 'dig in one hole' had been reserved for correspondence with Lobengula. But the Pioneers' act in 'taking possession' of Mashonaland was not recognized by the Crown; indeed, it was felt in Cape Town and Whitehall that the next step was to get Lobengula's formal consent to the Company's exercising jurisdiction over Europeans in his territory—a right blandly assumed in the Queen's letter of 15 November 1889. Just a year later, in November 1890, Moffat presented the King with a document that would give the Company this authority and at this Lobengula 'entered at length into the whole question of the concession', protesting that he had never meant to give such a concession and that if he had, it was Lotje's fault, that he had clearly repudiated the concession and given Jameson leave only to 'dig in one hole', that the column should have come to Bulawayo before going to Mashonaland, and—a final grievance—that the High Commissioner and Rhodes had come to the borders of his country without coming to see him.[13] On 1 January 1891, he wrote to the Governor: 'Mr. Moffat has asked me to give Mr. Rhodes power to punish those who do wrong in Mashonaland. They ask for this now but they went into my country without doing so. Why do they come now and ask? When did we speak on this matter? Did not the Queen say that I should not give all my herd of cattle to one man? Have I given all my land to the people now in Mashonaland? Who has got the herd to kill today?' On 13 April 1891, the High Commissioner proclaimed that 'The country North and West of the South African Republic, West of the Portuguese dominions, and East of the German sphere of influence falls within the British sphere of influence', and that anyone entering this territory with a view to the occupation of land must observe the rules and regulations established by the Company. Ten days later, on 23 April, the Colonial Office told the Foreign Office that Sir Henry Loch had communicated to Lobengula 'his intention to govern and punish the whites in his [Lobengula's] country' and that there was therefore 'ground for assuming the existence of "sufferance" ' on the part of Lobengula, this giving Her Majesty jurisdiction in his country within the meaning of the Foreign Jurisdiction Act of 1890.[14] Next came the Order in Council of 9 May 1891. 'Whereas', it began, the territories of the Charter are 'under the protection of Her Majesty', and 'whereas . . . Her Majesty has power and jurisdiction in the said territories', the High Commissioner may 'from time to time, by Proclamation, provide for the administration of justice, the raising of revenue, and generally for the peace, order and good government of all persons within the limits of this Order. . . .' There followed the High Commissioner's proclamation of 10 June 1891, by which he empowered himself to appoint Resident Commissioners, Inspectors of Police, and Magistrates. It was under this proclamation that Dr. Jameson was gazetted Chief Magistrate of Mashonaland on 18 September 1891.

But the Queen's jurisdiction was based on Lobengula's supposed 'sufferance', and he was in fact protesting as vigorously as words would permit. 'There is no probability,' Sir Henry Loch had told Lord Knutsford on 20 November 1890, 'of Lo Bengula granting any concession of jurisdiction.'[15] His sufferance perhaps lay in his holding back his young men from fighting, perhaps in his own knowledge that words would do no good.

When Duke William of Normandy landed in England, he professed to be claiming what was his own, and there was talk of an oath Harold had sworn renouncing his Kingdom. But William has always been known as the Conqueror; his true claim to England was established at Hastings by the sword—and a very good thing for England it turned out to be. Mzilikazi took Matabeleland by the sharp blades of his assegais, and held it by the same title-deeds. In the events that have just been related, an elaborate structure of legality was erected, mainly for the satisfaction of English public opinion. It rested on the fiction of Lobengula's consent. But though Lobengula delegated certain sovereign powers at Tati, nowhere else did he cede or even delegate any authority that had to do with sovereignty. 'Leave to dig' was all he gave; even that was only wrested from him by

Jameson's clear threat of force. In the whole series of transactions, only Rhodes and Lobengula are consistent, Rhodes in a conviction that he was 'under an obligation to develop and open up to civilization that part of the country dominated over, not inhabited by the Matabele', Lobengula in a determination to cede no sovereignty but to avoid war, to give up the least that would enable him to keep what remained.

Lobengula could not adopt the policy of Khama, who had unreservedly allied himself to England; his people would not have let him and in any case the whole nature of his state forbade it; there was no room in the *pax Britannica* for a people who lived by raiding their neighbours. He was accused by Europeans of being vacillating and unreliable, but in truth he was like a hooked salmon trying to take out as much line as he could whenever the chance came. The charge of inconsistency might as truthfully be preferred against the salmon, which strives to avoid the gaff and comes towards it only when compelled. And Lobengula proved himself a noble salmon who put up a good fight.

III. The Pioneers

Section 1: The March of the Pioneers

The flag was hoisted at Fort Salisbury on 12 September 1890. The march from Macloutsie had been a considerable achievement. Over 400 miles had been covered in little more than two months and the road made as the men advanced; the wagons had rolled slowly forward over ground painfully cleared of trees, over rocky stream-beds and outcrops of granite, while mounted scouts kept up a ceaseless patrol in front, on the left flank and to the rear of the party. These were no idle precautions; it was barely eleven years since Isandhlwana, when a Zulu *impi* had surprised and destroyed a regular battalion of British infantry* and Lobengula was believed able to put 18,000 warriors in the field; the column consisted of 200 Pioneers and 500 police.

Selous, who was guide to the expedition, went first, marking the trees to be cut; next came the road-making party, of which every other man was employed with the axe, while the rest held the horses and kept a look-out. After every half-hour they changed, and the horse-holders took the axes; when they came to a stream they must cut a slope down to the water's edge at the best place for a ford, sometimes they must shift a boulder or make a corduroy track with logs; at the end of that day's progress they must clear a space big enough for the wagons to 'laager'—that is, be linked shaft to tail in an enclosure defensible against attack. There were still fires to build, food to cook, weapons and saddles to clean; someone must start the steam-engine that worked the searchlight; there were guards to be kept.

It was an achievement of courage, energy, and discipline. But of that enough has been written; what is important for the purpose

* The 24th Foot: 1st Bn. the South Wales Borderers.

146

of this book is to know what kind of men made the column and with what purpose they came, with what illusions and what expectations. They were picked men; 2,000 applied to join the Pioneers of whom less than 200 were chosen. That in itself gives them a certain uniformity; since they were picked for a purpose, they conform in varying degrees to an ideal. They were to be strong and active, young but not raw, say between twenty-five and thirty; though they were to include a wide variety of trades and backgrounds, all must be versatile and ready to work with their hands at anything. There must be masons, bakers, carpenters, and printers among them as well as farmers and miners; they must be soldiers and wear uniform on the march but on arrival they were to fall out of the ranks and fall to as individuals, each to be the creator of a farm, a business or a mine that would be one of the units adding up to make a country.

They were to come from every district of South Africa and they were to include speakers of Afrikaans as well as English; thus 'both the races' of South Africa—in the language of the day —would be involved and, at one level of Rhodes' thought, if anything should go wrong, every element in the electorates of Natal and of the Cape would join in the clamour for England to intervene; at another level, and if things went well, 'the two races' would be joined in partnership, a United South Africa would be one step nearer—and one more step would be taken towards that state above all states, that apotheosis of the British Empire, that was to end wars in all the world.

They were as mixed in speech, nationality, class, and education as they could well be: British artisan and ex-private soldier alongside peer's younger son and Oxford graduate, Texan cowpuncher beside Canadian Mountie and Afrikaner transport-rider. 'Such a mixed lot I never saw in my life, all sorts and conditions, from the aristocratic down to the street arab, peers and waifs of humanity mingling together like the ingredients of a hotch-potch',[1] wrote Arthur Leonard. But all had some experience of South Africa, even if only as a country once travelled through; most had lived in South Africa as colonists, burghers, or settlers.

None had any illusions as to the real nature of their enterprise in relation to Lobengula and the Matabele. The legal fiction of his willing consent had no currency here. 'Personally Lo Bengula probably never wanted to fight', wrote Selous,[2] 'though it is the most absolute nonsense to talk of his ever having been friendly to the expedition. But he had a very difficult part to play and it is wonderful that he managed to restrain his people as he did.' And again: 'We cut the road to Mashunaland in defiance of the Matabili.'[3] And Arthur Leonard probably spoke for all when he wrote: 'It does not seem to be within the bounds of common sense to suppose that a nation of ferocious savages, whose all-pervading, all-absorbing instinct is blood and rapine, will allow us quietly to take possession of a country which is virtually theirs by right of conquest without in any way resenting it. To imagine it even is a direct insult.'[4]

The bloodthirsty Matabele—the timid Mashona, delighted to be rescued from oppression—those were the two pictures of the people of the country general among the Pioneers. The second picture responded to something not perhaps quite universal among the Pioneers, certainly present in many and reflecting an aspect of Rhodes' own character. They had come to make their fortune—yes, but a fortune is not only gold. Many of them could have made money in London or Cape Town; making a fortune implied physical danger, nights in the veld beneath the glittering stars, biltong and the camp-fire, hardship and adventure before the prize was won. Ease after toil, port after stormy seas, these they wanted, but not yet; it was the storm and the toil that would give ease its value. In a word, they were romantics, with the strenuous Puritan romanticism of the Victorians, of Charles Kingsley and Arnold of Rugby. 'As to the romance of our present undertaking', wrote Arthur Leonard, 'I cannot speak. Even the halo of it is [today] dimmer and shadowier than a rainbow on a misty day . . . but there is no doubt that . . . [in the future it] will stand out in all the beauty and richness of colour. . . .' To such men as this it was necessary to believe, when they had time to think about it, that the march of the column

Cecil Rhodes outside his railway carriage, Vryburg Station, *c.* 1900

Sir Starr Jameson

would bring protection and the blessings of civilization to the Mashona, as well as bringing one step nearer that beatific and apocalyptic state towards which 'progress' was leading, when Rhodes should lie down with Kruger and wars should cease.

There are two clearly defined stages in the march of the Pioneers; in the low veld, they were in forest country, much broken by rocks and ravines, and were in real danger of a surprise attack on the model of Isandhlwana. Lobengula, more clearly than any of the Matabele—now that Lotje was dead—knew that Isandhlwana had led to the end of the Zulu kingdom, that it was no good to win one battle and that he could not hope to win more than one. The low veld country that was favourable to him in a military sense was for just that reason dangerous to him politically; he was concerned that the column should be safely through it without his being forced to give the word for an attack and there is evidence that he used all the means he could to temporize and delay. His anxiety matched that of the leaders of the column; once on the plateau, on the open downs of Mashonaland, they felt confident that their well-armed mounted men could deal with the Matabele, but Selous, their guide and director of intelligence, was far from sure he could find a way passable for wagons up the escarpment and he dreaded the prospect of a long delay in the thick broken country at its foot. When he found the gentle ascent to the plateau that was christened 'Providential Pass', 'a weight of responsibility that had at times become almost unbearable' fell from his shoulders. From now onwards an attack by the Matabele became less likely to occur, because the column had passed its closest to Matabeleland proper and was increasing its distance every day; at the same time, by the nature of the country it became still less likely to succeed.

Section 2: The Tribes to the East

The danger was passed; the flag was hoisted at Fort Salisbury, the Fort was built, the Pioneers received the order: 'Dismiss!' They broke off and stood, no doubt, for a little, in groups, discussing the past and speculating on the future, before they dispersed, citizens of a new realm, each to stake out his fifteen gold claims and his farm of 3,000 acres. Each man must have been aware of an acute problem of his own, how to begin making his fortune; as a community, they were concerned, perhaps without being equally aware of them, with three problems—their relations with the peoples to the east of them, their relations with the Mashona among whom they proposed to live, and their relations with the Matabele.

Those to the east included the people from the Zulu South who now lived in Gazaland, descendants of Soshangane's horde, and certain Mashona tribes, people who had once been subjects of the Monomotapa, now broken by the passage of Zwangendaba's Nguni or by the neighbourhood of Gazaland or the Portuguese, yet not shattered and demoralized so completely as those nearer to the Matabele. Mtasa of the Manica people was one of these, Mangwende of the Wa-ungwe another, and Mtoko of the Babudja a third, a chief who could still muster 5,000 warriors. Embassies were dispatched to these chiefs; Selous as guide and Colquhoun as plenipotentiary went to Mtasa; later Selous went to Mtoko in both capacities. They met chiefs who delayed and temporized, as Lobengula had done, who consulted the Mhondoro or tribal spirit, and took counsel with their elders—but not for Lobengula's reasons. The chiefs of these tribes discussed ways and means but had no intention of avoiding the protection now offered to them. They feared another danger: to the east were the Portuguese, whose rule, at this peripheral fringe, they had experienced only at the hands of raiders mixed in blood and tradition, such men as Matakenya or Gouveia, leaders of banditti who might not be seen for several years but who, when they came, must be bribed or fought, hunters for slaves and ivory, whose allegiance to Portugal might alternate with periods of rebellion and seldom influenced their behaviour to their African neighbours. Gouveia, for instance, also known as de Souza, was a Goanese mercenary captain, who had established himself as chief of a tribe and had been given the title of Capitão Mor of

Gorongoza; he waged war in the name of Portugal but for his own purposes.

Gungunhana of Gazaland, much the most powerful of the eastern chiefs, wrote to Queen Victoria: 'My desire is now, as it was my father's, to get the protection of the Great White Queen, so that I may be troubled no more by these Portuguese and may myself govern my people in peace.' Neither he, nor the Mashona chiefs, Mtasa, Mtoko, and others, could hope to maintain their independence. What was clear enough to the Kings, but not to the people, of powerful Bantu states such as the Barotse or the Matabele, was apparent to all among these lesser tribes, and the chiefs had no difficulty in bringing home the idea to their people. Mtoko had fought Gouveia and beaten him off only a year before but cannot have wished to repeat such a triumph. All preferred what they had heard of the Great White Queen to what they knew of Gouveia. 'You must belong,' they had said thirty years ago to Livingstone, not far from Mtoko's, 'to the tribe who love the black man'; they had heard something of Livingstone and Moffat, some faint rumour perhaps of the goodwill and good intentions of such men as Shepstone in Natal and Grey at the Cape; the English hunters and explorers whom they had met or heard of had been, as Moffat said, gentlemen, men like Selous. They rejected the devil they knew for an enigmatic being they certainly did not know but who so far did not sound like a devil at all.

Treaties were signed with Mtoko and Mtasa; for reasons no doubt valid in Europe, less apparent at the time in Africa and certainly beyond the scope of this book, Gungunhana and Gazaland had to be surrendered to the Portuguese. Nor is it possible here to recount the adventures of the party who foiled the Portuguese attempt to assert authority over Manicaland, of the skirmish at Massa-Kessi, and the arrest by Major Forbes of Colonel Andrade and the fabulous Gouveia. All these events, stirring and exciting though they were, are part of the contest between England and the other European powers, of whom Portugal was one; they helped to draw the boundary between

Mozambique and Rhodesia, they are part of the story of Rhodesia, but did not much influence the way that white settled down with black inside Rhodesia.

Section 3: The Mashona Tribes and the Legal Fiction

To that process of settling down, however, the other two problems of the pioneers contributed directly. Consider next their relationship with the Mashona who surrounded them. There was the fundamental difficulty that the Mashona groups—tribes, clans, and sub-clans—were economically self-sufficient and wished only to be left alone. They were willing to be protected against the Matabele but saw little to recommend working for wages on a white man's farm, still less going down a mine. They did not want to work for someone else; the settlers thought of them as a potential labour force.

To this basic incompatibility of object was added the question of law and order; the Mashona understood a law that operated within the tribe but they were aware of no law—though of some considerations of custom and equity—that governed their conduct towards strangers or other tribes. There had been no authority from which such a law could be derived. Lately they had had no external relations except with the Matabele, and Lobengula had certainly not concerned himself with justice between the various tribal elements of the Mashona. Was this new authority, the Company, to supply a body of law that would operate between tribes, and the means of administering it? Without some such system their pioneers could hardly live there; whether in England or South Africa the settlers had been accustomed to the protection of law backed by police. As between themselves, the consular jurisdiction of a British authority had been assumed from the time of Queen Victoria's second letter to Lobengula; he had again been told what was happening and his sufferance had been taken for granted. He had not been told that the Company proposed to assume jurisdiction among the Mashona, yet the Order in Council of 9 May 1891 provided for 'the good government of all persons within the limits of this order'. To impose and enforce law is a sovereign right, which the Company was in theory empowered to exercise only when the right had been delegated by a native African chief. And, emphatically, Lobengula had delegated no such power.

The labour difficulty as well as the judicial was made more acute by the weakness of the Company's legal position. This appears very clearly in the discussion about hut tax. After a long argument, the Company restated their position to the Colonial Office early in July 1893, just before the beginning of the events that were to lead to the Matabele War; their letter sums up a point of view they had put before and of which much was to be heard later: 'Setting aside the indirect but very great advantages of a ready market for produce and labour', their secretary was instructed to say, 'the Mashonas are now relieved of the constant liability to raids by the *impis* of . . . Lo Bengula, and are able to gather in their crops with reasonable safety; in fact the administration of the British South Africa Company gives them security for life and property. It would seem to be prima facie just that they should contribute to the support of this administration.' And he continued: 'One of the principal difficulties in dealing with African races is of teaching them habits of settled industry and . . . in a country . . . with a considerable demand for native labour, the necessity of paying this small annual tax will . . . furnish an incentive to labour. . . .'[5]

This was a double argument that had always a strong appeal to the Rhodesian employer; a few months earlier, however, the Acting Resident Commissioner at Palapye had expressed to the High Commissioner another view sometimes put forward by missionaries and officials: 'We are often reminding them', he wrote, 'of how indebted they are to us for our protection and for the keeping among them an expensive police force. Unfortunately the advantages of the arrangement are less obvious to them than its disadvantages. . . .'[6] Sir Henry Loch had also before him a legal opinion of W. P. Schreiner, Attorney-General in Rhodes' Ministry and later to be Prime Minister. 'In Mashonaland', wrote Mr. Schreiner, 'there has not yet been any grant, concession or treaty by which the ownership of land, as against the natives, has been vested in the British South Africa Company. The proposal now savours of taxing the real owners of the soil for the support of a Government which is in the country only by permission from the native sovereign.'[7] In the light of this opinion, the Imperial Secretary at Cape Town had written: 'The natives are probably in law and equity the real owners of the land they occupy and it would be difficult to charge them hut tax for the occupation of their own lands.'[8]

Thus the legal fiction—on this occasion in alliance with equity —stood in the way of what to almost every European in Rhodesia seemed an obvious and necessary course. And it was the same with law and order. Take for instance the case of Moghabi; on 29 February 1892, Jameson wired to Cape Town: 'Moghabi had raided another Chief who appealed to us for protection. Moghabi refusing to submit to our authority, Chaplin and a few men were sent to assist the raided chief and give Moghabi a lesson . . . Moghabi resisted so his kraal was burnt and Moghabi killed.' The High Commissioner informed Lobengula: 'My friend, I wish to let you know that a collision has taken place. . . .' Lobengula replied: 'I don't like the action you have taken with the Mashona. What does it matter if the Mashona fight among themselves? It is bad if you mix yourself up with such matters. . . .' Yet Lobengula was the King.

In Mashonaland, there had arisen the kind of situation that arose at different times in Central India, in Hellas, in Northern Italy, in the Balkans; if there is no strong central government to hold the scales between hostile chiefs, towns, or states, the weaker will turn to any power that seems likely to afford protection. And rare is the power that will resist such an invitation. Once in Mashonaland, Jameson could not stand aloof and watch the chiefs kill each other's people. Humanity forbade indifference; self-interest argued that anarchy is infectious, that warring chiefs make uncomfortable neighbours. Yet because of the legal fiction, there was hesitation and uncertainty which sometimes led in the end to a severity that might have been avoided.

One story illustrates the point; it tells itself naturally in the words of the time and deserves some detail. 'A Mr. Bennett', begins the Acting Secretary to the British South Africa Company, 'who occupies a farm near Manguendi's kraal and is on very friendly terms with the Chief himself, had some of his goods stolen by natives from a neighbouring kraal which belongs to a Chief named Ngomo; he complained to this chief, but the only result was a repetition of the thefts and an altercation in which Bennett and his boy (i.e. servant) were repeatedly struck by the Natives. Bennett then came in and complained to Dr. Jameson, giving what Dr. Jameson considered a truthful story, and as he had behaved with considerable forbearance, Dr. Jameson sent Captain Lendy and a small party out to Manguendi's, demanding that this Chief should be sent into Salisbury for trial. Manguendi said that he was not strong enough to compel him to come but hoped that we would visit him and punish him ourselves.'[9]

Lendy, the story continues, went to Ngomo and told him he would get a fair trial in Salisbury; Ngomo refused to come and was 'very impertinent'; Lendy came back to Salisbury for instructions and was sent a second time with more men, a seven-pounder and a Nordenfeldt-Maxim 'to take summary measures'. Some volunteers, though not called upon to do so, joined the expedition. 'The Chief and his son and twenty-one other natives were killed. . . . Upon learning the result, Manguendi sent a message to Captain Lendy, warmly thanking him for what he had done. All the natives in the vicinity are peaceful and thoroughly satisfied.' To this report, the Imperial Secretary replied: 'His Excellency desires me to invite your attention to the importance of keeping within the law in all dealings with the natives. I am to add that the punishment inflicted in this case involving the loss of some 23 lives, appears utterly disproportionate to the original offence, which was the theft of some goods from a Mr. Bennett.'

In reply to this came a fuller report from Lendy of his second visit. 'Day had fully dawned', he wrote, 'before the natives became aware of our presence, and catching sight of some of the mounted men, one man in the kraal, presumably Ngomo himself, shouted out to the others to come on and kill the white man. A well-directed shot from the seven-pounder was the signal for the firing, which was pretty general on both sides for some minutes; the shooting of the natives however was very erratic and they made but a very short stand, the shells from the seven-pounder bursting in amongst the huts thoroughly demoralizing them, all who were able escaping. . . .' On this, the Colonial Office comment was that: 'Lord Knutsford cannot avoid the conclusion that Captain Lendy acted in this matter with recklessness and undue harshness.'

Jameson himself now wrote at much greater length, listing various troubles that had arisen. A driver of one of the Company's wagons had been killed near Manguendi's and Ngomo's kraals; there had been complaints of the 'threatening and impertinent attitude' of the natives in that district; there had been the murder of a trader, reported separately; in the Victoria District (far to the south of Manguendi's country), a newly appointed chief had 'refused to acknowledge the white man's authority' and had raided another friendly chief, killing some of his people; a skirmish had followed in which the recusant chief had been shot. In this district there had been more unrest, but this had been settled by the visit of an interpreter, with one policeman, who had explained 'what the occupation of the country by white men meant'. The disturbance at Ngomo's had followed; travellers in the area had 'one and all quoted the natives as speaking in a contemptuous way of the white man's authority, "That they only talked and did nothing".' Lendy had gone to summon Ngomo for an enquiry, with an assurance that only the guilty would be punished. 'The death of the natives was due to their armed resistance to the carrying out of the law' and military opinion was unanimous that to have attacked the kraal by small arms only, or by assault, would certainly have led to casualties among the police and volunteers. 'Since these severe lessons, the natives willingly submit to the decision of an officer accompanied by a couple of policemen.' In view of the High Commissioner's instructions, a circular notice had been sent to all Justices of the Peace and field cornets ordering them not to interfere in inter-tribal disputes or in cases in which only natives are concerned, except so far as is necessary for the preservation of the peace.

In reply to all this, His Excellency professed himself satisfied with the course adopted by Dr. Jameson but still entertained 'doubts as to whether the fire of Captain Lendy's force was not maintained much longer than was absolutely necessary', since 'he must have been early aware that the resistance offered by the natives was feeble in the extreme'.

The story of Lendy and Ngomo illustrates very clearly the difficulties inherent in the situation. The Company could not tolerate attacks on their wagons or the murder of settlers they had invited into the country; they were bound to take steps to preserve the peace. According to the legal fiction, to which regard was still paid in Cape Town and Whitehall, the Company was there by permission of the native sovereign. But Lobengula thought the Mashona should be allowed to fight among them-selves—a view in which the Company could hardly acquiesce without cynicism; they had after all come to promote 'civiliza-tion and progress'. Ngomo was said to be Mangwende's vassal and to have defied his authority as well as the Company's; Mangwende said he was not strong enough to compel Ngomo to come in, a statement which may or may not have been true but was certainly wise. The truth was that once the Company had occupied Mashonaland, they were in fact sovereign, and the pretence that they were not could only cause confusion. The settlers saw this clearly; the phrases about 'the white man's authority', and the presence of volunteers with Lendy show, if proof were needed, that they at least had no illusions.

Occupation was an act of conquest which in fact established sovereignty; it was surely both inevitable and desirable that the Company should end fighting between chiefs, establish them-selves as a central authority, and enforce respect for property and person. That is one question; whether Captain Lendy was justified in what he did is quite another. When a soldier uses force at the request of a magistrate 'in aid of the civil power', the principle to be followed in a settled community is that he should use only so much force as is needed to establish the local situation—that is, preserve the lives of the men under his command and bring the crowd to a frame of mind in which it will submit to the ordinary control of magistrates and police. He should stop when the crowd ceases to threaten. By this standard, one is bound to share Lord Knutsford's view that fire was continued much longer than was necessary.

But that was not the standard Lendy applied. He ends his report with the words: 'I am sure that a very wholesome lesson has been given to all the Chiefs in the district.' He was not thinking only of the local situation, and he was not, of course, dealing with a crowd used to law and temporarily out of hand. He was asserting that Mashonaland had been conquered and one may feel confident that Jameson and all the settlers meant him to do so. It could hardly have been done without loss of life—and in affairs of this kind it is a sad law that the price mounts steadily; if severity is inevitable, the longer it is delayed the more is needed. Lendy's affair must be seen not as 'aid to the civil power' but as an assertion of sovereignty; in this light, it should be judged in perspective and placed beside similar assertions by other conquerors, Chaka, Cortés, and Napoleon. Perhaps closer parallels are to be found in the prairies of the Mid-West. There were few such incidents in Rhodesia, and that is really the best that can be said; Lendy's methods were less wholesale than Lobengula's, but the main difference between killing women and children with seven-pounder shells and killing them with assegais is that in one case the blood is shed at a distance from the killer; it is hard to believe he could not have achieved the same result by less firing and more patrolling.*

The story has been dwelt on at length because it tells so much of what is to come and what has already happened. The Company forwarded to the Colonial Office a representation about it from Mr. Charles M. Rolker, who was probably right in thinking

*Hole, an administrator as well as a historian, thought as I do.

that he 'echoed the feeling of every white man in Mashonaland'. 'Ngomo', he wrote, 'made open boast that he did not fear the white man nor care for him and his laws. He made threats to kill Bennett . . . and that he would fight the white man if he came to arrest him. If . . . rigorous action had not been taken . . . it would have been unsafe for prospectors to traverse the country. . . . The feeling of defiance would have spread and culminated in . . . worse trouble. . . . To have met Ngomo . . . with small arms, would have been folly, since a great many lives of white men would have been sacrificed. . . . It was simply a question of enforcing law and order or inviting rebellion by allowing defiance against the white man to spread. . . .'[10]

'The white man'—'the white man's law'—'the white man's occupation of the country'—these phrases recur, the personification of an ideal, an abstract, a type; individual differences are forgotten when 'the white man' is contrasted with 'the black man'—and it becomes the same on his side. That personification of a type will continue. There is, too, the assumption that it is justifiable to spend a number of black lives rather than one white life. And already the man on the spot, ready to be firm and to make an example, is opposed, hampered, nagged at, by the man in Whitehall, the man who 'continues to doubt', and 'cannot avoid the conclusion', a man who has scruples about another set of abstractions, not about 'the white man' and 'the black man', but about common humanity and liberty and forced labour, a man who 'does not know the country' and has no idea how different things are in Rhodesia.

With all this, perhaps, the average settler was not yet much concerned. He was at the end of a very long and slow line of communication. A pot of jam that would have cost 6*d*. in England might fetch £3 in Salisbury; whisky, in England 2*s*. 6*d*. a bottle was here 10*s*. 6*d*. a tot; there would be a month when the store had nothing but tinned salmon, another when there was nothing but *foie gras*. There were very heavy rains that first year, from the autumn (in English terms) of 1890 to the spring of 1891; the rivers were unfordable for weeks together, mails were lost, parties were stranded, waiting till their oxen or mules could get across the drift or ford; huddled on the bank in the pouring rain, with no protection but the tilt of their wagons, man after man went down with fever. So did the lonely prospectors in their tents or the huts hastily put up for them by the Mashona, and many did not recover; malaria is one thing in a modern hospital, quite another sixty years ago for a man with no one to look after him in a hut with a thatched roof that leaks. 'For years afterwards the outspans at these rivers bore melancholy records in the shape of little heaps or crosses and initials rudely carved on treetrunks of the last resting-place of many a young adventurer. . . .'[11]

There was disillusionment because it rained, because supplies were so few and so expensive, because gold did not lie about on the surface in lumps, because 'the Mashona were lazy and the Matabele dangerous'. The first Administrator has written, a trifle bleakly: 'Among the first steps taken by me were the formation of a headquarters at Salisbury, the establishment of postal communication, the laying out of townships, the creation of mining districts with Mining Commissioners, the dealing with applications for mining rights and licences, the adjustment of disputes among the settlers, the establishment of hospitals, the preparation and introduction of mining and other laws and regulations, the initiation of a survey, the opening out of roads to the various mining centres, the despatch of missions to native chiefs, the diplomatic action with the Portuguese. It must also be borne in mind that the settlers were naturally very impatient for rapid progress. . . .'[12]

So Rhodesia began. At Fort Salisbury and Fort Victoria, a few shacks, a hut for the Administrator, a store; at Charter and Hartley Hill, not even so much; dotted about, fifteen, twenty, thirty miles from each other, the farms. A house of poles and mud with a thatched roof might stand on a kopje; below it, in a clearing, the first mealies, the first stalls for calves. Or one might come on the shaft of a mine; a hole in the ground like a well; a windlass at the head, a bucket to go down in, and to work it three or four Mashona, barely understanding a few words of the prospector's Kitchen Kaffir—a kind of pidgin Zulu; a heap of reddish gravel at the mouth of the shaft and close at hand, wherever there were shade and water, the prospector's camp—a tent, six feet long, a packing case for table, a bucket to wash in, a tin plate, a knife and fork, a roll of bedding. From the photographs of those days before the snapshot, the pioneers look out rigidly, with a touch of defiance in the heavy beard or long moustache, in the set gaze below the wide-brimmed hat, a hint of swagger in the pose of crossed legs or hand on hip; they have defied Africa and the forces of nature and so far they have been victorious; they have a right to swagger.

The legal uncertainties facing the pioneers were made a little clearer during 1891 by the Lippert Concession. In the Rudd Concession, Lobengula had given no rights over land to Rudd and his friends but had promised not to part with such rights to anyone else. In his own eyes he had repudiated the Concession more than once, while in the eyes of the Company he had several times reaffirmed it, chiefly by silences or acts of omission. True to his policy of getting as far from the gaff as he could, he now broke the land term of the Concession and granted the German financier Lippert the exclusive right for a hundred years to make grants of land to Europeans throughout his dominions. The Company had been making grants of land since the arrival of the Pioneers; the Lippert Concession, unless itself held to be invalid as a breach of the Rudd Concession, invalidated these grants. But it was little use taking Lippert and Lobengula to the Courts —and to what Courts should they be taken? Rhodes bought the Lippert Concession and regarded the grants of land so far made as now legitimized. But the Company was not by that means any nearer a solution of the problem of law and order among the Mashona.

The Order in Council of 9 May 1891 provided that the High Commissioner should 'respect any native laws or customs by which the civil relations of any native chiefs, tribes or populations under Her Majesty's protection are now regulated . . .'. Dr. Jameson's order to 'field-cornets and justices of the peace' after the Ngomo affair went further; they were 'specially warned not to interfere in inter-tribal disputes or in cases in which natives only are concerned. . . . Natives should therefore be allowed as far as possible to settle their own disputes in their own way among themselves. Should any inter-tribal dispute arise which threatens to endanger the lives or property of Europeans, field-cornets and justices of the peace will communicate with the magistrate of their district before taking any action . . .'.

This step was taken in deference to opinion in England as represented by the High Commissioner at the Cape. It was far from satisfactory from any point of view; it was impossible to settle down in the country, thrusting farms of three thousand acres each into the tribal lands, and to disregard 'disputes among the natives' entirely. Theories have a way of being too late for the events to which they were best suited; if the concept of indirect rule had at this time been formulated, now would have been the moment to apply it, to give each chief the authority to rule by his own customary law, to back him and support him, at the same time to guide him. To disregard tribal disputes could not be a lasting solution; it served however until next year, when things came to a head with the Matabele.

IV. The Matabele War

Section 1: The Victoria Incident

A beginning had been made, but there were too many vital contradictions of purpose left unresolved for things to last long as they were. In particular, both Lobengula and the Company looked on the Mashona as their subjects; to one they were a source of cattle and women, to the other a source of labour; the Mashona, reluctant to fill either role, could hardly fill both.

Lobengula's state was founded on annual raids on the Mashona. To have given them up would have involved a complete change of direction in the spirit of his people, a complete economic reorganization. He was not big enough for that; even if such an idea had appealed to him, he could not have carried it through. And in fact it did not appeal to him; he had not made up his mind to give away any element of sovereignty; he had no intention of reforming his kingdom on lines that would fit into the new world. His raids then would go eastward, as they always had done, not only because he must raid somewhere, but to assert his sovereignty over the Mashona—the very thing that Lendy and Jameson had just done in the case of Ngomo. Two such raids went out in 1892; the *impis* must have had strict orders to touch no Europeans, but the 'labour supply', always precarious, dried up altogether; mineworkers, farm labourers, and domestic servants alike fled to rocky and inaccessible fastnesses.

On the European side it was not surprising that the settlers felt there was no hope of any real progress so long as the Matabele threat hung over their heads, and over the heads of the people on whom they must depend if farming and mining were to be a success. There was also disappointment that there was not more gold in Mashonaland; there were rumours that there was far more to the West. The Matabele cattle were famous and were believed to indicate rich pastures. Matabeleland, a present danger, might be a future source of wealth; more and more it came to be felt that the end to all trouble would be a settlement with the Matabele.

To say that Rhodes and Jameson shared that view is not to say that they coldly determined on war, chose the moment, and engineered the means. Indeed, it is clear they did not choose the moment, because Jameson (who succeeded Colquhoun as Administrator) had recently carried out a sweeping reduction in the police force—the only permanent military force in the country —cutting the strength from 650 to 150 by the end of 1891, and reducing the annual cost to one-third of what it had been. In July of 1893 he said he had barely 100 horses in the country, and horses were regarded as essential for dealing with the Matabele. Even so he was confident that, given three months to collect more horses, he and his volunteers could beat Lobengula—but his reduction of the police is not the act of a man who means to force a conflict within a year. The truth is, surely, that Rhodes and Jameson believed war would come and would not be sorry when it did, but were ready to wait for the right moment; the right moment would be when even Whitehall would be forced to concede that the Matabele had passed all bounds.

The incident thus awaited with a mixture of anxiety and impatience took place in July of 1893. Provocation occurred— and the general situation was not one in which provocation was likely to be disregarded. In May, 500 yards of telegraph line between Tuli and Fort Victoria were cut and taken away; not a trace could be found, but on enquiry it became clear, and has never been disputed, that the wire had been taken by a Mashona group under a headman called Gomalla, a vassal of Setoutsie, a petty chief. A police officer was instructed to tell Gomalla's people they must hand over the culprits for trial and punishment or else pay a collective fine of so many head of cattle. They chose the collective fine and paid at once—but in cattle which it later appeared were Lobengula's.

Copje at Salisbury, in 1891 (from H. Thomassett's *Sketches of Scenes in Mashonaland*)

Mashona village, 1891 (from H. Thomassett's *Sketches of Scenes in Mashonaland*)

Laager at Bulawayo (from a sketch by R. Curtis Brown in the *Illustrated London News*, 2 May 1896)

The Mangwe Post (from a sketch by Melton Prior in the *Illustrated London News*, 30 May 1896)

In Matabeleland proper, most of the cattle were in varying degrees the King's cattle; there was perhaps a sense in which all cattle were the King's, as all land was the King's, but in a narrower sense there were private herds, which must not grow too large, and larger herds belonging to the King, guarded and milked for him by his indunas and their people. But they might not be slaughtered without his permission. Setoutsie had presumably submitted to Lobengula and promised tribute in return for immunity from raids; as a sign of his submission and the King's faith in him he had been entrusted with royal cattle—which may even have been originally his own and allotted to Lobengula as tribute. At any rate in Lobengula's eyes they were his, and it must have been with malicious pleasure that Gomalla reported to him through Setoutsie that Jameson had taken them as a fine.

Lobengula sent an indignant message to Jameson: why had his cattle been taken? Did *he* cut the wire? Jameson replied: 'Now that I find that the cattle belong to the King, of course they shall be returned to him . . . at the same time I cannot allow this crime to go unpunished and shall send my police . . . to find the actual culprits and chastise them, or failing that . . . will punish Gomalla as I think fit.'[1] In June, the High Commissioner was able to write to Lobengula: 'I understand that this matter has now been satisfactorily settled and that the cattle have been restored to you. I desire, however, to explain to you that the telegraph wire is the property of the white man and that it should be protected by you. . . .'[2] It was perhaps already Lobengula's intention to punish Setoutsie and Gomalla himself; if so this letter cannot have discouraged him. News came that another petty Mashona chief had taken liberties with his cattle; he dispatched an *impi*. On 12 July, the British South Africa Company telegraphed to the Colonial Office: 'Lo Bengula sent Matabele punish Mashonas near Fort Victoria at same time friendly message all Europeans. Some Mashonas killed and cattle taken . . . no cause for anxiety.'

There seems no doubt that Lobengula did tell his *impis* not to interfere with Europeans. But such orders were not easy to enforce or obey. The two regiments sent were about 2,500 strong and were joined by about a thousand Maholis, that is to say people not counted as Matabele proper, less disciplined and less organized. The discipline of a Zulu or Matabele regiment in battle, for drill purposes, or in a dance, was impressive, but when they were turned loose upon a Mashona or Ba-toka population, they acted in little groups and their behaviour does not make pleasant reading; once that kind of thing had begun it would be difficult to control. Lewanika wrote of a Matabele *impi* who had been sent across the Zambezi in this same cold weather (or in English terms, summer) of 1893: 'They scoured Ba-toka for three months, destroying property and killing many of my people in the most revolting manner. Women were ripped open and impaled, men and children made targets of and roasted alive like meat. Nothing, not a dog, escaped where they passed. . . .'[3] There is of course an element of resentment in this because Lewanika looked on the Ba-toka as his in the same sense that the Mashona were Lobengula's, but what he says tallies with the accounts given by the settlers near Fort Victoria.

The *impis* had been told not to attack Europeans but they made no distinction between the Mashona who worked for Europeans and those who did not; they carried off cattle from European farms, and if the farmers left for Fort Victoria, as was often the case, they seem to have smashed their furniture and taken anything that was of use to them. Later, in a report made on an enquiry ordered by Parliament in the United Kingdom, Mr. F. J. Newton wrote: 'I take it as proved and accepted that the Matabele were in possession of the whole countryside, that they entered the precincts of the town of Fort Victoria . . . that they squatted on the commonage . . . and that mining, agricultural, and pastoral pursuits were at a standstill owing to their presence. The chief Manyao entered the town . . . and called upon Captain Lendy, who was magistrate, to hand over to him the Mashona refugees—men, women, and children—whom he saw had obtained sanctuary in the fort.' He assured him that his men would not spoil the water by killing them near the river but would take them into the bush where their bodies would give no offence. 'Captain Lendy gave the only reply which it was possible for an officer in his position to give. . . .'[4]

This was on 14 July; the first Matabele had been seen in the neighbourhood on 9 July; it was the 17th when Dr. Jameson arrived from Salisbury to find that for a week all business had been at a standstill, that volunteers were called out and armed sentries posted, the town in a state of siege. He saw villages burning on both sides of the road and mules (which must have been stolen from the farms of Europeans) 'laden with plunder' being driven off by Matabele with shields and assegais. He sent for the indunas in charge of the *impi*, of whom Manyao was the senior, Umgandan, a Matjaha or unmarried warrior, the second-in-command. He told them that in no circumstances would the fugitives be given up to them and that they must go back to Matabeleland proper. He would give them an hour to go; he pointed to the sun and made it clear how far the sun would have moved when their period of grace had expired. Then he should drive them. This message Manyao seems to have accepted without committing himself deeply, but Umgandan was defiant.

There was controversy later as to what Jameson told them; it was alleged that he had given them an order to do something impossible, to be back in Matabeleland proper within an hour. That would be quite out of character and was clearly not what he meant; he meant that they had an hour in which to start moving, to show that they seriously meant to go. He gave them an hour and three-quarters and then sent out Lendy with a patrol of mounted troopers. His instructions to Lendy were, he later deposed: 'You have heard what I told the Matabele; I want you to carry this out. I don't want them to think it is only a threat; they have had a week of threats, with very bad results. . . . Ride out in the direction they have gone. . . . If you find they are not moving off, drive them, as you heard me tell Manyao I would, and if they resist and attack you, shoot them.'[5]

There can be no reasonable quarrel with these instructions; placed as he was, Jameson was bound to keep the neighbourhood of his settlements clear from raids of this kind and one may agree that, from their point of view, the settlers had shown forbearance in waiting a whole week. Whether Lendy carried out his orders properly is another matter; Jameson's silence on this point may mean no more than that he was loyal to a subordinate. Lendy walked his horses three miles or more before he came up with some Matabele, straggling slowly towards the north-east; this would be about an hour after he started, nearly three hours after the ultimatum. There is reason to believe that there had been a sharp difference of opinion between Manyao, who wanted to avoid a conflict and go back to Lobengula for orders, and Umgandan who was all for defying Jameson. Manyao had admitted to Jameson that he had not full control over all the young warriors; it may well be that he believed he was doing his best to withdraw, and that from his point of view what now befell him was a breach of faith; it would not to him seem inconsistent with his best that his men had burnt two Mashona kraals that afternoon.

Lendy, however, saw those two kraals so recently set alight, saw that the Matabele had only covered three miles in the three hours since the ultimatum, concluded that they were defying Jameson and continuing the raid. For a week he had been restraining his men—and no doubt himself—in the face of great provocation; he was not, as appears from the affair of Ngomo's kraal, the man to be squeamish about loss of life; now he felt he had clear orders. He extended his line, gave the order to fire and advanced at a canter. The Matabele fired a few desultory shots but offered nothing that could be called resistance; one of the first to fall dead was Umgandan. Mr. Newton believed that nine Matabele were killed in the pursuit; it was certainly not a massacre. There was a conflict of evidence as to who actually fired the first shot, but Mr. Newton's conclusion was that the Matabele made no hostile move till they were attacked; on the evidence he records there can be no doubt he was right.

Jameson's verbal orders sound as though he had thought of two possibilities—'driving' without firing, and shooting if this process was resisted. Lendy does not seem to have tried the first;

it may be that even a more patient man might have found it necessary to shoot Umgandan but one is left with a feeling that that might have been all that was needed to quicken the retreat and put resistance out of the question.

Section 2: *The Approaching Storm*

The *impi* went back to Bulawayo and told Lobengula they had been called to an *indaba* and treacherously attacked. Until he received this report, Lobengula had been acting as if he was prepared to go a long way to preserve the peace; as late as 30 July, Sir Henry Loch, the High Commissioner, cabled to the Colonial Office that Lobengula had expressed regret that he had sent his *impi* so close to Fort Victoria but he added: 'impossible to say what Lobengula may do after hearing of fight'.[6] This was based on news sent from Bulawayo on the 22nd; on the 20th Loch had sent a message in the following terms: 'My friend, . . . the *impi* in the neighbourhood of Victoria has transgressed your orders . . . entered the streets of the settlement, killing the black and native servants of the white people before the doors of their houses, . . . the whole country is smelling of the blood shed by your people. These acts . . . cannot be permitted. . . . They will bring on you the punishments that befell Cetewayo. . . . I wish to control the anger of the white people . . . but I shall not say stop to them unless you at once withdraw your *impis* and punish the indunas. . . .'

To this Lobengula replied: 'I shall return no cattle nor compensate anybody until Rhodes returns to me all the captives, wives, children, cattle, goats, and sheep which were given protection by the Victoria people and had I known at the time when I sent my *impis* what I know now I would have ordered them to capture and loot all they could lay their hands on belonging to the whites to compensate myself for the people and their property which were withheld from me.' And two days later he sent another message, this to Dr. Harris, Secretary to the British South Africa Company: '. . . you did not tell me that you had a lot of Amaholi cattle hiding with you together with their owners and that when my Indunas claimed them from Captain Lendy he refused and told my Induna that the Amaholis and their cattle did not belong to me any longer and then turned his cannon on my people. Are the Amaholis then yours? . . . I thought you came to dig gold but it seems that you have come . . . to rob me of my people and country as well . . . you are like a child playing with edged tools. . . . Captain Lendy is like some of my own young men; he has no holes in his ears and cannot hear; he is young and all he thinks of is a row, but you had better caution him carefully or he will cause serious trouble between us. . . .'

In the messages that followed, there were angry references by Lobengula to Jameson's talk of a boundary between them. 'Who gave him the boundary lines? Let him come forward and show me the man that pointed out to him these boundaries.' Jameson answered that the King knew very well that 'ever since we have been here, the Umniati and the Shashi rivers formed the boundary across which we would not allow our white people to go . . .'. In all this discussion, there are wide assumptions on either side which the other does not accept. Lobengula assumes that the whole of Mashonaland and all 'the Amaholi' are still his; Jameson that he has been given a portion. apart. In particular, Jameson assumes that the prohibition about crossing the Shashi applies to Lobengula's men crossing to his side, but it sounds even in his own account as though all he had agreed with Lobengula was that the settlers would keep to their side.

From the Colonial Office, Lord Ripon sent strict instructions to Sir Henry Loch that the Company must be made to understand that 'their duty must be limited to defending their occupied territory and Her Majesty's Government cannot support them in any aggressive action'.[7] Lobengula recalled the *impi* 6,000 strong that he had sent across the Zambezi towards Barotseland and talked of sending another to Fort Victoria that would not have orders to spare white people; he refused to accept the Company's monthly payment and referred to it as blood money. Rhodes bought horses and sent them north; he told the High Commissioner that in a month he would have 1,000 mounted men in strong positions; he and Jameson exchanged laconic telegrams; what King, asked Rhodes, going to make war against another King, sitteth not down first and considereth. . . . Jameson replied that he had considered and it was all right. Lobengula sent a message to Moffat at Palapye: 'Son of Umshete, why don't you speak, why do you keep quiet, what great wrong have I done? . . . I was only sending for my own stolen cattle among the Amaholi', and Loch answered him: 'You ask Mr. Moffat what you have done . . . your *impi* entered the settlement of the white men and killed their servants. . . . I do not desire war, I wish for peace. . . . I will tell Dr. Jameson provided you keep your *impis* away from the vicinity of the white people, that . . . he should be content with restoration of any cattle and other property. . . .' The Imperial Secretary wired to Rhodes: 'Demand for compensation should not be pressed. . . .' Lobengula moved his regiments to positions on the roads from Bulawayo to Salisbury and Victoria.

Meanwhile, the inhabitants of Victoria met and passed resolutions as to the absolute necessity of settling once and for all the Matabeleland question; crops have been destroyed, homesteads wrecked, and 'on nearly every farm', they urged, 'the natives in the employ of the farmers have been killed by the Matabele, and in many cases these cold-blooded murders have taken place in their presence. They state most emphatically that as they fully believe these raids will be of yearly occurrence, they are fearful not only of losing cattle and crops in the future but the very great probability of they, their wives and children being murdered as well as the natives. . . .'

On 21 September, Loch reported that he believed Lobengula was personally anxious for peace, and that Europeans in Bulawayo thought the movement of *impis*—which now covered the three approaches from Salisbury, Victoria, and from Bechuanaland —were defensive; as to this he was not himself wholly convinced. But, he continued, the Company, having now collected horses and made their preparations, cannot afford to let the present suspense continue indefinitely; they and their settlers cannot feel secure as they are nor concentrate on developing the country if they must perpetually be standing to arms. He thought it would be right to let them demand the withdrawal of the *impis* and move forward to push them back if they would not go.

Lobengula sent an induna,★ Umshete, with a present for the Queen and orders to see her personally, but Umshete was not empowered to give way on two essential points: he could not agree to any boundary between Matabele sovereignty and the Company's, and he could not agree to give up raiding the Mashona. To whom do the Mashona belong? he asked indignantly and Loch sent him back. But on 5 October, a change occurred in the situation; Loch reported that a party of about thirty Matabele had fired on a patrol of the Bechuanaland Border Police— employed of course not by the Company but by the Crown; at about the same time, another party of Matabele fired on some of the Company's police on what the police considered their side of the Shashi; these incidents, Loch thought, indicated that the *impis* had got out of hand and meant to force a war.

Loch accordingly told Goold-Adams, commanding the Bechuanaland Police, to take what measures he thought necessary for the safety of the Bechuanaland Protectorate and sent a similar message to Jameson. He believed that the Matabele would attack Tati and threaten Khama's country and authorized Goold-Adams to push forward on to the high veld, ready to advance on Bula-wayo if necessary; Goold-Adams had 220 police, and Loch told him to take command of some 200 troopers temporarily en-rolled by the Company, who had been intended in Jameson's original plan to operate independently; Goold-Adams had also 1,000 of Khama's men. On 7 October, Loch ends his cable to the Secretary of State with the words: 'I have just learnt by telegram from Jameson that two columns of the Company's men are advancing from Salisbury and Victoria to press back the *impis* on their front.'[8]

The High Commissioner summarized the situation as he saw it in a telegram to the Marquess of Ripon on 30 October: 'All hope

★This man, of course, was a Matabele; Umshete was also the nickname of Robert Moffat.

of an amicable settlement between Lobengula and the British South Africa Company had to be abandoned when he continued to keep his *impis* close to Victoria and when a patrol party of the Company's police were fired on not far from the station, but the strongest reason that led me to believe that no hope could be entertained that friendly relations could . . . be restored . . . was that he never abandoned his claim . . . to have handed over to him the Mashona men and women who had sought the protection of the Company, who, if given up would either have been put to death or reduced to slavery. When I questioned Umshete on this subject . . . his only reply was "Who then do they belong to?" speaking of the Mashona as if they were only cattle and to be treated as such. . . . Under the circumstances, I authorized Dr. Jameson . . . to force back the Matabele *impis* to a safe distance from the neighbourhood of Victoria, and also take any other measures he might consider necessary for the security . . . of those . . . within his administrative authority.'[9]

Jameson and the settlers had been troubled by no doubts as to whether the movements of Matabele *impis* were defensive; they were all of one opinion that the present situation was intolerable and must be ended. But a certain distrust of the Company was already showing its head; before enrolment, the volunteers demanded that their rewards should be set down in writing. There was nothing unusual, in South Africa, in the understanding that a Commando did not ride for nothing; what was unusual about 'the Victoria agreement' was that the terms were expressed in what was intended to be a formal document. Each trooper was to have the right to a farm of 6,000 acres, 20 gold claims, and a share of half the loot—that is to say, of Lobengula's cattle. The agreement makes it clear that when the inhabitants of Fort Victoria passed resolutions about a settlement with the Matabele, it was a settlement they meant; it has no bearing on the question of whether the Company had deliberately provoked war, because it was signed in August, when there is no question that preparations were being hurried forward as quickly as possible.

Jameson's original plan had been that three columns, each of about 250 mounted men, each with some quick-firing Maxim guns, should advance from Salisbury by Charter, from Victoria, and from Tuli. After the Matabele's brush with the Bechuanaland Police, the last force from Tuli was put by Loch under the command of Goold-Adams; this became on paper the strongest force of the three. The shots fired on the police thus brought Imperial forces into the war; they also served as the trigger that released the Company's two columns.

Lobengula knew now that what he had always feared was happening. But he still tried to prevent the worst. Loch cabled on 20 October: 'Lobengula sends messages denying he has *impis* on borders; offers to send anyone I may appoint to see; says he hears of advance on part of whites and knows they want to fight and asks why they do not say so.' Loch thought it too late to do anything about this, but Lord Ripon, now Secretary of State, told him that if he could get any message to Lobengula in reply, he should do so, telling him that he could have peace if he would withdraw his *impis* and agree to arrangements that would provide security against future raids.[10]

It is possible at this stage to sum up very briefly. The Pioneers, or most of them, were firmly of the opinion that only a settle-ment with the Matabele could end their troubles. But the Com-pany did not plan and provoke war; Rhodes and Jameson were however not sorry to receive provocation and after the Victoria incident they went ahead with their preparations. Lobengula would do anything to avoid war short of renouncing sovereignty over the Mashona; Loch wished to save him but only at the price of his recognizing that he had a boundary with the Company— which meant that he had given them half of what he thought his kingdom. And this he would not do.

Section 3: The Last Ironies

In all these events, as in those leading up to the signing of the Charter, there is a time-lag between the dispatch of a message to Bulawayo and its receipt, a time-lag often longer than the interval between the messages. On 1 October Loch had written to Lobengula asking him to send to Cape Town a party of indunas empowered to treat (as Umshete had not been). 'Be wise', he wrote, 'keep your *impis* away from the white people and send some of your chief indunas to talk things over with me. . . .' This reached Lobengula on the 14th, after Jameson had begun to move against him. He at once dispatched his half-brother Ingubogobo and two other indunas with the trader Dawson; they were to go to Cape Town to see Sir Henry Loch. They reached Tati on the 18th; this place, it will be remembered, was where Sam Edwards had been given powers to act on behalf of Lobengula; it was theoretically part of Matabeleland. Dawson and the Indunas were surprised to find that Tati had been occupied by Goold-Adams and his police; this had happened after the firing on the 5th, when Goold-Adams had been told to make Bechuanaland safe. In what followed, no one meant to be cruel or brutal; the incident gave an extra turn to the screw, an added touch of tragic irony to Lobengula's tragic story; it sprang quite simply from bad manners, which in their turn arose from the South African habit of thinking of 'the black man' and 'the white man' as though all black men were alike, all white men alike, as though there were no differences of rank or character between them.

Dawson arrived with the three Indunas—envoys to the High Commissioner; he saw a friend and went off to have a drink, telling a mine foreman to look after the 'three natives'. He went on from his drink to his dinner—and one wonders whether he had taken more care of his horse than of Lobengula's envoys. Meanwhile Goold-Adams heard from an interpreter that there were three Matabele in the camp who had come with Dawson and were talking of getting their horses and escaping. They were no doubt frightened and uneasy at their reception; Goold-Adams supposed Dawson was leaving Bulawayo to be safe and that these men had come with him as guides. He did not want them to go back and tell the Matabele his numbers and where his sentries were posted; he sent orders that they were not to be allowed to go. The guard moved on them to take them into custody; one of the three in a panic seized a bayonet from the nearest man's belt and stabbed him with it; he was shot, and another, also bolting, was killed with the butt of a rifle. Only Ingubugobo, the King's brother, stayed motionless and lived.

It would have made no difference to the war if this had not happened. It was too late to stop the war. But that his envoys had been murdered—and as it must have seemed to him treacherously murdered—this added a last bitterness to the last days of Lobengula, who had seen so clearly what was coming and had yet cherished so long a shred of faith that somewhere among the countrymen of Robert Moffat justice was to be found.

There is a postscript to this story. Dawson reached Palapye on the 22nd and gave Moffat a letter from Lobengula which he telegraphed to the High Commissioner: 'I am tired of hearing the lies which come to me every day. How many of your people have my people killed? You say my people have fired on yours twice. How many are dead? Are your people stones that bullets do not kill them? You hear what your people say . . . send two men of yours and I will give them assistance to find out who has done this shooting . . . your people must want something from me—when you have made up your mind to do a thing it is not right to blame it on my people. . . .'[11]

It was the last cry of a tragic figure overcome by events:

> . . . As flies to wanton boys, are we to the gods;
> They kill us for their sport.

Not much need be said of the war itself. It proved that Jameson was right, and some of the professionals wrong, as to the strength needed to defeat the Matabele. It proved that in open country there was no need to fear another Isandhlwana for a force of mounted men who knew how to shoot, who were used rather as mounted infantry than cavalry, and who took reasonable trouble to send out continual patrols and get information. Goold-Adams and his column advanced from the south but had no fighting apart from one skirmish, when an isolated party was attacked while trying to catch up the main body. The Salisbury column of 258 Europeans joined the Victoria column of 414 on 16 October, two days before the affair of Dawson and the Indunas, at a point not far from the modern town of Que-Que; they crossed the Umniati River which Jameson had previously told Lobengula he regarded as the boundary between them. The united force had two seven-pounder guns, five Maxims and some other machine-guns; they advanced steadily on Bulawayo, laagering every night, keeping out scouts; they were heavily attacked twice, at the Shangani River, some seventy miles beyond the Umniati, and at the Imbambezi. On both occasions, the enemy attacked with courage and determination, but their tactics were as unsuitable to the weapons of their antagonists as those of the French at Poitiers. Their traditional battle formation was still Chaka's—to advance in a crescent, with a mass of troops in the centre or 'chest' of the *impi*, and two horns curving forward on either flank. Shell-fire usually broke this formation before it could get within rifle range; the Matabele understood shells so little that they were seen to fire their rifles at shellbursts; indeed they did not understand their rifles very well and are said to have believed that the higher they set the sights the harder they would hit. But it seems much more likely that they did not understand sighting at all and simply discharged the piece in the general direction of the enemy. When they came within small arms range they had to face well-aimed machine-gun fire and rifle fire. Their casualties were believed to have been very heavy; 'it would appear', wrote an observer, 'that the Umbeza and Ingubu regiments were practically annihilated', and the Insukamini, which was at both battles, lost almost as heavily; 'I must record', he continued, of the first two at Imbambezi, 'the pluck of these two regiments which was simply splendid, and I doubt if any European troops could have withstood for such a long time as they did the terrific and well-directed fire brought to bear on them.' On the side of the settlers, losses were at the Shangani one white trooper and one 'Cape Boy' driver killed, six white men wounded; at the Imbambezi, four killed and seven wounded.

It was not, then, a war that soldiers would find very interesting.

The fire-power on one side was so much superior that the Matabele never came to close quarters and never used their assegais. Jameson entered Bulawayo on 4 November; he was joined ten days later by Goold-Adams from the south. Lobengula had fired his kraal and gone away north-westward. He had till the last been scrupulous to preserve the lives of the white men he had known; some he had helped to escape but the traders Fairbairn and Usher had stayed till the last and he had taken care they should not be hurt. He had said there was a hedge about the word of a King and in his own way he was a King to the last.

But the problem must be seen from Jameson's point of view. The rains were beginning and the rivers would soon be rising; malaria would get steadily worse and it would from now on be more and more difficult to move men, and still more supplies, about the country. The object must be to disband the force and settle the country as quickly as possible. But no settlement could begin till Lobengula was captured; so long as he was at liberty there would always be Matabele to obey him. Jameson sent him a letter: 'To stop this useless slaughter you must at once come and see me at Bulawayo, where I will guarantee that your life will be safe and you will be kindly treated. . . .'[12] The answer was written by one John Jacobs, a coloured man who had some education in English; spelling and grammar are poor and it is plainly a bad translation, but an echo of what Lobengula may have said can be heard behind the words: 'I . . . have heard all what you has said so I will come. But allowed me to ask were are all my men who I have sent to the Cape?' He mentions Umshete, James Dawson, and the three Indunas. 'And if I do come were will I get a house for me as all my houses is burn down?' Perhaps the whole tenor of the speech on which this letter was based was ironical; perhaps it meant: 'Said the spider to the fly . . .'. At any rate he did not come; he moved away from Bulawayo northwards.

Jameson sent after him a mounted force under Major Forbes that was organized to move quickly. There were still two last tragic turns to be given to the screw. The pursuing force came on the remains of a camp near the Shangani River; Lobengula was only a short day's march ahead. He knew the hunt was close and there is evidence, which did not come to light till much later, that he sent for the Commander of the Mbeza Regiment, the Induna Mjan, and gave him a bag of gold sovereigns. Again no one can say exactly what he said, but it is agreed that he gave orders that a message should be sent to his pursuers to the effect that he was conquered, that they should turn back. And the bag of gold, said to have been a thousand pounds saved from the monthly 'blood-money' which the Company had paid him since the Rudd Concession—that he may have added with some such ironical words as these: 'Give the white men this. It was gold they said they came for. It is gold they love. Can it be for this they are following me?' And the deeper thought behind might be that this would convince them that he had no more hope.

Whatever he said, his messengers left with the gold and the message, but they either misjudged the column's position or were frightened of approaching the main body; they spoke only to two stragglers behind the main column, to whom they gave the gold and the message. To these two, only the gold was comprehensible; they kept it and said nothing till they were brought to trial a year later. If the message had been delivered, Forbes must have parleyed; his horses and men were very tired, he had already been faced with something that among regular soldiers would have been very like mutiny. But it was not delivered; he knew nothing about it and his instructions were to capture Lobengula if he could.

The last incident in the story thus arose from the theft of the bag of gold. On the afternoon of 3 December, Forbes formed his camp for the night and sent out a mounted patrol of volunteers under Major Allan Wilson with orders to find out which way the King had gone and bring back news before nightfall. Wilson disobeyed these orders and did not come back. Instead he sent back first two, and later three, men to report that Lobengula had crossed the river, that Wilson, hard on his heels, had taken up a position in the bush near his camp and that he hoped that Forbes and the main body would follow across the river and join him before daylight.

This was the kind of Nelsonian disobedience which a commander of irregular troops must expect. Forbes had meanwhile received information, which proved to be greatly exaggerated, that Lobengula had gone on with a few men and that the Induna Mjan with the main *impi* of about 3,000 men had circled back, like a wounded buffalo to catch its hunters, was in fact near him in the dark and might attack him at any moment. Unless he was quite sure that this information could safely be discounted—and he could not be—it would have been madness to break his camp in the dark and advance as Wilson asked him. To order Wilson back was the solution for a staff college exercise; but it might mean six weary months of chasing Lobengula through the scrub—and all the time sour looks from men who thought he had thrown away a chance. He compromised and sent twenty men on to join Wilson; as has been generally pointed out, this reinforcement made Wilson's party into something more than a patrol for reconnaissance but was not enough to enable it to pursue Lobengula effectively or defend itself against a serious attack.

It seems that the intelligence which reached Forbes had been partly true; there were Matabele parties threatening him as well as Wilson. When the twenty reinforcements reached Wilson, there were already Matabele between him and the river and to get back, even with this added strength, would not have been easy. Wilson determined to go on, to make a desperate dash for the King's camp and try to capture him. He attacked the camp and came close to the King's wagon, but met with such heavy opposition that he had to fall back; he then tried to cut his way through to the river but was forced to stand, surrounded and greatly outnumbered. Forbes advanced at dawn but was attacked; he found the river had been rising all night and was now impassable and had to fall back to his original position of the previous night. He could thus give no help to Wilson, who, with all his men, died fighting with great gallantry.

The Matabele War

This tale of high courage and some folly is necessary to an understanding of Rhodesia. It has become a legend, perhaps an inspiration, certainly a symbol. There is the monument to Allan Wilson and his men at the national Valhalla in the Matobo Hills where Rhodes lies buried; there is a memorial at Zimbabwe; walk into any public building in Rhodesia and the odds are that you will see a painting of the last stand of the Shangani patrol, the dead horses serving as cover to the riflemen, the piles of bodies, the charging savage stopped with a revolver shot; you will see the same picture in many private houses too, and the name of Allan Wilson is remembered in medals, in prizes, in sermons.

To ask why this should be so is not to decry the valour of these men nor the sincerity of those who honour them, but the question needs to be asked; there have been other brave men who died fighting, both before and since, in the wars of 1914 and 1939, men whose name does not live in the same way. The names of these men are not forgotten, first, because their fate was for long un-certain; there were rumours that they had escaped to the North and were still alive. This uncertainty came to an end but not their fame. That lived on because the legend of their death was needed for this new country. The Matabele war had completed the founding of Rhodesia but it had till now been a war with few losses on the winning side. There is something in mankind deeply suspicious of a free gift, of anything too easily won, of a city not founded on a sacrifice; there have been peoples, both black and white, who have buried a victim below the cornerstone or the gate-post of any notable building. The tale of the Shangani patrol met this deep human need. And it stood as a symbol for the heroic few among the barbarous many, for the supremacy of the white man's spirit even in death, for the pride of the English in the last days of Queen Victoria, the period of 'Recessional' and 'The English Flag'.

Never the lotus closes, never the wild-fowl wake,
But a soul goes out on the East Wind that died for England's
   sake,

wrote Kipling, in a mood that in England survived Mons to die in the mud of Passchendaele but which lived on in Rhodesia.

Forbes fell back from the Shangani River slowly and painfully. Jameson had to decide that operations must stop for the rains. Lobengula moved north; it was not known for some time that he died early in January and that the war was over. It was said to be small-pox of which he died, but perhaps it would be as true to say with the fairy-tales that he died of a broken heart.

V. The Rebellions

Section 1: The Matabele Settlement

The war was over but the settlement that followed would make more difference than the war had done to the way white lived with black. One by one the Indunas came in to surrender; they saw Jameson and talked to him. Goold-Adams, of the Bechuanaland Police, an Imperial Officer, not a Company's man, was present at one of the most important of these interviews, with 'Gambo', who had commanded nearly half Lobengula's forces. He reported to the High Commissioner the gist of what Jameson had said: 'the great object was white and black to live peaceably together, the severe punishment of persons practising witchcraft . . . the parcelling out of cattle amongst the natives to provide them with food. . . . As soon as the country was quiet, the return of a certain number of arms to allow Natives to hunt and severe punishment of whites interfering with native kraals. . . .' This was in March 1894; in June, Dr. Jameson reported more formally, but in similar terms, the points he made at every interview: 'The King being dead, the white Government had taken his place . . . the laws would be the same for whites and blacks; the people through their indunas could always complain to the White Government, . . . their wives and daughters would be protected equally against whites and blacks. . . . This point was specially emphasized as the dread of interference is the main factor against the natives settling down in proximity to the whites. . . .'[1]

There was more than this; there were assurances about cattle and land, of which more later. What Jameson said was apparently judged to be enough; gradually the news spread that Lobengula would not come back and more and more of the Matabele came to terms. Meanwhile, a difference between the Imperial Government and Rhodes was working itself out by the process of being patiently committed to writing and argued over clause by clause, Sir Henry Loch as mediator showing unfailing good sense.

Loch had foreseen the difficulty before the beginning of the war and advised on it in the light of his general views. He did not much care for the Company as a political device. 'I consider it advisable on principle that the executive of a country should not be personally interested in the acquisition of the lands and properties of those they are called upon to govern . . .' he wrote in a secret dispatch on 18 October 1893,[2] but he was a sensible and fair-minded man and he recognized that Her Majesty's Government could not disclaim responsibility and yet retain control. 'Unless Her Majesty's Government are prepared to assist the Company with men and money and to accept all the responsibilities that now attach to the Company', he had cabled to the Marquess of Ripon in September 1893, 'I do not see how HMG can exercise the right of interfering with the Company's freedom of action.' This was to argue on the base of the facts with which he was faced. But what he thought right was that Her Majesty's Government should take more responsibility and more control; as soon as the border incident brought in Goold-Adams and the Bechuanaland Police, he cabled his opinion that 'all negotiations with Lobengula and the policy respecting the future administration of the country should be arranged by the High Commissioner. . . .' A few days later, in the secret dispatch already referred to, he was suggesting that the administration of Mashonaland and Matabeleland should be accepted as an Imperial responsibility until the British South Africa Company were in a sufficiently established position to take over the government—with due regard, of course, to Imperial interests. But by 12 November, the 'great success of the Chartered Company' made it in his opinion impossible to follow this course and he 'proposed to discuss the future government of Matabeleland and Mashonaland on the basis of their being treated as one country under the administration of the Company, with such safeguards as may be necessary for the security of Imperial and native interests'.[3]

Rhodes meanwhile had other ideas. 'I claim that people here have beaten the Matabele. . . . The Company never asked the British Government for any assistance. . . . We have paid expenses and I claim we should have settlement of terms of peace. . . .' The Colonial Office however were firm: '. . . the settlement will necessarily involve considerations . . . bearing directly upon the peace and security of South and Central Africa generally and it is therefore needless to point out that Her Majesty's Government are bound to keep the supreme control of that settlement in their own hands.'[4] So long as the difference was stated in terms of principle, it seemed insuperable, but when it came to drafting details the differences were not so great; Rhodes put the emphasis on swift decision, on trusting the man on the spot to be fair; the Colonial Office were concerned to protect the native against exploitation, to preserve the impartiality of justice, to maintain some shadow of Imperial control.

But these were differences of emphasis; compromise was possible. Agreement was reached on 23 May 1894; the main points, for the purpose of this book, concern equality before the law and the land commission. 'Natives', reads clause 23, 'shall not be subjected to any exceptional legislation save as regards liquor, arms, and ammunition', title to land, and a hut-tax. The Land Commission will consist of the Judge and two others and shall 'assign to the natives . . . land sufficient and suitable . . .' which is to include 'fair and equitable portion of springs and permanent water . . .'. This land will constitute Reserves exclusively for native use; elsewhere, natives may hold land in the same way as anyone else except that there are special provisions to ensure that a native shall not part with his land unless he fully understand what he is doing.[5]

The Land Commission duly met and heard evidence; they recommended the formation of two reserves to be known as the Gwai and the Shangani reserves. The total area was about 6,500 square miles; Loch, forwarding the Commission's recommendations, thought that in Lobengula's day the Matabele and their slaves had occupied about 10,000 or 11,000 square miles, and that as the slaves might be assumed to have deserted, and as some Matabele would stay on white farms or go to the mines, this was not an unreasonable area to keep for their exclusive occupation. The Commission themselves wrote that 'the evidence of the chief indunas inhabiting and well acquainted with the land lying in the Guay Reserve conclusively establishes the facts that it is well-watered and fertile and is regarded as being the best grazing veld in Matabeleland and has been and is still being occupied by natives'. But they did not go to see it themselves and they were, one must suppose, not yet sufficiently experienced in the mis-understandings that may arise from evidence given through an interpreter, or in the strange evidence people will give before a court they feel to be alien.* Marshall Hole, who served the Company twenty-three years and was an administrator of experience, writes that the Gwai Reserve 'proved quite unsuit-able, the bulk of it being waterless, and the natives never settled in it except on a small portion along the banks of the river itself . . .'. And there were considerable objections, though not so wholesale, to the Shangani area, some of which was infested with tsetse.

The Land Commission was also asked to pronounce on the problem of cattle. Jameson had said the King's cattle would be taken, private cattle not interfered with. The question was what this meant and how much the Company should take. It was a matter which for any Bantu people lay very near that core of self-respect without which a man or a people break down into degra-dation or desperate violence. Cattle were everywhere a prize to be captured or carried away in war as a sign of victory, but they were far more than that. Among the Mashona tribes—and many

---

* For some years I was fated to listen to evidence given in court by Indian villagers which was sometimes completely at variance with what they had told me in the direct and informal atmosphere of the village. Their evidence was usually more skilfully contrived, but could not be more irrelevant to the facts, than the sworn testimony I remember hearing from British regular soldiers in the same district, to whom my court, with its Indian pleaders and clerks, was even more unfamiliar than to an Indian villager.

of the so-called Matabele by origin belonged to the Mashona group—cattle are often dedicated or vowed to an ancestor and regarded as held in trust for him.[6] Among both Matabele and the Mashona—indeed, among any Bantu people who trace descent through the father—cattle are intimately connected with marriage and, when a woman leaves one group for another, cattle change hands and are usually distributed among her relations; cattle sustain the marriage as well as nourishing the holders with their milk; they may be handed back, or at least claimed, if there is a divorce. And among the Zulus, the Matabele, and the Angoni, there was a kind of feudal network of cattle-holding;[7] a rich man gave out his cattle to his feudal followers who used the milk but might not kill a beast without his sanction. The King's cattle were spread far and wide among his people, held in varying degrees of vassalage; some of them might be allotted to a queen, whose children had some claim to inherit the right to use them.[8]

In all this, there is to be seen just emerging, but not at all clearly defined, a distinction of a kind between ownership and the right to use; the King or the spirit of an ancestor may be compared to a proprietor, or the ward under a trust, the user or vassal to a kind of tenant or trustee. But there was no precise law; Sir Henry Maine pointed out long ago that, in an early stage of tribal development, there is no idea that land can be owned; it can only be used. Here in Bantu societies may be seen a stage later than that of the German tribes of whom Sir Henry was thinking; the idea of property is coming into being in relation to cattle—and for that matter people. But it is not yet exclusive individual ownership.

In a European feudal state it was not easy to say who owned the land, the King, his tenant-in-chief who held perhaps an earldom of half a county, the holder of the manor who paid a knight's fee, or the yeoman who paid a fee by bearing arms in war. In England after the Conquest there might be half a dozen men, from the King downwards, who might say of a particular strip of land, 'This is my field', and in each case with a different shade of meaning. So, among the Matabele, the King, an ancestral spirit, a married woman, an Induna, and the man who milked her, might have said of one beast: 'This is my cow.' To decide who owned the cattle of the Matabele was not a tangle to unravel in a few weeks. One thing only is clear: the cattle were one of the strands that bound the Matabele people together, the way they were held contributing to the royal dominion, to the cult of the ancestors, and to the stability of marriage.

The Company's view was certainly a simplification of all this. Almost all the cattle in Matabeleland had belonged to the King, many of them having been captured from other tribes in war. It was death, they believed, for any subject to hold many cattle, because he thus became a rival to the King. If therefore the Company now took, say, two-thirds of the cattle, leaving one-third to be owned by the people as absolute proprietors, they would be conferring a benefit. And it would be a further benefit if they left some of their own cattle for the time being in the hands of the natives, who would have the use of the milk until the cattle were required, just as they had in the old days.

The Commission on the whole accepted the Company's view. And so on the whole did Loch, who estimated the cattle Lobengula had possessed at from 200,000 upward. The Colonial Office however suspected that things were not so simple: 'experience in former wars, especially in Zululand', wrote the Marquess of Ripon, 'shows that distinction between King's cattle and people's cattle is fallacious, in all cattle being in some sense King's. . . .'[9] And he was insistent that 'ample cattle for their requirements should be secured to the Matabele'. The course events actually took was unfortunate; some 90,000 cattle were branded with the Company's mark and registered as belonging to the Company but for the present left in native hands to milk; from time to time some of these would be called in for slaughter, sale, or re-distribution. Later, when it was believed that some 70,000 were still in native hands, the Company decided to take two-fifths of these finally and confirm the absolute possession of the rest to the people of the country.

Selous, who knew Matabeleland better than most Europeans, thought that the Company's official view was based on a mistake;

'almost every man of any standing in Matabeleland', he wrote, 'had been a cattle-owner, some of the chief Indunas possessing large herds of private cattle.' Perhaps he too was simplifying and defining the distinction between 'royal' and 'private' cattle more exactly than the Matabele had done; if the feudal analogy I have suggested has any value, it would be quite possible to find good Matabele evidence for the Company's view as well as for Selous's interpretation. However, he goes on to say that this mistake was not in itself fatal; that if the Company had at once recognized, say, one-third of the cattle as belonging absolutely to the people, they would not have felt intolerably defrauded. What was fatal was leaving some with the people for the time being and sending for them afterwards. The Native Commissioner would receive orders to drive in so many head of cattle to Bulawayo; he would make up the number as best he could and, writes Selous, 'certain natives suffered wrong, especially owners of perhaps only three or four cows, who in some cases lost their all, both in cattle and faith in the honesty and justice of the Chartered Company, which they deemed had broken the promise* given them, as indeed was the case, though the mistake was made inadvertently and through not considering the investigation of the whole question of sufficient importance to take any great trouble about'. And he quotes Helm as being of much the same opinion as himself.

Thus uncertainty and distrust were brought at an early stage into the way the Matabele regarded their conquerors, while Matabele society was disrupted by tearing out one of the most binding strands in the whole fabric.

Land and cattle had been the questions on which the Commission had been asked to report; they reached their conclusions and action was taken. It is easy now to look back and see mistakes; at the time, they were moving in a fog of ignorance, above all in a fog of easy and often unconsciously contemptuous assumptions as to what Africans needed to keep them happy. How wide of the mark those assumptions were, events were soon to

* The promise given by Jameson that only the King's cattle should be taken.

show. But for the moment all were united in complacency. In came the satisfactory news that the Matabele were settling down happily. 'All report the civility and submission of the natives', wrote Dr. Jameson to Sir Henry Loch in January 1894, going on to argue that 'without some disarmament the natives would never understand that they were conquered' and that it was necessary to take not only the King's cattle, but 'a portion of the Indunas', 'as a salutary measure to ensure submission and future tranquillity'.[10]

Major Sawyer, Military Secretary to the High Commissioner, travelling in Matabeleland writes back: 'I was much struck at the kind and considerate treatment of the natives on the part of those in authority and cannot help thinking that it was greatly due to this that they had become so quickly reconciled to the new rule.' And in February 1894 Loch telegraphed to the Colonial Office: 'Very good sign of people accepting change of rule is number of cases amongst Natives themselves brought in to be settled by Jameson and Magistrate of Buluwayo.'

Section 2: The Reasons for the Matabele Rising

On the surface, then, all was well. It was the general belief among Europeans that though a few had regrets—the Indunas who had once ruled the country, the amatjaha who had so often washed their spears in innocent blood—most of the people were glad to be released from tyranny. When it became necessary to account for the rebellion, many theories were put forward; it is easy to list the factors that one observer or another believed were decisive, much harder to assign a relative importance between them. A man's own temperament and experience will guide him, one putting first the grievances about land, cattle and labour, another the deep injuries to self-esteem—to more than self-esteem, to all that complex system of emotional involvement with the world that is built up from custom and past history, a system from which man is no more severed without a shock than the unborn child from the *placenta*.

There was the land, there were the cattle, there was the labour

question. This had been touched on in Jameson's interviews with
those who surrendered; 'the people were now to settle down and
till their ground and the Indunas were advised to induce them to
work for the white people on their lands and in the mines, for
which they should all be paid. . . .' This is the language in which
Jameson reports what he said to the High Commissioner;
it is guarded language, because Jameson knew very well the sharp
reaction he might expect if any newspaper in England caught a
sniff of anything that smacked of slavery or forced labour.
But Selous was not a diplomat; aware that things looked different
under grey English skies, he yet described them as he saw them
in the harsh African sunlight. 'They found themselves treated',
he wrote of the Matabele, 'as a conquered people . . . who had
only been permitted to return to the country from which they
had been driven . . . under certain conditions, of which one was
that the indunas should, through the medium of the native
commissioners, supply miners and farmers with native labour—
all the able-bodied young men in the country being required to
work for a certain number of months per annum at a fixed rate of
pay.' He goes on to say that he thinks 'the boys' were usually
well treated, cruelty being a rare exception; but 'owing to the
excessive indolence of the people, there can be no doubt that the
labour regulations were most irksome to them'.[11] There were
not exactly official 'regulations' enforcing paid labour; but Selous,
who was managing a large estate in Matabeleland when the
rebellion broke out, thought there were, and that they were
not all of them committed to writing made no difference to the
Matabele. They found it just as hard to see why they should leave
their homes and live under discipline in alien surroundings, toiling
all day for what seemed altogether someone else's good.

There was a reluctance among the Victorians to discuss another
element in the situation, but there is good evidence of its
importance in Dr. Jameson's account of his interview with the
Matabele who came in to surrender. They were assured that their
wives and daughters would be protected—and the point was
specially emphasized because of their dread of interference. Three

years later, Rhodes himself admitted by implication that this protection had not always been given.[12] And 'it was very widely said in South Africa that the Native rebellion had, as one of its causes, the treatment of the Native young women by white men and also by Native police'.[13]

Selous probably spoke for the great majority of his fellows when he wrote: 'the Matabele broke out in rebellion because they disliked their position as a conquered people and imagined they were strong enough to throw off the yoke of their conquerors. . . .' And he goes on: 'We Europeans make the mistake of thinking that, when we free a tribe of savages from what we consider a most oppressive and tyrannical form of government . . . we ought to earn their gratitude; . . . we invariably fail to do so. . . .' What 'the savage' says, Selous writes elsewhere, is: 'hang your Pax Britannica; give me the good old times of superstition and bloodshed; then, even if I did not know the . . . hour when I might be smelt out as a witch and forthwith knocked on the head, . . . I could have basked in the sun till my time came; and then, too, when the *impi* went forth, what glorious times I had and how I revelled in blood and loot!' It was not a rising against intolerable injustice or cruelty, he believed, but a very understandable attempt to go back to the old days by a people who did not perceive the true strength of the conquerors.

This was the general view; the Matabele had not been dealt with severely enough in 1893; half their regiments had never been in action and they had not been so thoroughly disarmed as they should have been—due, of course, to interference from Whitehall. The opportunity had been provided—so the farmer or miner would say—when Dr. Jameson withdrew every armed man he could and stationed his police on the Transvaal border; when the Jameson Raid took place and ended ignominiously in defeat by the Transvaalers, then the leaders of the Matabele knew that the time had come. And they brought the rank and file, discontented already, to the point of rising, by working the oracle, inspiring the priests of the Mlimo, the Makalanga spirit of fertility, to prophesy success.

There is much in this, the view of common sense; it is true that no very elaborate explanation is needed for the desire of a conquered people to be free, that the police had been taken away and Jameson defeated and disgraced. Yet one may wonder—and the answer can only be conjecture, an opinion that can never be tested—whether the rebellion would have occurred if personal humiliation and uncertainty about the future had not been added to these more tangible grievances regarding land, labour, cattle, and women. On one aspect of the humiliation, there would be general agreement; Selous, Colin Harding, Marshall Hole, all speak of the bullying and insolence of the black police, recruited immediately after the war and, naturally, not recruited from those who had been fighting, therefore from the despised Maholi. Selous speaks of a visit to him at his home in Essexvale by Umlugulu, an important Induna under Lobengula, who 'complained bitterly of the high-handed manner in which the "Ama-Policey-Minyama" behaved. I have no complaints,' he said, 'against the white policemen; but the black police, *wa duba, wa duba sebele*, they give me trouble, they really give me trouble.' The same cry was raised again and again. It was the recruiting of labour more than anything else that gave them their chance;[14] they would arrive in a village and until they had taken their pick of the young men and led them away, would—so the complaints ran—take their toll of the daughters and the wealth of the homestead. To this active oppression the inexperience and sometimes indifference of their officers must have contributed. It is not easy for an administrator to encourage the confidence and pride of his police without licensing brutality; he must walk a tight-rope between a suspiciousness, a meddlesomeness that will paralyse initiative and a trustfulness that will encourage oppression. In those first three years, the Company's earliest administrators in Matabeleland would have been more than human if they had always kept their footing.

After the rebellion, when Rhodes went alone into the Matopo Hills to parley with those who still held out, they told him their grievances and one of the Indunas told how he had come in with his advisers and young men, as befits a chief, to pay his respects to the Chief Magistrate in Bulawayo. He had waited all day; towards evening he had sent a polite message. He did not wish to hurry the great man but his people had not eaten all day; when a white man came to visit him, he killed a beast and gave him a meal. The answer came: there were stray dogs in the town; he might kill those and eat. That answer must have come from a policeman or a messenger, not from the Magistrate, but the insult would not have been given to a man whom the Magistrate delighted to honour. It grew from a soil of indifference.

Uncertainty contributed perhaps almost as much as humiliation. The Matabele had been defeated; if Rhodes himself had come to live among them—and a Rhodes unhampered by either voters or shareholders, either in England or in the Cape—perhaps they would have been quiescent, if not content, with a rule that was direct and personal. It was for this they asked him in those long talks in the Matopo Hills: 'We want one, not half a dozen heads,' Somabulana said to him. And Faku added: 'Give us a head and we are satisfied.' But the leaders they had been given were divided among themselves; and within themselves; they were partly controlled from a distance by a will alien to their own, so that they must draw back as soon as they had stepped forward; they alternated between the firmly paternal and the mildly trusting. And there were differences between one Native Commissioner and the next; even a rule that is both strange and harsh can be borne if it is certain in its operation; a man becomes reconciled to what he knows is inevitable. But when the new order is unpredictable, every manifestation of it strikes home with the impact of the first.

On top of all this came natural disasters. Locusts and drought had come when the Pioneers entered Mashonaland and never gone; next came rinderpest and the cattle died; those the rinderpest did not kill the Company's veterinary officers shot to prevent its spread. Cattle were the life-blood of the country, providing transport as well as milk and meat; it is not surprising that the Mlimo, the Makalanga godling of the Matopo hills, began to prophesy that nothing would go right so long as the white men were in the country.

The Mlimo was one of many spirits who were in the country before the Matabele came. There are many kinds of spirits at work among the Mashona,[15] having in common the attribute of seeking from time to time a human host or medium, the *svikiro*, in whom the spirit chooses to dwell. This spirit may take up residence permanently in one human host; this is what happens in the case of a *mhondoro* or tribal spirit, when the man too is called the *mhondoro*, as well as being the *svikiro* of the spirit; when the human host dies, the *mhondoro* spirit will after a time take a new residence, who will be recognized by various signs, rather as a new Dalai Lama is recognized. There are other spirits* which possess a man or a woman for a few hours at a time and who again are recognizable by the strange behaviour of the host.

The Mlimo was a god of harvests and fertility who spoke from a cave; Selous says his chief priest was also called the Mlimo and that there were other human Mlimos in other parts of Rhodesia; others say that in this case the distinction between the invisible spirit and the host was always clear. Charles Bullock describes him as a god whose jurisdiction extended over the whole of Mashonaland and Matabeleland, called Mwari as well as Mlimo, not interested in individuals or even tribes, being too far above them, 'a god of the Cosmos, ordering it in its course'. This does not agree with what others say and may be a confusion, but all are agreed that Mlimo was a god of this country before the Matabele came; perhaps just because he did not concern himself (until 1895) with war or politics, but only with the course of nature, Lobengula consulted the Mlimo and he had a following among the Matabele. Now, when natural disaster piled itself upon political, he turned to a new role and began to prophesy that nothing would go well until the Europeans were driven out of the country.

'Faced with a grain famine, robbed of their newly-acquired cattle, importuned in season and out of season to provide

* These are called Shave spirits and are very like the voodoo gods of Haiti; see *Divine Horsemen of Haiti*, Maya Deren: Thames and Hudson, 1953.

unaccustomed labour, bullied by their former tribesmen and
slaves who had enlisted in the Police Force . . . what wonder
if the Matabele Indunas began to seek a short cut out of their
troubles. . . .'

The words are not those of some theorist from Whitehall but
of Marshall Hole, who for a quarter of a century was the
Company's servant in Rhodesia. The short cut was a conspiracy
of a kind not very carefully co-ordinated or thought out, a mere
determination to rise and kill every European in the country;
it arose from and linked itself to the prophecies of the oracle,
the one feeding the other. It was in October of 1895 that Jameson
moved his police to the Transvaal border; it was on 2 January
1896 that they surrendered to the Transvaalers at Doornkop. The
first steps in the short cut took place in March, a little more than
two months later.

Section 3: The Nature of the Matabele Rising

There is little need to dwell on what happened. A determination to kill—that certainly was wide-spread. But there was little
more planning to it than that. As a military operation, it was
hardly planned at all; the Matabele never grasped the dependence
of the Europeans on lines of communication; their policy, if they
had thought one out, should have been to cut the roads, particularly to the south, to avoid battle, to cut off stragglers, to starve
out the Europeans. In fact they ambushed an occasional wagon
but made no determined attempt to keep the roads shut; there
was even talk of their having deliberately left the road to the
south open so that the Europeans might have the opportunity of
escaping. They let themselves be brought to battle, were defeated,
and from then on were simply hunted. All they could do was to
hold out in the tangle of granite kopjes that is the Matopo Hills.

There is no point in any detailed description of the rising.
What is important is the feelings it aroused, which it was bound
by its nature to arouse. The Europeans were scattered about the
country at farms or mines; during the last week of March news
came to Bulawayo, first, of a native policeman murdered, then

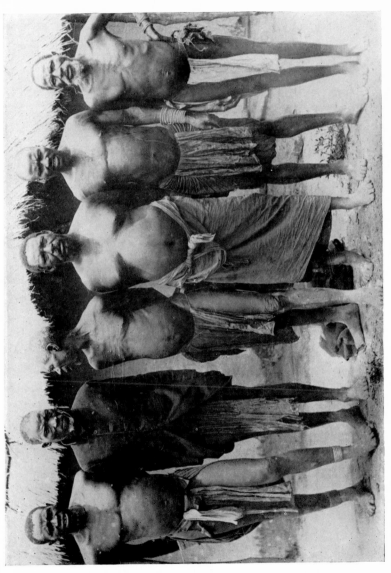

Councillors of Makoni as they were captured at the end of the Rebellion, 1896. 'The faces of the chiefs . . . wear a discarded look'

False Alarm in Bulawayo (from a sketch by Melton Prior in the *Illustrated London News*, 6 June 1896)

Relief of Inseza (from the *Illustrated London News*, 3 May 1896)

of a miner, Thomas Maddocks, and then, thick and fast, murder after murder. It was murder, not fighting; there would be an approach on some pretext, a beginning of conversation, perhaps a request for help or advice, then the sudden attack, a blow on the head with an axe or a knobkerry. Sometimes the man of the family would be led away from the homestead on some pretext and killed when far from guns or horses, the wife and children being then murdered at leisure; sometimes this precaution was not considered necessary and all were killed together.

In the last week of March 1896, 122 white men, five women, and three children were murdered, nearly all in isolated homesteads or camps; during April, five men, three women, and five children. Three months later, when the rising spread to Mashonaland, about the same numbers were killed there; the total was about one in ten, considered against the whole European population of Rhodesia. In Matabeleland, considered separately, the proportion of Europeans killed would have been higher; everyone who was left alive must have lost a friend. That was enough to make men bitter; to the bitterness of personal loss, to the closeness of peril, must be added anger at the treachery of the attack and an outraged astonishment that it should come from a people who had been trusted—or was it only that they had been disregarded as likely to be a danger?

That women and children had been killed roused men to an even fiercer pitch of fury. There were not in fact many women, as the figures show, but not many were needed; any people worth the name will fight for their women, but the Victorian English and the Afrikaners were both particularly vulnerable here. One had made an ideal of chivalry and set a picture of the women of his own race on a pedestal apart from the masculine brutality he acknowledged in himself; the other had behind him long generations of a conscious endeavour to preserve racial purity. Both were shy of talking seriously about sex, uneasy in the presence of any women not relations; both were inclined to project on to the masses by whom they were surrounded all the instincts they had themselves succeeded in repressing or directing to other channels.

Selous can speak for most of the settlers; he was a fair-minded man, a good observer, and in both his face and his writings one can discern something of that compassion and gentleness that sometimes go with courage in men who have spent much of their lives in danger, hardship, and fighting. 'For breaking out into rebellion against the white man's rule', he wrote, 'I should have borne them no great animosity. . . . I should of course have lent the services of my rifle to help quell the rebellion; but had it not been accompanied by the cruel murders of white women and children, I should not have been animated by the same vengeful feelings as now possessed me, as well as every other white man in Matabeleland. . . .'[16] That was what all would have said; it would have been inexplicable at that time to any of the Matabele. He writes elsewhere of coming to the place where 'a Dutchman named Fourie', with his wife and six children, had been building a house for a Mr. Ross, who with his wife and an adopted daughter, were living in temporary dwellings near by. All these eleven people had been killed. 'The remains had been much pulled about by dogs or jackals but the long fair hair of the young Dutch girls was still intact and it is needless to say that these blood-stained tresses awoke the most bitter wrath in the hearts of all who looked upon them, Englishmen and Dutchmen alike vowing a pitiless vengeance against the whole Matabele race.' Just such words had been used by those who came to Cawnpore in 1857 after the massacre of the women and children who had surrendered on promise of safe-conduct. Selous trusted that his readers would not judge him and his followers too harshly: 'be charitable', he wrote, 'if you have not yourself lived through similar experiences . . . you probably know not your own nature nor are you capable of analysing passions which can only be understood by those Europeans who have lived through a native rising, in which women and children of their race have been barbarously murdered by savages, by beings whom, in their hearts, they despise; as rightly or wrongly they consider that they belong to a lower type of the human family than themselves.' 'I have seen', he adds, 'many gruesome sights and have with my own hands collected together the broken skulls of murdered women and children . . . to give them Christian burial. . . . I have hidden nothing but have told the naked truth and related not only how white men, women, and children were murdered and their senseless bodies afterwards mutilated by black men but also how black men were shot down pitilessly by the whites, no mercy being shown or quarter given by the outraged colonists.'

To come back to the sequence of events, in March there were the murders of isolated parties; by early April, the survivors were in fortified camps at Bulawayo and Gwelo. They were strong enough to defend themselves and to send out a patrol of twenty or thirty troopers to a farm or a mine from which no news had come in; they were not strong enough for offensive operations. There was a great shortage of horses and, because of the rinderpest, of oxen for transport; there was no military striking force and not enough rifles for the few hundred men capable of bearing arms. But patrols could go out in a circle, visiting two or three outlying farms, to rescue survivors or get news, meeting sometimes a little resistance on the way out, sometimes having to fight hard on their way back.

But help was coming: a column of volunteers—150 strong— was organized in Salisbury and started for Bulawayo on 6 April. On 2 April, Major Plumer, an imperial officer, was appointed to raise in Mafeking and to command the Matabeleland Relief Force, and by the end of the month this irregular force of volunteers, 800 strong, was on the way; the Imperial Government had offered regular troops amounting to nearly 1,000—though at first there was some reluctance on the Company's part to accept a present that would not only eat but have to be paid. Taking all together, by 2 June, when Sir Frederick Carrington assumed command, the total of Europeans under arms in Rhodesia, so far all irregulars, was in the neighbourhood of 2,000. The numbers are tiny and it is always difficult to remember the vast scale of the country, the minute scale of the forces involved.

The tide turned on 28 April, hardly more than a month after

the first murders, with the first engagement that was more than a skirmish. On that day 115 volunteers with 70 'Colonial natives' (that is, Africans from Cape Colony, not locals), drove back the Matabele from positions near Bulawayo; till now the Matabele had drawn closer and closer, surrounding the city with growing menace, growing self-confidence. Now for the first time they were brought to battle and pushed back. Now it was possible to send out a strong patrol to meet the column from Salisbury; this was done and the united forces made a circle southwards and were back in Bulawayo by 1 June. They had had no serious fighting; Selous describes a brush near Thaba Induna: 'The sight of the long line of cavalry thundering down upon them seems to have turned the hearts of the savages to water . . . for having fired a few more shots they turned and ran . . . [they] never made any attempt to rally but ran as hard as they could, accepting death when overtaken without offering the slightest resistance. . . . No quarter was either given or asked for. . . .'

Section 4: The Mashona Rising

It must have seemed that the rebellion would soon be at an end, but a few days later came news of the risings in Mashonaland. These began on 15 June and followed the same pattern as in Matabeleland; on the lonely farm or mine, pretext was sought for conversation and then a sudden and wholly unexpected attack and skulls cracked by clubs or axes; 'within a day or two they had hacked to death practically every isolated family and individual within a radius of eighty miles of Salisbury'.

The reaction was even more bitter than in Matabeleland. The Mashona had been so utterly despised that the shock was even more stunning here and besides it was felt that they were un-grateful; they had been saved from the Matabele and given the blessings of peace. No one said of the Mashona, as Selous had of the Matabele, that he bore them no ill-will for trying to recover their own country; it had not, the settlers felt, been their own country for several generations. And if the Matabele had legiti-mate grievances about cattle, the Mashona had no right to any complaint; they had, on the contrary, been secured in possession of such beasts as they had.

Why then did they rise? Hole, who spent some months examining witnesses and enquiring formally into just this question, thought that those who had worked the oracle of the Mlimo in Matabeleland sent messages in June to their professional brethren, the priests and tribal oracles throughout Mashonaland, to say that the Matabele were destroying the Europeans, that they had eaten up the column sent from Salisbury to help Bulawayo, that they would soon be masters in their own house and before long would be on their way to Mashonaland to resume their old sway, and that they would know how to treat those who had not helped them; the Mlimo had ordered everyone to join in driving out the Europeans and nothing would go right until they did. This was Selous's view too, and was supported 'by a mass of corroborative evidence from every part of the country'.[17]

No doubt this was what they said when it was all over. But the reasons people give afterwards for sudden acts of violence are not always what influenced them most at the time; indeed, they may never have been conscious of what made them behave as they did, still less able to put it into words. Hole's version was convenient for everyone; the Mashona put the blame on someone else, those who collected the evidence were reassured that the rising was not due to any Mashona grievance nor to any shortcoming of the settlers. But it must surely be assumed that before the messengers came there was deep among the Mashona some emotional readiness to take the course of action the Mlimo suggested.

There was much controversy in the British press about the causes of the rising. The spokesman for the anti-colonial view was Henry Labouchere, the editor of *Truth*; both in his paper and in the House of Commons he expressed, often in the most intemperate language, a horror of atrocities and a belief that atrocities were constantly being committed by settlers in Rhodesia upon the natives. He was reckless in his allegations and often disproved as to facts, but a doubt is bound to be raised in any enquiring mind as to whether a substratum of truth did not remain. In general terms, his charge was that the Mashona rose against oppression and cruelty and that there was even greater cruelty and injustice in the methods used to suppress the rising. It is the kind of general charge that cannot finally be proved or disproved; there will always be some cruel and evil acts and it is a question of what proportion they bear to the normal course of events; one can only form a tentative opinion. But there is a sense in which the best evidence is of a negative kind; it is the admissions of the defence and the omissions of the prosecution that are most convincing.

Disregarding Labouchere (who fulminated from England but did not visit Rhodesia), hear the prosecution evidence of John White, Methodist Missionary, whose life was written by C. F. Andrews, the friend of Gandhi.[18] White had come to Africa to work for Africans, he was committed as wholly to their protection as any man could be, and had in fact met with hostility and dislike for that reason. He was emotionally committed, but a man whose word is to be believed; there are deductions to be drawn from what he does not say. He wrote a long letter to the *Methodist Times*: 'Now that the back of the Mashona Rebellion is broken, we are better able to give a dispassionate opinion. . . . I have refrained hitherto from committing myself publicly, because I wanted to hear what would be assigned as the cause of the rebellion. . . . The local press has now spoken. . . . The contention that cruelty to the Mashona has anything to do with the rising has been described as "a cruel, cowardly and wicked lie". We are thus compelled, even though reluctantly, to state the truth as we believe it.'

Here then is a prosecution witness, but a temperate and reliable one. He cites a case of an official who by threats compelled a chief to give him his own daughter for immoral purposes. White reported the matter; the official was found guilty and dismissed; he left the country. But, White continues, 'so trivial seemed the offence that within nine months he was back again and held an official position in the force raised to punish the rebels'. This is the first item in White's charge; to some, as clearly to White, the original offence will seem so shocking that it blinds to all else. But if the incident is to be used in a historical discussion as to the cause of a rising, the first conclusion to be drawn is, surely, that the administration was ready to hear and punish a complaint against one of its servants. And it is not surprising that in the heat and danger of the rebellion anyone, whatever his record, should have been accepted in the forces raised. But a man will risk the displeasure of a Government more readily than the disapproval of his fellows and it does sound as though public opinion was tolerant of native concubines if procured discreetly.

Next comes a story of police callousness. A Sub-Inspector of Police sent to investigate the murder of a white policeman put under arrest seven chiefs—presumably meaning to hold them for interrogation—and told them they would be shot if they ran away; three did try to run away and were shot. This was reported to the Government but 'nothing was done', or in other words no public action was taken. One can have no doubt that there ought to have been a formal enquiry, but it seems unlikely that it could have had any result but a serious warning to the officer that he ought to have explained his intentions to the chiefs and to the escort much more fully and carefully. Taken at its face value, the story indicates a profound suspicion and mistrust on the part of the chiefs, a rigid obedience to orders by the native police, callousness rather than cruelty on the part of the Sub-Inspector.

These two are the only specific charges White brings; he goes on to three general charges, that the hut tax was levied inequitably and collected unjustly, that the native police were tyrannous and molested women, and that, though many of the European farmers and miners had been humane and just, others have 'given the Mashona a very poor opinion of civilized justice and propriety. Many of them have bought, according to African custom, Kaffir girls whom they regard as their property. The girls consider themselves . . . the slaves of these men.'

That is the sum of White's indictment, a more temperate one than Labouchere's and more reliable; it presents a picture far indeed from one of wholesale atrocities, but containing nothing to diminish a predisposition to revolt. It may be read with the opinion of Colin Harding, himself a policeman, which has been quoted before; his words are these: 'I would here remark that the Mashona still declare that they preferred the raids of the Matabele who, when they came, killed them and purloined their women and other cattle [the literal interpretation] and then went away, to the occupation of their white masters who did neither and simply remained as irksome governors.'

A rider should be added to White's charges. He speaks of police tyranny but does not mention the chief occasion for it, which here as in Matabeleland was recruiting labour. It was bound to be so; the Mashona had been content with his round hut, his pumpkins and millet, and an occasional meal of meat; his homestead was self-sufficient; all he wanted was to be left alone. But to the bustling European it seemed self-evident that man must work and he wanted men to dig and milk and plough for him. He expected the Native Commissioner to find him labour; he was infuriated because the labour, when found, ran away, misused its tools or idled. And there was really, he would say, only one way of punishing a native. A traveller describes difficulties with labour on the road; but if you find a native unwilling to work you have only to say to him: 'Twenty-five!' and 'he gives you a sickly grin' and gets on with his work. They all understand what 'Twenty-five!' means.

There was then a predisposition to be rid of their new masters, to which was added incitement by the Mlimo and the Matabele. The events of Mashonaland were those of Matabeleland over again; the murders of isolated parties; concentration in laagers or forts; patrols to bring in survivors; and then the turning tide and offensive operations to punish the rebels and to end opposition. The offer of imperial troops was accepted as soon as the trouble spread to Mashonaland and it was a matter of two months only before it was possible—in August—to break the laager at Salisbury. Meanwhile, in July, in the biggest single operation of the whole rising, Plumer with 750 men had attacked successfully the main Matabele stronghold at Thabas Imamba; from that moment onwards few Matabele can really have hoped to win. But among the tumbled boulders and caves of the Matopo hills they could hold out a long time and a long guerrilla war would not only be directly very expensive to the Company but would delay the country's development.

Rhodes, in his finest hour, went with only three companions into the Matopo hills, met the Matabele chiefs, sat surrounded by their armed men and far from any help, and patiently, hour after hour, day after day, discussed the terms on which they would make a settlement. They told him their grievances and why they had rebelled. Was it not better to die than to live as dogs? And at last after many weeks he brought them to accept his terms. Those who had been guilty of murder were to be handed over for trial and all arms were to be surrendered; on the European side the forces, except for police, would then be disbanded; certain chiefs would receive salaries and would be recognized as holding authority; the people would be given food.

It was Rhodes' finest hour; he forgot for a time the arrogance and the impatience the years had laid on him and recovered one of the best of his qualities, that readiness to recognize the other side of a question and come to terms with it; he showed again the patience, the dramatic insistence on one point vividly illustrated, that had so often overcome opposition before. He had to persist against the fears and obstinacy of the Matabele; against the fears and obstinacy of the soldiers, their talk of security and unjustifiable risks; against the fears, the obstinacy, the anger, and desire for vengeance, of those behind him who wanted no terms but unconditional surrender. He persisted and the terms were made. As for the Matabele, there is a photograph of the chiefs who accepted the terms in Hole's book; Sarah Gertrude Millin has written of that photograph in her life of Rhodes, a life told in a series of scenes rather than in a consecutive story, a book with flashes of perception and insight which the more scholarly accounts miss. 'The haggard chiefs', she writes, 'wear old military hats and caps; bits of second-hand uniform, second-hand—fifth-hand—coats, overcoats, waistcoats. Some have trousers . . . some an apron of leopard-skin, monkey-skin or leather thongs. . . . The faces of the chiefs, like their clothes, wear a discarded look. . . . The past is gone and there is no future. . . .'[19] It was true; these were no longer the plumed warriors, shining with health, insolent in savage splendour, but shabby old men with no hope, with no more resemblance to what they had once been than a faded old tiger-skin to the splendid beast it once adorned. The same look is on the faces of Makoni's councillors, of whom a photograph is included in this book.

But with the Matabele peace could be made. With the Mashona it was more difficult, because they were not a single people; each chief must be dealt with separately. And with the Mashona, there were no battles after the first month; it was a matter of going to each chief's country, calling on him to surrender and, if he refused, chasing him till he was cornered. The country is much of it very broken, strewn with piles of gigantic boulders, full of caves; the Mashona had long practice in hiding from the Matabele; the process of cornering was not easy and usually ended in a cave from which it was impossible to eject the fugitive except by dynamite. Most of the regular soldiers were withdrawn in December, but the business of reducing chiefs one by one lingered on till September of 1897, nearly a year after the settlement with the Matabele.

'Fast in their caves, which had previously been filled with water', wrote Colin Harding of one of these incidents, 'rebels, women, and children remained until shaken nigh to death by the explosion of dynamite. But at last the women and children voluntarily though reluctantly came out of the caves, dusty and weary of eye, each woman carrying her child, . . . but in no other way suffering from the shocks. . . . Seeing their women kindly treated, 200 of the men also surrendered and they also were treated humanely. There was none of the shooting of prisoners of which we have read and I say now and advisedly that never have I seen a Mashona prisoner shot without a fair trial.'[20]

This is an allusion to Labouchere's allegations. Harding was a liberal minded man, whose life had been saved by two Mashona in what was nearly an ugly mining accident and who wrote at the end of his career that he hoped 'many of his native friends would say that by justice and patience he had to some extent repaid the gallant deed of their three untaught and unclothed Rhodesian brothers'; all the same, it is clear that when he says a fair trial he means a trial in which the accused had a formal opportunity to speak and in which the sentence was inflicted for some legally punishable offence; he would possibly not have argued that the courts were impartial. Indeed, they could not be, as Selous has made clear. Sentences were usually by a board of officers, most of whom remembered friends or relations who had been murdered; the proceedings were scrutinized later at Cape Town and in London. Two regular officers, Major Watts and Lt.-Col. Baden Powell, were placed under arrest by the High Commissioner and were subject to an enquiry for carrying out a sentence of death without waiting for confirmation. In both cases, they argued that the prisoner was a well-known leader caught in the act of rebellion and that to have delayed carrying out the sentence would have been misunderstood by the natives generally and might have caused danger to the men under their command; in the case of Watts, there was the additional point of some doubt as to whether the prisoner, Makoni, had not surrendered on conditions. But in neither of these cases was the officer found culpable and it is hard to argue that under the circumstances they should have been; in neither case was there the least likelihood of delay altering the sentence and if these things have to be, they are surely less horrible done quickly. One other case however may be cited because it was discussed at length in correspondence with London and because it does give an indication of the kind of evidence on which a court-martial of irregular officers might convict.

A party of soldiers was engaged in building a fort. Till the fort was built, they believed they were in danger; an escort of forty-three armed men had been attacked not three miles away in the last two days and there had been fires in the hills all round every night, presumed to belong to hostile forces. A patrol saw a native woman with a child near the camp and caught her, though she tried to run away. Questioned, she said there were no natives in the neighbourhood, an obvious lie; she also said she was going to a chief whose kraal was in the opposite direction from that she was taking when caught. She was judged, on the ground of these two statements, to be a spy. 'There was no means of keeping her in safe keeping, escort could not be spared to take her to Gwelo; if released, enemy would have at once full information of weakness of force. After full consideration Board of Officers condemned her to death.' In a later and fuller report, the story continues: 'In order to have the sentence carried out in the most humane manner, I told the adjutant to have her taken out of camp by colonial boys without being told the decision and to send the orderly non-commissioned officer to see this order carried out without her knowing anything about it. . . . As regards the child, it was only after the return to camp of the escort that I learnt, on asking where it was, that it had been shot.' The High Commissioner reported to the Colonial Office that 'the proceedings indicate a disregard for human life . . . and were irregular to an extent which amounted to a parody of justice' but 'in view of the wide discretion granted by military rule and custom to officers commanding isolated detachments' he was not prepared to say a crime had been committed and considered that 'grave animadversion' and 'a severe reprimand' would meet the case.[21]

This was an exception; it would not otherwise have come to the notice of the Colonial Office. But it has been dwelt on because it is an example of mixed standards and ideas. That a peasant woman captured by armed men of another race and of an utterly alien culture should blurt out that none of her own people were near, that she should give an unsatisfactory account of her movements, was not really surprising; to regard this as evidence that she was a spy was to judge her as a rational creature capable of considering the effect of her answers. But in deciding on the sentence of death, the court was influenced largely by the inconvenience of disposing of her in any other way; in deciding not to inform her of the sentence, they had clearly ceased to think of her as the prisoner of a court martial capable of defence, still less as a human soul able to communicate with a Deity; they thought of her rather as a cow which should not see the butcher before he struck. And as for the child—no doubt everyone on the board of officers had been shocked by what he heard of what the Matabele did to the children of the Mashona. But this child, like its mother, had not really been thought of as a human being.

The reduction one by one of Mashona fastnesses dragged on; it was not till October of 1897 that Kagubi, the chief purveyor of the Mlimo's oracles in Mashonaland, surrendered uncondition-ally and the Rebellion could be said to be over. What followed will be discussed more fully later; it is enough for the moment to quote Marshall Hole's words to indicate the essence of the task as it was locally conceived. 'The Company', he wrote, 'was in a position to devote its attention to the settlement of the natives in areas where they could be kept under supervision and deprived of the opportunity for hatching further plots. Large tracts of country were selected for reservations. . . . The constitution of the native department was overhauled and commissioners of proved capacity sent to all the principal centres of population. . . .'

A new era was certainly beginning. The occupation of what is now Southern Rhodesia was complete and the newcomers firmly in the saddle. They had shown that they meant to stay. They were incomparably more advanced than the native inhabitants in the making of tools, weapons and houses, in knowledge of agricul-ture; they had behind them 5,000 years during which men had recorded in some form of writing their discoveries and their perceptions of truth, 5,000 years of exchange between peoples, —peaceful exchanges of thought and goods, violent exchange by invasion and conquest which had caused human misery but had permitted ideas to breed. Here was another conquest, the last in that immense series which included the invasions of Greece by Dorians and Achaeans and the exile of the Jews in Babylon, the conquests of Alexander, the rise and fall of Rome, the conquests of Mexico and Peru, the Norman Conquest of England; this last conquest in Central Africa would no doubt be as fruitful of unhappiness as those others—but in none before had there been so great a gap in technical achievement, in understanding of each other's moral and legal standards, religion, and family organization; in the long run the question it posed was whether that gap could be bridged and any fruitful advance in thought be achieved as a result.

Part Three

MASTERS AND CONQUERED

I. Parental Persuasion

Section 1: Two Kinds of Rule

The rebellions were over and the first days of adventure. Now the two races, black and white, had to settle down and find a way of living together, a way that would take into account certain facts which began to seem immovably established. South of the Zambezi, there were no more independent African States; Southern Rhodesia was white man's country. The settler had come to make his home and stay; he ruled the country by right of conquest and he had made it very clear that he was not going to be turned out.

The two races, masters and conquered, were poles apart, not only in tool-making techniques and in social organization, but in what they expected life to bring them, in their attitudes to leisure, work, and money. And to neither did it seem likely for the moment that this separating gulf could be bridged in any future that need concern them. To bring progress to the natives— that had always been an object; but few indeed had seriously considered what exactly progress meant nor what would happen when it had been acquired. In the meantime—that is, for several generations at least—the natives would be servants, farm workers, labourers in the mines.

This was south of the Zambezi. To the north-west, across the great river by the Falls, northward towards the as yet unravished copper fields, but leaving Barotseland as a backwater, would flow a thin trickle of men who took for granted this same simple relationship of masters and conquered and assumed that it would last indefinitely. But to the north-east, in Nyasaland, and spreading their rule and influence northward and westward, were men of European stock who came from the sea instead of by land from the south, men who brought with them a distinguishable set of ideas and intentions. Their acts might not always accord with their intentions; their intentions themselves were imperial—they pictured themselves as ruling; it was however an imperialism with a difference. The tale of their first coming and their early wars with the slavers round the Lake will be told elsewhere; for the moment, all that is necessary is to assert briefly the point, later to be made good by evidence, that most of these men came in the first place not as settlers, but as missionaries or administrators, not to make their fortune and their home in Nyasaland but to perform a task which would benefit the natives of the country and to go back when it was done to the land of their birth. No doubt they too hoped to earn a living, no doubt they too looked forward to adventure and enjoyed the exercise of power. But, when all allowance has been made, their outlook was different; even the traders came in response to a missionary appeal.

The difference was put in words by Sir Harry Johnston, who may be thought of as first among the founders of Nyasaland. 'Africa South of the Zambezi and North of the Atlas . . .', he wrote, 'must be settled by the white and whitish races and that Africa which is well within the tropics must be ruled by whites, developed by Indians, and worked by blacks.' This was on 10 October 1893. And a few years later he expanded the point, in a letter to Lord Salisbury dated 31 May 1897: 'British Africa between the Zambezi and the Mediterranean [must] in the interest of the native races . . . be ruled from Downing Street. . . . In districts where . . . climatic conditions encourage true colonization, there undoubtedly the weakest must go to the wall and the black man must pay for the unprogressive turn his ancestors took some thousands of years ago; there . . . the direct rule of Downing Street may cease. But where, as throughout all tropical and Muhammedan Africa, we merely impose our rule to secure a fair field and no favour for all races, and inferentially for our own trade, there the local government must depend directly on London.'

Here then the stark impact of Darwinism is tempered by some awareness of the concept of the dual mandate and the recognition that the rulers are trustees, an idea in which, surely, is implicit the likelihood that the wards will some day come of age. That consummation, at least in India, had been clearly envisaged seventy years ago by the greatest of the East India Company's servants. And Sir Harry referred to India as a model. But south of the Zambezi 'the weakest must go to the wall'.

That is not how it would have been put in Southern Rhodesia. In Livingstone's time, it was true, there had been speculation about Southern Africa on strictly Darwinian lines. In North America and Australia, the original inhabitants of the country had virtually disappeared, not without some active assistance from the invaders: was it perhaps a law of nature that a people backward in the technical arts should melt away beneath the assaults of gin, tuberculosis, and syphilis, not to mention bullets and arsenic? Would the Bantu too vanish from the face of the earth? But this possibility could no longer be entertained by the end of the century; the Bantu were clearly not going to disappear. Like the settlers, they were there to stay; they displayed, indeed, a persistence and a virility that began to be disturbing.

In the relationship between the two groups there was, as has been said, a basic and overriding simplicity; they were masters and conquered. But within that simplicity was a complexity, a whole web of contradictions between conscious ideals and fears often unformulated, between general rules of human conduct and a new set of rules, the special rules that were in process of being evolved to meet this new situation. There were memories of the rebellions and of South Africa's long tale of Kaffir Wars; there were fears for white women in lonely places; there was white supremacy to be upheld, and there was a beginning, here and there, of rivalry in certain employments, of which the skills could be learnt more easily than their white practitioners liked to think. And there was the occasional man in whom the natural streak of cruelty was too strong to resist the temptations of power. But leaving such men out of account, a white Rhodesian as a rule liked to picture himself as a parent, strict but kindly, looking after his employees and bringing them up in the way they should go, bringing them the benefits of knowledge and of useful and industrious habits; he would tell amusing stories of their backwardness and their ludicrous mistakes, as parents do of their children.

Children, yes; but not perhaps children who had been greatly desired or in whom much pride was felt. It was a mixed kind of parenthood. The father would show in a dozen ways how lightly he esteemed his offspring, how slight he thought the danger of rivalry or rebellion, how benevolent were his fatherly intentions, and yet every day, and in one breath with his scornful superiority, would betray by some precaution an anxiety he was careful not to acknowledge. As to other natives, not his employees, the typical settler saw little of them and was content to ignore them; he had freed them from the tyranny of the Matabele if they were Mashona, of Lobengula if they were Matabele; he would see that no more disastrous wars befell them, they would be prevented from falling back into the worst of their old superstitions; apart from that, the less seen of them the better.

There were, too, settlers less typical, men to whom Africa had come to mean more than the land of their origin. They shared much with their fellow settlers, but with the difference that when they thought of Africa, they called to mind something more than the physical heritage both loved—something more than the majesty of a sky starred with fires unfamiliar to northern eyes, the tawny grass of the veld, the sweep of a hundred acres of red soil glistening stiff and new from the plough, blesbok, duiker, and sable antelope; the sharp aromatic scent of blue gums at dawn, the scent of dust as darkness falls in the dry cold weather of June. They thought also of the rhythm of drums at night and the sound of African voices in laughter, petition or bewilderment; they remembered nurse, herdsman, chief or messenger as friend; they delighted in curious knowledge of African custom and belief. But of such men there were not many.

Section 2: Parental Persuasion

As if there were not enough complexities in the way the Rhodesians themselves looked on the captives of their bow and spear, there was also what Rhodes called the Imperial factor. This again was falsified if it was seen, as so often it was from Rhodesia, in the shape of a single bogy labelled Downing Street or White-hall. It was not one factor but a bundle of factors, to which a varying importance would be attached by a succession of Colonial Secretaries. The way each exercised authority depended not only on his personal views but on his estimate of public opinion; the question was whether there were enough people in England who minded what was happening in Rhodesia sufficiently to exert themselves in a particular cause. Before considering the form pressure from England took most often, let us pause for a moment to consider the machinery by which control could be exercised.

We are thinking of the period from the end of the Rebellions to the end of the First Great War. During this time, the country was governed by an Administrator appointed by the British South Africa Company, who took the place a Governor would hold in a colony directly administered by the Crown. The Administrator was helped by an Executive Council of four, also appointed by the Company, their appointments, like his own, being subject to approval by the Secretary of State. Under the Southern Rhodesia Order in Council of 1898, there was also a Legislative Council of the Administrator and nine other voting members, five nominated by the Company and four elected by inhabitants of Rhodesia who could muster certain qualifications. The composition of the Council was changed in 1903, in 1911, and again in 1913; the details do not matter, but by the first change the Council was enlarged and the elected members became equal in numbers to the nominated; by the second, the number of nominated members was reduced, so that the elected could outvote them; by the third, this tendency was carried further and there were twelve elected members to six nominated.

The Administrator would normally act on the advice of his

Executive Council, but could overrule them; it was lawful for the Administrator to make ordinances for the good government of Southern Rhodesia with the consent of the Legislative Council, but these were to be submitted to the High Commissioner at Cape Town for assent or disallowance. The High Commissioner acted in this respect as agent of the Secretary of State, to whom he was responsible, and he was guided by the advice of a Resident Commissioner, a permanent watch-dog at Salisbury, who was a member of both the Executive and Legislative Councils but could not vote in them. The Resident Commissioner's report went to the High Commissioner at the Cape with every ordinance sent for approval; in the debates in the Legislative Council, the non-official members sometimes begged him to state his views in the Council and give them an opportunity to answer, rather than send a hostile report of whose content they might be ignorant.

It was a main object of this appointment of a Resident Commissioner that he should make sure the High Commissioner was aware of any prospect of legislation that was discriminatory against Africans. 'No conditions, disabilities or restrictions', ran Section 80 of the Order in Council of 1898, 'shall, without the previous consent of a Secretary of State, be imposed upon natives by Ordinance which do not equally apply to persons of European descent, save in respect of the supply of arms, ammunition, and liquor.' Thus the Resident Commissioner as watch-dog was one means by which the Imperial factor, which was really a bundle of factors, made itself felt.

In this bundle there was one stick that no minister of the Crown, indeed, no member of Parliament, could ignore, and one that was of immense importance in Africa. This was the conviction of a majority of the voters in Britain that it was their country's divine mission to fight the slave trade and anything that smacked of slavery or forced labour.

This is not the place to show how this feeling had first grown during Wilberforce's long struggle to end a profitable trade, nor how it had continued till slavery was abolished wherever the

Crown had jurisdiction. Nor shall I speculate here on the inconsistencies of a nation so morbidly—as it seemed to the Rhodesian—concerned that the law should not be used to extort work from an African and yet so tolerant of grinding poverty as a means of getting work from an Englishman. It does not matter, for our purpose, how far this concern proceeded from a desire to appease an English conscience uneasily aware of the sharp differences of class. What does matter is its reality for English Members of Parliament and its effect in Rhodesia. Here it was an irritant; it created in the European an aggressive readiness to get on the defensive when he looked towards England, an apparent confusion of purpose towards the African. That confusion made the Rhodesian English seem hypocritical to Afrikaner and African alike; it increased African suspicion and distrust.

Concern at any suspicion of forced labour was then a constant factor in English politics; concern with the need for labour was as constant in Rhodesia. Open any Rhodesian newspaper—and *The Rhodesia Herald, The Bulawayo Chronicle,* and *The Livingstone Mail* appeared very early—skim through the columns for a month, looking at letters, resolutions of public meetings and leaders, and the odds are that you will find as many on the shortage of labour as on all other subjects put together. The reason is very simple; settlers wanted labour and Africans did not want to work. They had been used to an economy in which money played no part; they saw no reason for change.

The position as it appeared to almost every European in Africa was put with disinterested detachment by Sir Alfred Milner as High Commissioner:

I have never shared the objections, which are so strongly felt at home, to a well-regulated system of state compulsion, whereby natives of a certain age, fit for labour and not otherwise engaged in it, should be compelled to do a certain number of months' work every year, under proper securities of good treatment and for adequate remuneration. . . . The black man is naturally inclined, much more than the white, to do nothing at all. As the economic compulsion which is found in European countries does not exist here, he will, if left to

219

himself, generally live in absolute idleness. . . . I cannot conceive that, under any except the most distorted code of morals, it can be thought right for us to encourage him in this attitude, or even not to dissuade him from it by all reasonable means. . . .[1]

There is no need here to analyse the implication that work, in the sense of a rather unpleasant activity, has positive moral value, but it is worth pausing to wonder how many people in the history of the world have shared this assumption, so blandly taken for granted in the nineteenth century by Anglo-Saxons of the wealthier sort. But there is no question that Sir Alfred spoke for his time. The same thoughts were expressed in more settler-like language in a hundred letters and speeches; here, for instance, is Colonel Napier speaking in the Fourth Session of the Third Southern Rhodesian Advisory Council in 1907:

. . . they were not going to get the natives out of their kraals whilst they had wives to work for them and they must use coercion. They were like children and must be treated as such, and a little parental persuasion in the shape of a caning might have a good effect. They did it to their own children and it should be done to the subject races.

Nor was the view confined to employers. Here is Father Daignault, S.J., writing to the Deputy Administrator at Bulawayo in 1897: '. . . natives of this country . . . in reality are but grown-up children . . . given to many vices, conspicuous among them being . . . idleness . . . men in authority who have the true interests of the natives at heart ought to treat the natives not only as children but ought also to do all they can to make them acquire habits of work. As this cannot be obtained by mere moral persuasion, authority must necessarily be used. . . .'[2]

Thus, in varying degrees, almost every European believed in parental persuasion, but a good deal of circumspection was needed in the way it was applied. Mr. Taylor, Chief Native Commissioner, not long after the Rebellion, told the Matabele that they 'must understand that this was now a white man's country. . . . He did not expect all to turn out to work. . . . They would please the Government very much if they only went to work for three months and had nine months to rest in . . .'.

This was gentle persuasion indeed, but it was not, unfortunately, enough. On another occasion he was more explicit: 'There could be no forced labour; the Government would not allow it. At the same time he wished them to go out willingly. . . . He would have the Indunas realize that they were Government officials. They were paid so much and in return the Government looked to them to assist in supplying labour. They must see that the boys turned out to work. . . .' Here one of the Indunas asked to speak. 'Masongo . . . did not quite understand the Chief Native Commissioner's reference to force not being used.' In reply, 'the Chief Native Commissioner said that . . . the messengers would not go to the kraals and say to this or that boy: "Here, you must come to work." The Indunas must tell the boys to go. If they refused, then those who did so must be reported at once to the Native Commissioner, who knew what to do.'[3]

These instructions, so confusing to Masongo, did not escape the all seeing eye in Whitehall and Mr. Chamberlain wrote: 'The system of obtaining a supply of labour through the Indunas, as set forth by the Chief Native Commissioner, appears to be liable to a form of compulsory labour and I desire therefore to request you to call the attention of the Resident Commissioner to the language used by Mr. Taylor and to instruct him to furnish a full report. . . .'

The British South Africa Company, in their reply, were of the opinion that 'A system more judicious, more humane in intention, and better guarded against the evils of forced labour on the one hand and uncontrolled competition on the other could scarcely be conceived. . . .' They thought that 'it would be exceedingly discouraging to humane and experienced officials like Mr. Taylor . . . if the spirit and purpose of their dealings with the natives were inadvertently misconstrued by the Imperial authorities at home . . .'.

And here one may be confident that the Company were right. Criticism from England must have been most discouraging, because every Native Commissioner was conscious of being sniped at from the other flank, and for reasons directly opposite. For the settler, he did not exercise enough force. Meetings of local farmers' associations and the like passed resolutions at regular intervals calling on the Native Commissioners to be more active in getting them labour. Here is one taken at random from *The Rhodesia Herald* of 12 December 1907: the meeting resolved: 'That the Government be approached to instruct Native Commissioners to assist the industries of the country by persuading the natives to work. . . .' And as this was a meeting typical of many, it is worth noting other resolutions passed at the same time; they asked for summary trials by local courts with power to order corporal punishment for insubordination and 'acts of defiance'; the poll tax on natives to be £2, with a remission of £1 for six months' work; and there should be more inspectors of native labour, in particular medical and sanitary inspectors.

To return to the quandary of the Native Commissioners, Mr. Wilson Fox, in his detailed report to the British South African Company on Problems of Development and Policy, notes the general feeling of 'the people' (that is, the Europeans) that it is 'the object of the Native Department to segregate the natives, to keep them apart from the general life and work of the country and to cry "hands off" when any attempt is made to get into touch with them for industrial purposes'. And on 7 January 1910, *The Rhodesia Herald* spoke of the charge against the Native Department that it 'has allowed the indigenous natives to become, in the security afforded them, an idle and useless race'. This appearance and this charge were inevitable if the Native Commissioners were to behave as the Colonial Office thought proper; if they did as the Rhodesian employers wished, they were at once exposed to reprimand from the Colonial Office.

Orders from the Administration as a rule inclined to the Colonial Office view. 'Under no consideration whatever is any compulsion to be exercised' and 'when messengers are dispatched to seek labourers, they are not to be given any powers whatever. They are simply to deliver your message through the Chief or headman and return with such as are willing to work.'[4] On the

other hand, Native Commissioners were to lose no opportunity
of pointing out the advantages of work. It was not only Masongo
who was confused by these instructions, which could hardly be
explained to a messenger or Chief without being made contradictory. 'See that people come to work but don't force them.'
What could anyone make of that? In fact, of course, it could
only mean that the Native Commissioner must close his eyes to
what happened when he sent his messengers to a kraal—unless
of course something happened which he could not overlook.

In 1900, Captain Lawley, Administrator of Matabeleland, had
to report that native messengers, 'sent to collect boys', had used
force. 'The offenders are now in prison awaiting trial', and this
occurrence will be 'ostensible proof . . . that the Government
will not sanction anything in the way of force being used in the
collection of labour'.[5] One may suspect that in most African eyes
it was an instance of inconsistency and hypocrisy.

'When a Chief repeatedly fails to send men for work', wrote
the Deputy Administrator of North-Eastern Rhodesia in 1899,
'the Collector calls the Chief to the Boma and tells him that if he
wishes to be friends with the white man, he must make his people
work. The reply is usually . . . that he has no control over his
people and they won't work.'[6] In Southern Rhodesia, too, the
Native Commissioner tried as far as he could to work through the
Chief; if the Chief could not produce labourers, the messengers
were sent to remind him. And they applied parental persuasion as
best they could, steering carefully between the dangers of being
found out and of producing no results. 'While undoubtedly
strong moral pressure is brought to bear on the natives to induce
them to work in the mines and elsewhere, no case of actual
compulsion has come to my knowledge . . .', wrote the Resident
Commissioner in 1901.[7] No doubt much care had been taken
that no case should.

There were changes of system, one new device laying emphasis
on the main object of procuring labour, another on the preven-
tion of abuse. The Native Commissioners had at first been the
official agents, but in Whitehall this was felt to be dangerous.

The native, persecuted by the Native Commissioner's messengers, would have no one to turn to; suppose, too, that he was ill-treated by his employer—would he appeal to the very man who had sent him to work under such brutal direction? He would not be able to distinguish between the Commissioner's two capacities, as labour agent and as fountain of justice. And indeed, they might be confusing to the Commissioner himself.

In 1899, Labour Bureaux were therefore formed; five special agents were appointed by the Chamber of Mines whose sole duty was to recruit labour; if their messengers proved oppressive, it was hoped that their victims would come for redress to the Native Commissioners. But the result of this was 'a marked falling off in the labour supply', and once more 'the Native Commissioners were ordered to do all in their power to comply with the requirements of the mine managers'. 'Neither the Matabele nor the other Rhodesian tribes take kindly to labour in the mines', wrote the Resident Commissioner in April 1900, '. . . and they work in the mines either from direct pressure brought to bear on them by the Administration, a pressure only short of force, or the necessity of earning enough to pay their taxes. . . . The Native Commissioners induce the natives to work and afterwards collect taxes from wages unwillingly earned. . . . This detracts from their influence. . . . There is undoubtedly discontent among the natives . . . due primarily to the constant pressure exercised by the Administration and to the often arbitrary and illegal methods adopted by native messengers. . . .'[8] This was written when the Bureaux were functioning. On 1 July 1900, a Labour Board was formed for Southern Rhodesia instead of Bureaux, but after nine months' working it was found that in Mashonaland less than 4,000 natives had been engaged through the Labour Board while nearly 10,000 had sought and found work direct and more than 18,000 had sought work through the Native Commissioners.[9] And the working of the Board was no more satisfactory in Matabeleland. In 1901 the Board first separated into two Boards and then dissolved, when once more 'the Native Commissioners naturally become recruiting agents'. 'Practically the recruiting of native labour continues to be directed by the Chief Native Commissioner. . . .'

This was not the end of the matter; an independent Rhodesian Native Labour Board was set up as a commercial venture in August 1903; it ran at a steady loss and was reconstituted from time to time with fresh capital and fresh hopes. One of its many difficulties was a distinct difference between the views of farmers and mine owners; the latter paid higher wages and wanted labour in bulk; the farmers wanted individual farm hands who would stay with them and take an interest in the stock on the farm. Another difficulty was competition from the south. There was for a time an agreement with the Witwatersrand Native Labour Association that the latter alone should recruit in Portuguese East Africa, and should provide Southern Rhodesia with 12½ per cent. of the Portuguese recruits, leaving to Southern Rhodesia as a recruiting field their own country and the Zambezi territories, that is Northern Rhodesia and Nyasaland. But by 1903, this had produced 'not a single native for Rhodesia', while the Rhodesian organization had sent as many to the Rand as it found for Rhodesia.

All this time the problem was growing in size. In 1905, it was calculated that Southern Rhodesia needed no more than 25,000 labourers all told; by 1910, the mines alone wanted 39,000 and the farmers another 23,000. By a calculation based on three assumptions, any of which might be inaccurate by as much as 50 per cent., it was reckoned that 210,000 Rhodesian Africans ('indigenous natives' as opposed to 'foreign natives') should be available for labour altogether, of whom 70,000 at any one time ought to be working on a basis of four months on and eight months off. Yet not even half these numbers could be found.

It would be tedious, and not really to the purpose, to go through all the changes that were made in the system of recruiting; there are however certain constant factors. The Colonial Office was always jealous that the Native Commissioners should be impartial; the Rhodesian employer was always anxious that the Native Commissioner should use all his influence to make natives work; the Native Commissioner walked his lonely tight-rope between them as the one effective element in the situation.

The various attempts to set up separate labour agencies were thus ineffective; 'the nearest thing to labour this country gets from the Labour Bureaux', Major Irvine is reported by *The Livingstone Mail* as saying, 'is the smell of natives in the coaches.' It was also confusing; in the *indabas* the Matabele complained, as so often before, that they liked one head to deal with, one man who would give them clear orders; to have two departments, with two sets of messengers, was the last thing they wanted. In this at least they got their way; the Native Commissioner remained the head of the district; the labour agent and his messengers were seldom looked on as more than a subordinate department of the Government. Complaints therefore were rare. But it did sometimes happen, particularly in the north, that the messengers of private persons went into the kraals to fetch labour and complaints were then sometimes made.

Thus in February 1900, a Chief reported that 'three of Messrs. Posselt's boys had come to him and asked for labour; he sent round to collect his people but the messengers became impatient . . . went round themselves to the kraals, and took women and cattle and kept them until husbands and owners came and offered to go and work in order to release their wives and cattle. They also flogged the headmen of several kraals . . .'.[10] And in 1901 the messengers of a trader Pretorius 'went about calling themselves police' and one of them threatened to report a Chief for 'declining to give him one of his daughters'.[11] One may deduce from this how Government messengers might have behaved if they had not been forbidden to use force; still more speculatively, one may wonder how often they did behave like this and were not reported.

Section 3: Acquiring Wants

Everyone concerned with the question of labour was agreed that the real need was to persuade the African to want more and therefore to earn more. Taxation would force him out of the kraal to earn money to pay his tax; once out, he would acquire the taste for blankets and bicycles and he would come back again to the white man's world to earn more. In the matter of the tax too, there were changes, proposals, counter-proposals, yet certain constant factors. The Rhodesian employers with few exceptions considered that the Africans of the territory were too lightly taxed and that it was far too easy for them to earn enough to pay their taxes. Further, they did not pay their fair share of the cost of running the country, which would be much less if they had not happened to live in it.

As a result of resolutions passed by the Farmers' Associations and the Chamber of Mines, and of discussion with these bodies, the Administration of Southern Rhodesia proposed in 1900 that the hut tax should be changed to a poll tax. Every male native capable of labour was to pay an annual tax of £2 unless he could show that he had been in employment for four months of the previous year; once he had been in continuous employment for three years he would be exempt for ever.[12] It was believed, at this time, that the average earnings of natives throughout the territory were 30s. a month;[13] it would be possible then, for a man who came to work without his family and who lived on the rations provided on the mine or farm to earn the £2 of the tax in two months, or in four months to earn immunity from the tax and have £4 or £5 to take home with him. It is however possible to doubt whether even doubling the tax would have had the desired effect. In 1903, the Inspector of Native Compounds reported that a native woman cultivating an extra acre or so can earn her husband more money in a month than he can earn in three months on the mines. If the Inspector was right in this, no increase in tax would make the Rhodesian African come to the mines; only better wages would do that.

The proposal to double the tax no doubt seemed moderate to a Rhodesian employer; it would not, with the exemptions, have done much to meet his second point, that the native did not pay the full expense of keeping himself in order. This was constantly expressed; as one sample, the Salisbury Chamber of Mines resolved in 1903:[14] 'That owing to the necessity of a large mounted police force in the country for the protection of the whites from a recurrence of the '96 rebellion, the natives be directly taxed for the maintenance of this force.'

The administration did not put forward to the Imperial Government this part of the argument; they were no doubt aware that in England, far from making the poor pay for the police on the grounds that criminals usually came from the poorer classes, people of influence were coming to feel that those who were protected by the police should do most of the paying. On the proposals that were put forward, The Aborigines Protection Society expressed another and quite contrary view: 'the residue of the natives from whom, in the advance of "civilization and British rule", the most profitable parts of their land have been taken has, at the very least, a right to quiet occupation of the less valuable parts and to immunity from attempts to force upon it uncongenial pursuits. . . .'[15] The Secretary of State, steering between the two opinions, pointed out that 10s. instead of £2 had been considered the right sum in a similar proposal put forward from the Cape Province and the proposal was dropped.

In spite of constant proposals to raise it to £2, with remissions for those continuously employed, the tax in fact remained at £1, but it was sometimes paid by recalcitrants in the form of labour on the roads, for which the remission was at the rate of 6s. 8d. a month. In some cases, Chiefs obstinately refused to pay taxes. In a special report sent to the Administrator on 14 July 1902, Mr. Byron, Assistant Commissioner, reported: 'The Chief Gosi failed to realize the gravity of the situation. . . . I informed him that for several years in succession no hut-tax has been paid . . . as I could not obtain any satisfactory assurance, I was determined to show him that the Government intended to be firm. . . . I therefore informed him that I would destroy a portion of his crops and after he had moved his personal property, I requested Lt. Myburgh to destroy his kraal.' 'This patrol, as carried out', commented the Resident Commissioner, 'appears to have assumed more the character of a raid than the methods ordinarily employed by police for the enforcement of law.'

Section 4: Parental Protection

To sum up, the natives were taxed, mainly to make them work, and during this period, from 1897 to 1918, the Imperial Government kept the tax at a lower rate than Rhodesian employers would have wished. But while the employers were almost unanimous in wanting some form of compulsory labour, the more responsible among them, those who went to meetings and passed resolutions, were agreed that conditions of work should be levelled up and the standards of the worse employers brought nearer those of the best. There were several resolutions in favour of more government inspection; it was often emphasized in reports to the Colonial Office that mines where the men were well looked after had no difficulty in getting labour, and it was sometimes suggested that in the experienced native's list of what he looked for when seeking employment, a fair and understanding manager came first, diet second, housing third, and wages last.

The diet supplied by a well-known mine in the Hartley District was reported in 1908 to be:[16]

Meal—3 lb. a day, with a choice between maize and millet
Meat—1 lb. a week
Monkey-nuts—1 lb. a week
Beans—2 lb. a week
Coffee, with sugar, 1 pint per shift.

Another mine offered 1½ lb. of rice or 2½ of maize meal every day; meat, 1 lb. a week; vegetables 2 lb. a week; lard or monkey-nuts ½ lb. a week; salt ½ oz. a week. These are not so well-balanced or varied as Copper Belt rations today, but must be judged in the light of the knowledge of the time; they do not compare badly with rations taken on Scott's expedition to the Antarctic.* And

* See Apsley Cherry-Garrard, *The Worst Journey in the World*, and the experiment there conducted by three men, each of whom travelled on foot in the Antarctic midnight on a ration containing only biscuit, chocolate, and fat; to see what would happen, each took the three in a different proportion.

they are better than a few years earlier, when the usual ration was 3 lb. of meal a day and ½ lb. of meat a week, sugar and vegetables being given only at the best mines and regarded as a luxury.[17]

The complaint was less often of the diet than that men were badly housed; they greatly preferred their own mud and thatched huts to corrugated iron sheds which were too hot when it was hot and too cold when it was cold; the Inspector of Native Compounds thought they were right. Some employers began to provide wooden stretchers to keep men off the ground at night with good results on health. It was complained that there were no arrangements for warm clothes—showers were not yet thought of—when they came hot from the mines into a winter night. It was no doubt the men's own inexperience that contributed to the deaths from pneumonia; from the Premier Diamond Mine in Kimberley it was reported that in 1907 the deaths among 'British Central Africans' were 106·6 per thousand, while the figures for Basutoland were 21·5 per thousand and from Zululand, only 10·9.[18] Earlier it was said that 12 per cent. of men who worked at Selukwe died at the mine or on the way home; this area had a particularly bad reputation and the mines were thought to be bewitched.[19] But Selukwe paid high wages, perhaps for this reason; truck and shovel boys getting 35s. to 50s. a month, compared with 20s. to 40s. at the Surprise Mine, and so right up to the aristocracy of labour, drivers getting 100s. at Selukwe compared to 60s. or 80s. elsewhere.

In 1902, the Resident Commissioner, Sir Marshal Clarke, wrote to the Colonial Office that in general wages were 'fair, considering the quality and amount of work given in return', and that as a rule, 'the native is fairly treated, in many cases with consideration'. Native blacksmiths sometimes earned 7s. or 8s. a day, finding their own food, as early as 1902. Bad employers, of course, there were; some for instance always paid wages a few weeks in arrears so that the boys would not desert;[20] but on the whole these bad employers found it difficult to get labour and began to see their mistake. On the whole, progress, thought Sir

Marshal, had been encouraging and the natives were 'fast acquiring wants and voluntarily go to work in increasing numbers'.

But there was still a shortage of labour and many complaints
that the natives would not work for more than three months at
a stretch. And there can be no doubt that the African of those
days and of that part of Africa proved very often a maddening
employee; 'no less than eight boys failed to put in an appearance
this morning, being found later in a hopeless state of intoxication',
complains one employer,[21] and many others harp on the same
theme. As domestic servants, they were at first even less satisfactory; 'it took a long time', wrote Marshall Hole,[22] 'for a savage,
unused to tableware, brushes and crockery, and satisfied in his
own home with one or two bowls or platters . . . to grasp the
different uses of the multitude of strange utensils and appliances
with which even the most frugal Englishman surrounds himself,
to realize that a sock . . . should not be employed as a coffee-
strainer and that it is an offence against good taste to clean out the
inside of a saucepan with his master's hairbrush'.

The reaction to this kind of thing might be irritation or contemptuous good humour; for Marshall Hole, at any rate in
memory, the latter was more frequent. It was the custom to
re-name the servant or farm-hand as soon as he was employed,
abandoning his own name as too difficult and calling him instead
Lobster or Monkey; Hole recalls the piquancy of an official
document beginning: 'Victoria, by the grace of God, Queen,
Defender of the Faith, unto Jackass, Greeting. . . .' He describes
engaging a servant; 'a nondescript would arrive . . . and tell you
his name was Sixpence or Pumpkin and that he wanted £2 a
month. Scornfully you would offer him 15s. . . . To the accom-
paniment of much chaff a bargain would be struck at £1 and
there and then he would begin work and stick to it at any rate
until the first month was up. . . .'

When Marshall Hole came to Salisbury in 1891, he had travelled through country where the Mashona were 'a miserable lot,
still in the state of thraldom to which they had been brought by
fifty years of Matabele raids and persecution'. 'The only coin they

knew was a shilling' and this was the price quoted equally for a goat or an egg. 'But they much preferred bartering for . . . red beads with white eyes, coarse blue calico known as limbo, cheap cotton shirts and blankets, and brass cartridge cases. . . . They were . . . easily scared, taking flight like wild animals at any suspicious movement. . . .'

'For a long time', wrote Marshall Hole, 'they [the Mashona] appeared unable to rid themselves of the suspicion that underneath the sudden irruption of white men there lay some sinister design against themselves, and even if, greatly daring, a boy engaged himself to wash up the dishes and sweep the hut of the *Mlungu*, he was almost certain to decamp as soon as he had achieved the adventure of a month's service.' It was not surprising that there should be scorn for the attempts of these people to fit themselves into a new world and irritation at the inconveniences that resulted; Marshall Hole was an educated man and perhaps not typical. By his side as an employer may be set a correspondent of *The Rhodesia Herald*, probably more representative, who wrote: 'The farm is absolutely at a standstill. Fifty things want doing . . . and here adjoining us is a native reserve with hundreds of able-bodied men . . . and yet for goods, words, and money we cannot get one. I have been in the country fourteen years and admit having a bad name among boys of old. Still so far I am proud of myself, as I have not yet been hauled over the coals, and trust I never shall be, for leaving marks or not paying and feeding my labour. But it must be remembered that it was the pioneers who had to learn the language and teach the boys, who were then not much better than baboons. . . . Where there is no fear of the master there is no work done. I do not mean we should be cruel but I remember it was a little bit of a stick now and then that made a man of me. . . .'[23]

Legislation in this early period was proposed by the Chartered Company, in consultation with elected representatives of the settlers. There were of course many respects in which the interests of the settlers clashed with those of the Company directly, in the matter for instance of the royalties to be paid to the Company on minerals; there were others in which the Company was in the unfortunate position of being the buffer between the settlers' desire for 'a free hand' and the restraining influence of 'Whitehall'. But there was also a wide field in which the settlers' interests coincided with the Company's; both, in general, hoped for the development of the country, both needed a plentiful and reliable source of labour. They could agree, in general if not in every detail, on the proposals made, in November 1901, to the Colonial Office, to regulate contracts made between employers and employed.

These were designed to give the employer some hold on the man who had agreed to work for him and at the same time to protect the employed. Contracts were to be in writing and could not be for more than three years; a servant or apprentice engaged under a contract might be punished by a court of law for various offences. The punishment might be a fine of up to £4 and in default of payment imprisonment up to one month; the offences included being absent from work, intoxication during working hours, performing work carelessly or improperly, being 'abusive or insulting to his master's wife or children', or 'departing from his master's service with intent not to return'. There were double penalties for a second offence. On the other hand, a master might be fined £5, or in default sent to prison for a month, for withholding wages or failing to supply suitable food, and the contract might be cancelled if he brought a charge held to be groundless or unlawfully assaulted the servant.[24]

All this would sound a little odd to an English employer in the reign of Edward VII, who was used to relying for discipline on the harsh compulsion of economic necessity and on that alone. In England at the time a man out of work would come near to starving; he would therefore take good care not to lose his job by abusing his master's wife or coming to work drunk. But it would not have seemed odd to an Englishman in the reign of Henry VIII or Elizabeth I, when England was emerging from a Middle Age which had been relatively static, in which serfdom had been not far distant, and in which unless he went into the church a man's position in society had been usually governed by his birth. In Tudor times, as this static society broke up, sturdy beggars were whipped to make them work and apprentices disciplined in almost every aspect of their lives till they were twenty-three.

The analogy is far from exact; the transition from feudal manor to industrial society took 700 years in England and included much ebb and flow; Tudor England was one state in race and, leaving Wales and Cornwall aside, in language; it formed a bridge between the Middle Ages and the Industrial Revolution but did not bestride the immense crevasse between the early Iron Age and the Victorian, nor was it badgered and perplexed in its balancing feat by an outside authority planted safely and obtusely on the farther side. But it is broadly true that in the early sixteenth century, the state in England tried by legislation to regulate contracts which were taking the place of old fixed absolute relationships, just as, throughout Southern Africa, the state tried to regulate contracts which took the place of slavery, the only form of relationship between master and servant previously known.

Still less did the proposals seem odd in Rhodesia, where the employee did not mind losing his job; he still had his tribal self-sufficiency to fall back on, and, as for his tax, he could always find someone to employ him for another month; there was a shortage of labour. If the country was to be developed and labour to be provided, it was surely essential that some legal means of enforcing a contract should be found; almost any legal device was bound to be an improvement on illegal means. The Colonial Office objected to the proposals, on the grounds that the fine proposed for employees was too high in relation to the wages that could be earned; but after discussion and with modifications, the proposals became law. Even so, *The Livingstone Mail* could write in a leader on 18 July 1908:

A native knows that he can, with impunity, be as impudent, as lazy and as careless . . . as he likes; that the worst that can happen to him is dismissal . . . this is no deterrent. . . . There is no other provision for discipline, accordingly many a justly incensed man strikes a native and finds himself before the magistrate. . . . We recall the course adopted by an old friend. . . . Having been fined £5 for assault, he took the boy behind the Maxim Hotel and administered another sound sjamboking. He then pulled out of his pockets a couple of handfuls of sovereigns which he showed to the boy. 'Now go,' he said, 'to the magistrate and have me fined another £5. When the case is over I will give you another hiding worse than you have just had, and go on paying five pounds a time until you are satisfied.' . . . What is a man to do when his boy becomes unmanageable at a busy moment? Until a father is punishable for spanking his infant son, we shall find some difficulty in reconciling with justice . . . a native's protection by the Law from similar necessary discipline.

The problem continued. There was never enough labour; the 'boys', when they could be induced to work at all, continued to be careless and irregular in their hours. Attempts were made to provide labour from other sources; Chinese, Arabs, Indians, Somalis, Abyssinians were suggested, and even West Indians. But to the use of Chinese there were political objections from England; Arabs, Somalis, Abyssinians were not forthcoming in satisfactory numbers, while the Government of India wrote: 'The pioneers of colonial enterprise are naturally and necessarily masterful men, not very squeamish or tender-hearted; it is probable that for the control of Africans sterner measures than are needed for Indians are absolutely necessary and there is always a risk that the distinction between the two races may not be recognized when both are labouring side by side.' And they could not accept any system which would involve confinement to mine compounds and would not provide citizenship for Indians on a basis free from discrimination. The Rhodesian Government did not pursue the idea of bringing over Indians on these kind of terms.

From the first days of the Pioneers to the end of the Kaiser's War, it was always the case that employers were looking for more labourers than there were labourers looking for work; this was an inflationary situation—in terms of labour—which ought to have produced higher and higher wages. This happened only to a slight degree, because the African labourer came unwillingly to work and, as yet and as a rule, saw in better wages no inducement to improve his skill or to show much sense of responsibility for someone else's property; he went back to his kraal as soon as he had earned enough for his immediate purpose. His attitude to work proceeded, surely, in varying degrees and proportions from three causes: first, the simplest and most obvious, his wants were few; secondly, he felt himself completely alien from his employer and his employer's objects; thirdly, his culture and upbringing had not encouraged him to think of work as in itself natural or good and had on the other hand led him to seek satisfaction in dancing, music, and discussion; the Mashonaland farmer would have put it more concisely, that he was idle. The point sometimes made, that he could earn more money from his land, applied only to those who lived near a market.

Again, wages were pocket-money. Wife and children stayed in the kraal and lived on the pumpkins and millet they grew themselves, just as they always had done. The labourer—in Rhodesian terms, the boy—was housed, fed, and often clothed by his employer. He was a child and could not be trusted to feed himself; he did not understand the use of money and would starve if he had to buy his own food. This was the contention of the employers; it was undoubtedly true, in all but a very few quite exceptional cases, of the first Africans who came in to work—and is even true today of many if the established system is suddenly relaxed and they are suddenly left to look after themselves. But it meant that the truck system—the payment of wages in kind— became an accepted institution. In England, a half-century or more earlier, during the throes of the revolution that turned English farm labourers into townsmen, the truck system had been one of the first enemies alike of Lord Shaftesbury and other reformers from above, of the first Trade Unionists and other reformers from below. The English system did not even profess to be paternal; it was merely a means of adding to the employers' profit. The Rhodesian system of housing and feeding labour was without question necessary as an introduction to life in a competitive society; it prevented much misery in the beginning. But the basic objection in principle to both systems is the same, that an earner is denied the right of spending the money he has earned —and though that denial served a useful purpose with the first Africans, its continuance discouraged the growth of responsibility.

There was perhaps one other reason why wages did not rise more rapidly. Throughout southern Africa it had once been true—and here in Rhodesia very recently—that the African was more interested in goods than money; in Nyasaland in the nineties two yards of 'limbo'—coarse cotton cloth—would buy an old man and one yard a goat; beads and calico bought in England for a few pence would buy native produce sometimes worth pounds. Labour was at first paid for in trade goods; later, when wages were turned into money, they were reckoned in relation to the money value of trade goods. This was one reason why wages began very low in cash terms; soon throughout southern Africa there were many employers paying low wages and naturally reluctant to see them rise; a convention was established, backed by a vested interest. Native wages might be high or low within a limited range; there are references to wages of 5s. a month on farms in one district[25] and of skilled boys as drivers on £4.[26] But the convention limited them to that range and the inducement for the exceptional man to get out of the ruck was thus sharply checked.

II. At the Root of Strife

Section 1: The Decision to Keep Separate

Zan, Zar, Zamin—Women, gold, land—runs the Persian proverb; these are the three roots of strife among men, the motives of every crime, the springs of every story. In Rhodesia, and between African and European, gold had not been a direct cause of strife but in a negative way lay at the back of one recurring friction. The European wanted gold and needed labour to get it; the African did not want gold and therefore could not be induced to provide the labour. But women and land play their part in the Rhodesian story as directly as in any other.

When one people conquer another and settle in their country, they do not usually exterminate them altogether. The fate of the North American Indian and the Australian came near to extermination but a less extreme form of accommodation has been more usual. Conquerors and vanquished may slowly mingle, as Norman did with Saxon, till they are indistinguishable. They will perhaps be lords and serfs but they will buy and sell together, eat together, fight on the same side, pick up each other's speech; at last a pair will defy convention and marry. Telescoped into weeks instead of years, and reduced to the scale of one manor, the way this happened in England is told with poetic insight in *Puck of Pook's Hill*; marriage in that story came early and was the key to what followed; when the dispossessed Saxon lady accepted the Norman Sir Richard, hostility and suspicion disappeared. More often perhaps, marriage put the seal on a situation already existing. This kind of fusion was constantly taking place among African tribes; conquerors and conquered became in a few generations hard to distinguish. In Mexico and South America, it did not happen in the same way; in most states of

Latin America there are still people distinguishably Indian, some mixed and some to be classified as Spanish by descent. But not often do the two elements, conquerors and conquered, stay entirely separate for many generations; when this does happen it has usually been by a conscious effort, supported by strong sanctions in religion or public opinion.

This is not the place to go in any detail into the story of how and why this kind of conscious effort came to be made in what is now the Union of South Africa, the colonies from which so many of the first Rhodesians came. But something must be said because the Pioneers and their successors brought so much with them from the south. The gap between the newcomers to the Cape in the seventeenth century and the various people they found on the continent—Hottentot and Bushman rather than Bantu—was so wide that there was hardly room for any community of interests, any true partnership of man and woman. The invaders brought at first few women of their own and they were not all saints or monks; what sometimes took place between those first Europeans and the women of the hunting tribes they made servants, or of the slaves they imported, must usually have been a matter of physical gratification and no more, with no element at all of shared life or common endeavour; the experience was so far from satisfying to a people of conscience, whose only book was often the Bible, that they came to look on it with horror and repulsion and as soon as women of their own kind were in the country the community began a determined effort to keep themselves pure in race and in their way of life. To meet on any terms of equality, to eat together or talk as friends, came by the end of the eighteenth century to be forbidden between white and black;[1] thus by a paradox the prohibition of intercourse took a spiral form, each twist of the spiral more extreme than the last.

This spiral of prohibition must be dwelt on; to make it clear, it may be stated crudely, heavily over-simplified, using old-fashioned words. There was no love but only lust between that first official of the Netherlands East Indies Company and that first Hottentot servant-girl. Therefore he regarded what had taken place with remorse and repulsion and tried to forget it. He determined, when he married, that he and his wife and children should be kept pure from such contamination. There must be no more half-breed children and no more marriages between his people and these people; to make sure that there were no marriages, there must be no danger of the common interests, the shared misfortunes, that make love instead of lust. The gap between his mind and the woman's had bred his horror; because of his horror, the gap must be widened and fortified, so that he should not cross it again, so that he should never be reminded of what he disliked in himself. The horror had grown from lust instead of love; because of his horror, love, which might be lasting, had grown more horrible than lust. So marriage between black and white became more shocking than a casual encounter, provided, that is, that the casual encounter was between white man and black woman.

A book which may contain much that is spurious has described life at Kimberley after the first discovery of diamonds in words which put the point well: 'The subject, of course, was never openly discussed; but white wives and mothers were careful not to employ Kaffir women. With bland faces and knowing eyes, they ignored the presence of Kaffir women in the houses of bachelors, or even of men whose wives were away from Kimberley, but when a white man so far forgot himself as to marry a Kaffir girl, the public rose in its wrath and blotted him out of the social picture. . . .'[2]

Melina Rorke's autobiography is probably at least as fanciful in what relates to herself and the people she met as most autobiographies, but her descriptions of society often ring true. That her picture of Kimberley, though no doubt exaggerated, applied also to Rhodesia, there is good evidence. A letter in *The Livingstone Mail* of 1921 from the Secretary of the Rhodesia Women's League sums up the history of the previous twenty years. 'It is not generally known', she wrote, 'that in 1903 (before women of Rhodesia had the vote) the Immorality Suppression Ordinance was passed, making it a criminal offence for a white woman to cohabit with a native, while the reverse relationship of white men and native women continues to remain outside the cognisance of the law. All thoughtful people are agreed that such mixed intercourse is degrading to the white race and has a very evil influence on the black. Rhodesian women now demand equal legislation in this matter. If legislation has been considered necessary against women, then I need hardly state how very necessary it is that men, who are so much more frequently guilty of an act criminal in a woman, should suffer at least the same penalty.' And she quotes the resolution passed by the Rhodesia Women's League, that: 'The conditions of the country imperatively call for legislation making cohabitation between white men and native women a criminal offence, as by statute it is criminal for white women to cohabit with native men.'[3]

Such legislation had been suggested in 1916 and eventually rejected; the point is, however, that women were agitating not merely against the formal difference in law between themselves and men but were concerned about something that they believed did happen. 'Men are so much more frequently guilty' the secretary wrote, and no one seriously questioned either this statement or her judgement that what happens is 'degrading to the white race'.

Take again, chosen from much other evidence, a speech made by Colonel Sir Aubrey Woolls-Sampson, reported in *The Rhodesia Herald* of 10 May 1912:

He was convinced that the crimes of the native against white women were largely influenced by the infamous behaviour of a considerable class of white men in their relations with Kaffir women. . . . Two years ago, when in Northern Rhodesia, he found a great many of the white men living with Kaffir women. He had made enquiries of the natives and found that some women had been three parts paid for by Kaffirs and then the white man came along and offered some payment and the girl's father let them go. Whenever a Kaffir was treated in that way . . . he hated the white man. . . . He had been told that story in Seccoeni's country, in Swaziland, in Zululand, in Rhodesia and right away to the North. . . .

In Matabeleland, the number of white men living with native women was, he said, 'positively appalling'. And he went on to quote an old chief who had said:

There will never be peace between the black man and the white man . . . until you give our women the protection you demand for your own.

A year later, on the same theme, a correspondent to the *Herald* wrote: 'To my mind the guilt for this race crime lies at the door of the stronger race. It is a crime that goes unpunished and is perhaps the cause of most of the bitterness felt by the negro race. Can we wonder when we remember that for the slightest approach to intimacy with a white woman on the part of a coloured man, the penalty . . . might be death . . . while, for the contrary, a shrug of the shoulders, or at most a smile of contempt. . . .'[4] And, if the point still needs clinching, the Native Affairs Committee of 1910 received strong representations against miscegenation and the practice of concubinage, which they clearly considered no imaginary evil.

One may—doubtfully and with a recognition of exceptions —make distinctions. The practice was more common near a frontier than at the Cape, in the wilds than in a town, among poor whites than among the educated or well-to-do; perhaps the Afrikaner felt the greater horror and was more prone to the casual encounter, perhaps the immigrant Englishman was more likely to start a semi-permanent relationship. But if the English on the whole felt less strongly than the Afrikaners, the difference is a matter only of degree, and it is hard to detect much difference between English-speaking South African and Rhodesian.

It would be easy to exaggerate all this; it is not to be supposed that concubinage was so wide-spread as Melina Rorke suggests or that it was permanently in the minds of Rhodesian women. But it did sometimes happen, it was a possibility, something as a rule deliberately out of the conscious mind. 'His Honour the Administrator desires me to inform you that a report having reached his ears that Mr. M. E. Weale, the Native Commissioner, Chilimanzie District, has for some time past been cohabiting with native women, the Chief Native Commissioner of Mashonaland has been requested to call upon Mr. Weale to resign immediately. . . .'[5] That shows that the custom was not wide-spread but that it was common enough for it to be felt necessary to be severe with it.[6]

The very fact that the custom was not wide-spread—as it had been for instance in the early days in Bengal, as it was in the Spanish possessions—the very fact that it was disapproved of and not discussed, meant that the possibility had been relegated to a subconscious level of the mind from which emotions have a Jack-in-the-box way of bursting out suddenly in a moment of stress. In what follows, it is impossible, by the very nature of what is suggested, to provide absolute proof—in the sense in which one can prove a fact in a court of law, in the sense in which it has been possible to provide evidence about the fall of Lobengula. Those who most indignantly deny that the argument has any validity will be those least acquainted with the impulses and emotions that lead them to form their own opinions; they will probably be those to whom the argument applies most closely. They will not be convinced. None the less, there is evidence, though it is usually indirect, from which one may detect in some minds, and deduce in others, an element, seldom conscious, still less often expressed, of envy for a greater sexual freedom, an envy lying behind the disapproval which is expressed. I have quoted elsewhere, but must repeat because they express so exactly what is meant, the words of King Lear:

> Thou rascal beadle! Hold thy bloody hand!
> Why dost thou lash that whore? Strip thine own back.
> Thou hotly lusts to use her in that kind
> For which thou whip'st her!

Envy can be felt in the passage quoted from Melina Rorke, in her 'bland faces and knowing eyes', and again when she writes, of 'Kaffir women' as servants, that 'every white man became the immediate object of their amorous advances'. And perhaps with this envy went a tendency to exaggerate the extent of the freedom. All the world over, both men and women—though perhaps more often and more violently women, who have been kept in stricter bonds—attribute to some dark and shadowy figure which they fear and hate the desires they disapprove of most strongly in themselves. And for Rhodesians that dark and shadowy figure was ready made in the person of 'the native', at the same time scapegoat and shadow, while those cellars of the mind where rejected desires were stowed were also the repository for fears, fears that remembered the rebellions in Matabeleland and Mashonaland. And when desire emerged, fear was not far away.* So it was that almost every white Rhodesian spoke with horror of the African's lustful immorality, his utter lack of restraint. And he took elaborate precautions to safeguard his women against these tendencies.

No doubt on a hundred farms men went about their business without a moment's uneasiness or any knowledge of such dark realms of the mind as these. No doubt as a rule the natives did their work, came to the back stoep for medicine, were careful not to be cheeky when they spoke. And so there was no anxiety. They were justly ruled by kind parents. That is the kind of picture one gets from the account of most travellers. Take for instance one continental writer, M. Alfred Bertrand; all in his picture is energy, development, success. 'Men with bronzed energetic faces go through the streets and about their business in riding-breeches and shirt-sleeves wearing felt hats with huge brims. In the saddle they nearly always gallop', he wrote.[7] His Rhodesians are cheerful extroverts, far indeed from the neurotic; so most of them are today. But another observer, M. Henri Rolin, a lawyer of distinction, who visited Rhodesia in 1912, was more penetrating than most travellers; I translate from his French as literally as possible:

* A practising psychiatrist has told me that while patients in England used often to be tempted in dreams by a 'black man', since 1946, the 'black man' has often become 'a Russian'.

'Society is composed, so to speak, of two societies, one super-
imposed on the other, almost of two castes; an aristocracy of
white land-owners and capitalists, a proletariat of blacks. . . .
The whites conquered the country in 1893. They are established
there as masters, with the overwhelming superiority given them
by their intellectual and moral heritage from Greece and Rome,
from the achievement of Europe in science and mechanical
invention, in industry and the art of ruling, in accumulated
skill and capital. Below the whites, the blacks. . . . One
has to see them, in their sordid villages, half-naked . . . to
appreciate the immense distance which divides the victors
from the vanquished. . . .' And he goes on to speak of: 'Hate,
more or less concealed by the native since the last insurrection
was crushed; hate expressed by the whites with more or less
freedom, according to their level of education. A trader in a
small way [*petit commerçant*] will not hesitate to tell you that
the black is a "stupid animal"; a farmer whom you ask if he
is afraid of another rebellion, replies that "he would like it,
because it would make a splendid shooting-party". There are of
course exceptions. Educated men are naturally more prudent,
more discreet in their language; missionaries, officials of the
department of Native Affairs, occasional philanthropists, display
a sympathy for the blacks that is sometimes very effective.'[8]

M. Rolin was a shrewd observer who made a thorough study
of the laws and administration; he was an admirer of the
Chartered Company for its energy in developing the country, for
a power of decision the Colonial Office could never have shown,
and for its liberal policy '*à l'égard des blancs*', but he made reservations (to which we shall return) as to its native policy. His view
that 'hate' was the central emotion on both sides would be
contested by most Rhodesians who knew the country before
1918; they would indeed be shocked by the suggestion. And no
doubt for most of the time and for most men, humorous contempt or paternal benevolence or sheer disregard were more
common. But when there was any suspicion of approach to a
white woman, then the hidden bitterness appeared.

Section 2: The Black Peril

Consider first the legal fact that in 1903 the death penalty was imposed for attempted rape;[9] it was however left at the discretion of the judge to impose a lesser penalty. The law does not state that the penalty of death will only be inflicted when the attempt is made by a native on a white woman. But in practice the extreme penalty was not imposed for the substantive offence, that is, rape successfully achieved, if it was committed by a white man, whether on a woman of his own race or on an African, nor was it imposed on an African if his victim was African. To anyone with the least experience of criminal law, the dangers of such a provision will be obvious; rape—even the substantive offence—is notoriously difficult to prove with certainty, and that for a number of reasons. In the first place, the question of consent must usually depend solely on the evidence of the woman, and there are degrees of consent—of which one is a reality of consent with a pretence of resistance; next, there may have been provocation on the woman's part or false evidence given with the motive of Potiphar's wife; finally, in the most genuine case memory—being closely entwined with emotion—may play tricks and identification may be uncertain. These difficulties are of course far greater in the case of an attempt; the offence depends on the woman's opinion of the man's intentions, which may sometimes be clear but may easily not be at all clear.

But the fact that an offence is difficult to prove ought to have nothing to do with the punishment, and the importance of this provision of Rhodesian law is the severity of the punishment and its application in practice to a section only of the Crown's subjects. There can be little doubt that if some of the cases tried in Rhodesia on the capital charge of attempted rape had been reported to the police in another country—say in a country where there was one society instead of two—the charge would have been for some lesser offence with a lesser penalty; under the Indian Penal Code, for example, a code imposed by aliens but impartial, it might often have been 'assault with intent to outrage

246

a woman's modesty', for which the penalty could not be more than two years' rigorous imprisonment.

But this was not one society and the circumstances were special to the country. 'How were white people to live on isolated farms and in outside places', asked Mr. Holland in the debate on this question; 'how could a woman go into a witness-box and admit having been raped and live as usual afterwards? It was impossible, and that was why it was so essential that not only the accomplished rape but that the attempt also should be punishable with death.' And the Attorney-General, in the same debate, made very clear a point recognized by the laws and customs of Rhodesia. 'The law did not recognize', he said, 'that the black man was the white man's equal. . . .' He instanced the liquor laws; no child could be supplied with intoxicating liquor and 'the native was put on the same footing as the white child. If he were the white man's equal, why take from him the privilege of drinking himself to death? Why should they protect him if he were their equal. . . . The native might have a dozen wives if he pleased . . . a white man having more than one rendered himself liable to imprisonment . . . ; the law, the legislature, . . . and the higher authority in London recognized that the black was not the same as the white man. . . .'[10]

It was still clearer in the Immorality Suppression Ordinance, 1903, by which a white woman convicted of illicit intercourse with a native might be sentenced to two years hard labour, the native to five years. Another act in 1916 made it an offence for a white woman to make indecent suggestions to a male native, and for a male native to make such suggestions to a white woman. But between a white man and a native woman, such behaviour was not criminal.

A distinction had thus been made between the races in criminal law, the field in which a formal equality before the law is most often achieved. The distinction, it can hardly be denied, sprang from sexual fears and jealousies; how strong were the emotions these fears aroused could be seen when the High Commissioner at Cape Town refused to sanction the death penalty in two cases of attempted rape which occurred at Umtali, in 1908 and again in October 1910.

In the first of these cases, which occurred one evening when the complainant was walking home after dinner across a vacant plot on the main street, there were some peculiarities about the identification of the accused, and apparently little more than a presumption that the attack, if it was even an attack, was made with any sexual intention.

The complainant said she had been jostled and knocked down; she described her assailant to two police officers in vague general terms; he had eyes with prominent whites and dirty white trousers; they searched the servants' quarters in the neighbourhood independently. One of them saw Sinanga, later the accused, and let him stay in his quarter as he did not fit the description; the second arrested him because he did. The complainant failed to identify Sinanga at an identity parade, later saw him being taken to a police station by a constable and pointed him out. A jury could not reach agreement and was discharged; a second jury found him guilty and he was sentenced to death. It was not really surprising that the High Commissioner commuted the death sentence for ten years' imprisonment; shortly afterwards another African, a servant of a neighbour, came forward with a statement that he had been bringing home on a lead his master's pet baboon, which had attacked a dog and wrapped the lead round the complainant's legs; she had screamed, and the servant, having disentangled the baboon, fled in a fright as great as hers. When this statement had been sworn before a magistrate, the High Commissioner pardoned and released the man who had been originally accused and sentenced to death. One may have reservations about this second story and yet agree with the High Commissioner that it adds one more element of doubt to a case already doubtful.

In the second case, which was tried in October 1910, the accused, who had been a servant in the house of a European woman, came back to the house some weeks after dismissal and forced his way into her bedroom. His story was that he was hungry and had been drinking, that he had no money and broke into the house only to look for food; he was found guilty of rape—not the attempt—by a European jury and condemned to death. The High Commissioner thought there was an element of doubt as to what had in fact happened and commuted the sentence to penal servitude for life.

The point about these two cases in this context is the emotion they caused. There were meetings of protest, not only in Rhodesia but in the Union, where they were larger and more violent. 'Public feeling still runs high', reported *The Standard* on 9 February 1911. 'Mass meetings have been held in all parts of the country condemning the "ill-advised leniency" shown by Lord Gladstone.' An article in *South Africa* of the same week emphasized the point that the attempt should be punished as severely as the fuller crime, and advocated 'the public flogging of the culprit, to be followed by his public execution as near the spot of the outrage as possible . . .'. There were many letters to the papers, many columns of discussion headed: The Black Peril, The Social Curse, or The Great Offence. Many of these letters implied that sexual assaults on lonely women were more common in Rhodesia than elsewhere; only an occasional voice was raised to suggest that this was not so. But the figures available indicate an offence that was rare. Another implication in several letters, not explicitly stated but strongly felt, was that the crime was so abhorrent that a person accused of it ought to be punished even if the evidence was weak. And surely there had been an element of this in the jury's conviction of Sinanga, the first Umtali accused, on such doubtful evidence of identity.

It may be that this extreme provision of the death penalty served a useful purpose; there has been no case of lynching in Rhodesia, though two attempts at lynching have been described in published works.[11] In one case, the British South Africa police rescued the accused; in the other—a very early one—Jameson arrived in the nick of time and persuaded the crowd to think again on the curious ground that the country was in danger of a slump. But the argument was often used that lynching could only be prevented by severe laws; at the indignation meeting held in Umtali over the High Commissioner's action on the second of these two cases, *The Rhodesia Herald* reported that most of the speeches were moderate, but the statement had been made: 'That in the Southern States of America men had found it necessary to lynch and burn blacks who dared to molest women of the white race.' On this the editorial comment was indignant repudiation; 'it has never been contended by any sane person that appeals to the wild kind of justice which has on too many occasions been meted out to suspected offenders in the Southern States are necessary. On the contrary such methods are deplored by all right-thinking persons as a greater evil than that which they are mistakenly employed to remedy.'

Enough has been said to make the point that at any suspicion of intimacy between black man and white woman, an emotion was roused that was violent, though more controlled than in the Union. Indeed, Rhodesians could be a trifle smug when they looked South: 'No one can read the description of what happened at Turffontein, Johannesburg, on Monday night', wrote *The Rhodesia Herald* on 26 April 1912, 'without disgust and contempt for those who could be guilty of such hysterical folly ... a public meeting to discuss the recent native outrages was in progress when some excited person rushed to the door and shouted out that another woman had been molested, whereupon the assemblage broke up in disorder and a mob, armed with sticks and revolvers, rushed to the vicinity of the alleged outrage and proceeded to set upon every native in the neighbourhood. If it had not been for the protection of a couple of mounted policemen, two perfectly innocent natives would have been lynched on the spot. It subsequently turned out that the alarm was due to a lady informing her husband that she thought she saw a native's face at the window.'

Violent emotion then was roused by even the mention of a possibility, and though lynching had been avoided, the system of criminal justice went so far as to inflict the death penalty for an attempt when the offender was an African, while in no case was such a sentence imposed in the case of a European. And how, one may wonder, did Africans look on this? It is not easy to say because few Africans in the Rhodesias at this time could express themselves in writing. But there are other examples of the reaction already quoted by Colonel Woolls-Sampson—resentment that the law did not give the African for his women the protection that the European demanded for his. And, by hearsay, quoting the opinions formed by men who have long known the Mashona, and have gleaned a few grains of information on this subject in the course of talking about other things, one may hazard mention of varying forms of another reaction. There are, it is said, many among the unlettered Mashona who do not think it unreasonable that the white man should protect by the death penalty what he means to keep for himself. But why, they wonder, should anyone take so much trouble to keep a woman inviolate unless there is some peculiar virtue or magic influence to be acquired by sleeping with her? If we could eat the forbidden fruit, we should become as gods. . . . This can be translated into educated terms; there have been Africans brought up under this code to whom to achieve a white woman has seemed the crown of success—and success with a touch of revenge about it. And English-speaking Africans in Rhodesia today have been heard to let slip a phrase to the effect that the white trade unionist will always object to equal pay for the African because he is afraid that if pay is equal he will not be able to keep his girl.

This is uncertain ground, but surely all will concede that on the European side awareness of a sexual danger was one factor— and some perhaps will feel the most important—in the attempt to segregate and separate the native from the immigrant, an attempt that was so constant a feature of these years. In the newspapers, in discussions in the Assembly, there recurs again and again the assertion that the native must be kept in his place, that he should not be allowed to approach the status of the European, that a conscious effort must be made to maintain the gap. The social gap is as important as the economic; if the first is bridged, then there is one society and economic advantage will disappear too.

Thus the Salisbury Chamber of Mines in February 1903

recommended to Mr. Chamberlain 'that restrictions be placed on the present system of Christianizing natives, owing to injurious effects accruing therefrom, and the utility of labour and general economic principles be substituted'.² Three months later the entertainment of Booker Washington at the White House by the President caused considerable dissatisfaction. 'Whilst the Kaffirs remain in a raw state, the native question will have little significance beyond a difficulty to make them work. The black peril will only become a reality when the results of our misguided system of education have taken root and when a veneer of European civilization struggles with the innate savage nature. . . . In the Transvaal the native, who, before the war, walked humbly on the roadway now elbows you off the pavement. He has got out of his place. . . .'¹³ In the third session of the Second Council, in 1904, Colonel Napier, perturbed by the same tendency, moved that Municipalities should be empowered to make bye-laws 'to restrain natives of Africa from making use of such parts of streets and roads as are set aside for public foot paths'. And a year later, he suggested that the annual grant of £1,500 to Missions for native education throughout Rhodesia should be reduced to £1,000, as the 'uneducated native was the most honest, trustworthy and useful'.¹⁴ The argument was carried a stage further by a correspondent of *The Rhodesia Herald* who on 28 June 1912, objected to an item in the Budget: 'Grants in Aid of agricultural education of natives.' 'I will say at the outset', he wrote, 'that I do not consider it right that we should educate the native in any way that will unfit him for service. He is and always should be a "hewer of wood and drawer of water" for his master. If we educate him to plough, sow, and reap in the white man's way, we will very soon make him quite independent of the incentive to work, i.e. hunger. Our country will become a second India where there is no room for the white farmer or white man except as a civil servant.'

And again, hear *The Livingstone Mail*, whose pugnacious founder and editor, Leopold Moore, was usually at odds with the administration, denouncing the policy of developing Northern

Rhodesia as an 'estate in which race and colour . . . become . . . subordinate to the financial interest of the shareholders'. 'We shall consistently oppose', he wrote, 'the employment of natives where they compete with or are substituted for white men . . . it is better to pay a white man three times as much as a native than to run the risk of evolving a native, as contrasted with a white man's state.'[15] Two months later, after an interview, he reported that 'the policy we have advocated, viz. the employment of native labour for manual work only and of white wherever it can be utilized in preference to native labour, finds no sympathy with the Administrator and will not be adopted'.

Section 3: The Conflict Within

This was one strand of argument in the continuous debate. 'Preserve the gap—and to preserve it, make sure the native does not advance.' Many would have refused to subscribe to that extreme form of the doctrine. For many, conscience would recoil from the idea of denying the opportunity of education and of the Christian faith; others looked on public policy from a more detached and less emotional point of view and believed that to reduce the gap was in the interest of the country and everyone in it. 'How best to elevate and utilize its indigenous inhabitants is the most pressing problem with which Rhodesia is confronted today', wrote H. Wilson Fox in 1909.

Thus, in the first period of Rhodesia's growth towards maturity as a modern state, the conflict had begun within the white aristocracy. In Southern Rhodesia, almost to a man, the farmers and miners who meant to make the country their home believed that the social gap between themselves and the African ought to be maintained; they might wish to be kind masters—most of them did—but social equality of any kind was something too remote to consider. And if social equality meant sexual equality, it was not so much remote as morally wrong and repulsive in the highest degree. Some—and here the conflict arose—would add as a logical corollary that education of all kinds, even industrial education, should be withheld. Others, and in varying degrees, remembered Rhodes' mission to 'develop and open up to civilization' this country that bore his name; some of these, and again in varying degrees, perceived a discrepancy between keeping the native in his place and bringing him the blessings of civilization.

It was not a simple conflict between two sets of people, each using one set of arguments. Almost everyone on the white side sometimes thought that the native should sometimes be kept in his place, from the missionary at the pro-native end of the scale, through the Secretary of State and the Native Commissioner to the harshest mine foreman; throughout the same scale, almost everyone, at some other time, and again in varying degrees, believed he was a civilizing and uplifting influence. The great problem of Rhodesia, as they came to see it when they shook off for a moment immediate problems about labour, was how to maintain the social gap without denying the native all chances of education and development. It was a struggle within every white conscience as much as within the white community, between the professed ideal of paternal trusteeship and immediate short-term interests, the latter strongly reinforced on occasion by an assortment of lusts and fears that were normally kept out of sight and about which it is not polite to talk even today. These elements in the individual were represented in the community by individuals, but the cast was not always the same; the parts were occasionally redistributed. The more respectable elements in each individual, as in the state, were in search of a solution.

III. Red Soil and Granite Sand

Section 1: The Land

Rhodesia was settling down as it grew up; problems were being solved and relationships falling into conventional patterns. The settler cleared his patch of bush, grew his first mealies, raised his first calves, talked things over with his neighbours, and slowly, over the twenty years we are thinking of, his basic assumptions changed and moulded themselves into forms in which they were taken for granted. Every day, by a dozen of the acts, decisions, sayings, of each white man and woman in the country, these assumptions were shaped and strengthened; at the same time reason suggested, and sometimes proclaimed aloud, objects and a course of action that were wholly different. There is a wise and far-sighted doctrine or intention; there are in sharp contrast acts constantly performed that are short-sighted. In this process, the trio, gold, women, and land, each played their part, gold indirectly because the African did not yet want it, women negatively in that the white men were determined to keep them to themselves, land at first sight the most positively and directly.

Yet even as to the importance of the part played by land there can be different views. In 1957, an African writer[1] can state as a matter of course that 'the ownership of land has been one of the greatest points of division, if not the greatest, between African and European', not only in Rhodesia but throughout South Africa. Yet in 1915, the Native Reserves Commission reported that there was 'little evidence of conflicting interests as to the occupation of land between black and white'. This difference, partly due to changed circumstances, no doubt also owed something to the fact that the Commission was white; it can only be fully understood in the light of the peculiar conditions of southern Africa.

The first thought to strike anyone with the least knowledge of farming in English conditions might well be that surely in this country there is far more land than its population needs, enough surely for both black and white. But in Southern Africa one does not consider how many beasts an acre will carry, but how many acres will carry a beast; in the eastern parts of Southern Rhodesia, the answer is about ten acres to a beast and in the west it is about twenty, varying of course from district to district, and sometimes going as high as fifty. An improvement can be made if the land is fenced into separate paddocks which are grazed in rotation and if drinking water can be provided at scattered points, so that animals can drink near their grazing. But the basic fact is unlikely to be changed that it takes many Rhodesian acres to produce as much milk as one English acre, and more in the west of Rhodesia than in the east. And therefore, so long as we are thinking of a country mainly agricultural, it takes many more acres to support a man or a woman. In general, this is still true if one is thinking of Southern Africa instead of Rhodesia.

One reason, then, that farming tends to be extensive is the nature of the country. But this is not the only reason; convention too, has played a part. The first Dutch and Flemish farmers at the Cape were industrious peasants who had been brought to Africa to grow meat and vegetables for ships; they were used to a form of farming as intensive as any in Europe at the time. But as they spread outwards from the Cape Peninsula, they found country that to them seemed almost entirely empty of human beings; the Hottentots and Bushmen were few, roamed about in families or small bands, won their living mainly by hunting, by collecting roots and berries, by herding cattle, not by agriculture. It was much easier for the newcomers to the veld to send out herdsmen to watch their cattle than to go through the laborious business of ploughing, hoeing, sowing, and reaping, nor was there a market for surplus corn in any quantity. So the further he went from the Cape, the more the new South African tended to grow what was needed for himself and his family, his servants, and his beasts, but no more. And he grew little even for his beasts but relied rather on turning them out to graze on the veld; he came more and more to think of a farm as an area of several thousand morgen, a morgen being roughly two acres.

That was why the normal grant of land in Mashonaland was 1,500 morgen or 3,000 acres, while in Matabeleland it was double. And there was no incentive to find the labour and capital needed for intensive farming so long as the raw veld could be bought for ninepence an acre. Farming in Rhodesia, in the earliest days, says Marshall Hole, consisted mainly of cutting down the trees and selling them as wood. Missions which applied for land on which to build a church and school and start a station were often given 6,000 acres; there were grants of 18,000 or 24,000 acres for ranching.

This tendency to think in terms of great rolling landscapes is common to both Rhodesias. In Southern Rhodesia, there is next to be born in mind the question of height. There is the central plateau which is 3,500 ft. or more above sea-level, and therefore country in which white people can live comfortably; there are the fringes, which are lower and hotter, perhaps one-third of the total in area. Rainfall, and therefore fertility, on the whole gets less as one goes across the map from east to west and from north to south. There is also the division between country infested with tsetse fly and country free from it. Finally, there are in the broadest sense, two main types of soil, light and heavy, light granite sand and a heavy clayey soil which may be red or black.

The Bantu peoples had not confined themselves to the high veld or the low; they were to be found in both, but in Southern Rhodesia, the people in the low veld were unimportant, poorly organized tribes. Since cattle cannot live long where there is tsetse, the frontier of the fly country was also a frontier both for cattle-owning Bantu and for Europeans; as to soil, the various Mashona peoples, agriculturalists who had settled in the country many hundreds of years before, preferred the light sandy soils which were easy to work and which suited their standard grain (*ripoka* or Kaffir corn; a kind of millet; *eleusine coracana*). The red soils, and the less common black, stiff and clayey, hard to work but offering a richer crop when well worked and fed, were preferred by the mainly pastoral Matabele and the European. No Europeans are to be expected in the tsetse country or the low veld, while in the high veld they follow the stiff red soil. The Native Reserves Commission were able therefore to say that except round Salisbury, Bulawayo, and Gwelo, the natives lived on land of their own choosing; that there was no real conflict of interest, they attributed partly to the fact that the territory was large and the population small, partly to 'the amenable nature of the natives', and partly to the 'natural genius of the British for administration'.

As to who owned the land of Southern Rhodesia, there was continual controversy, from the death of Lobengula till after the First World War. It was a tangled question, but a highly simplified version of the dispute is all that is needed here. What was in question all this time was not the land actually occupied by natives of Africa in the areas reserved for them, nor the land which had been granted to farmers or miners; this last was 'alienated land' and it was the land that remained, the land still 'unalienated', that was the main subject in dispute. As to this, it was possible to take one of several views.[2] It was argued that the land belonged to the British South Africa Company, either as an ordinary commercial asset or, secondly, as an administrative liability for the expenses of which the Company were entitled to recoup themselves; on the other hand, it was variously held that it belonged to the British Crown, to the European inhabitants of Rhodesia (or perhaps to the voters, but the distinction is a fine one) or finally, and by a few eccentrics, that it had never been alienated from the native inhabitants of the country. Whatever view might be taken about ultimate rights in this residual land, it was unquestioned, during all this period, that the Company were in fact administering the land and making grants from it. This they did either on their own behalf or as agents, and if agents, either for the Crown or for the people of Rhodesia, who again might be variously defined.

From the point of view of a Mashona or Matabele tribesman this dispute did not at the time seem important; what did concern him most intimately was quite another set of categories. These were legal and administrative and his whole life might be changed if the land he happened to be living on was transferred to a new category. First, there were the reserves, in which he and his fellows continued for a long time to work the land much as they always had done; next, there were the lands alienated to Europeans, on which he could stay only as a labourer or tenant of the farmer; next, there were the unalienated lands, the residue not yet allotted, on which, whoever was the ultimate owner, he could exist for the time being on sufferance, paying a rent to the Company; finally, there were the urban 'locations', where he would be the tenant of the municipal authority.

Section 2: The Reserves

Take first the reserves. In 1913, there were, from the whole of Southern Rhodesia, over 9 million acres held by companies, and 12½ million acres granted to individuals, a total of 21,791,950 acres held by Europeans. Against this, a larger amount in total area, 24,877,150 acres were native reserves, and the British South Africa Company still held nearly 48 million acres of unutilized land, together with estates amounting to 156,209. But there is a wide difference in value between one Rhodesian acre and another. Of the land allotted to companies and European individuals, about four-fifths was within twenty-five miles of a railway; of the native reserves, less than one-third. At the other end of the scale came land over fifty miles from a railway and thus, from a European point of view, suitable only for ranching, by which is meant raising beef on a large scale; of this kind of land, little use to a peasant except for the barest subsistence farming, various companies had leased just over a million acres, individuals just under three-quarters of a million acres; of the reserves, over 8 million came into this category. Again, considered by height, nearly all the European individual land was over 3,500 ft. above sea-level, about two-thirds of the reserves.[3]

All this had come about very naturally. The first reserves had been those set aside at Gwai and Shangani for the Matabele;[4] they were largely empty at the time, and for good reason, as one was unhealthy and the other almost waterless. It was agreed, when the shortcomings of these first reserves were recognized, that further reserves must be set aside for natives and Native Commissioners were told to make their recommendations, not only in Matabeleland but also in Mashonaland. On the whole, their suggestions were followed and a good deal of variety was embodied in the result, not only because of differing local conditions but because not everyone interpreted the instructions in the same way. In one district, for instance (reported the Commission on Native Reserves of 1915), the areas reserved were those where natives happened to be tilling the ground in that particular season. But as, in varying degrees, all the tribes practised shifting cultivation, these small patches were less than they needed and much less than they had been in the habit of using over a longer period; in another district, where so far there were hardly any Europeans, almost all the land not occupied by Europeans was reserved. There were reserves so small as 5,000 acres; there was one of 3½ million; there were wide margins of error in the surveying.

Except in Matabeleland, and there only to a limited extent, it would be untrue to suggest in general terms that the Europeans had banished Africans to the lighter soils, the hotter regions, the areas remote from communications with markets. Africans had on the whole stayed where they were and they had not been particularly interested in markets and railways. They did not, when the Europeans first came, particularly want to sell anything. But to the Europeans, selling was essential; the railways came to European centres in the first place and Europeans chose land near the railways. Twenty years later, as the new economy developed and the African's desire to sell grew, the inhabitants of those 8 million acres of remote reserve found themselves heavily handicapped.

It is as well here to consider the theory on which the reserves had been set up. The theory was still unquestioned in 1915 by anyone in authority; it was part of the official framework of the state, but already the reserves were beginning to be regarded in a different light both by Africans and Europeans. The Commission stated the Doctrine as follows:

> The sudden immigration of a European community into a country previously inhabited only by African natives living in a state of tribal barbarism, and the rapid growth of that community, must have the immediate effect of dislocating the whole normal process of tribal development. . . . The native cannot at once be assimilated and it is necessary to set apart areas in which those not ready for the new order can live under the old conditions. . . .

The essence of the plan is a temporary shielding of the African till he is ready for assimilation; the words of the Order in Council are that reserves shall be set aside 'from time to time'; it is no-where contemplated that there shall be a permanent division of the soil. Having stressed this point, the Commission suggest that reserves should be looked on as an element in Rhodesia which ought to grow less as the old tribal system broke down; the 'open areas'—open to both races—should increase. The reservation of certain areas for Africans was not meant to preserve them for ever in segregation either from the new economy or from Euro-peans nor to ensure that in every generation every man should be entitled to a piece of land that would support a peasant family—a proposition absurd in Europe, but in tribal conditions taken for granted and still regarded by millions of Africans as em-bodying elementary justice and the first duty of Chief or Government.

The Commission condemned the idea as an absurdity yet were compelled to take account of it; it is implicit in their discussions of whether the reserves are sufficient. For those natives living in the reserves, there was still in 1915 an average of 50·55 acres of land to each person, and this works out at an average of 28 acres of land in the reserves to each native living in the territory, including those not in the reserves. These are not holdings, but averages to each person, man, woman or child, so to an average family in the reserves there may be available 250 acres. Much of this, however, will be rocky or desert; there is hardly anywhere in Rhodesia where it would be safe to reckon on more than a tenth of the land as suitable for arable cultivation—unless perhaps for a short period and with reckless disregard for the future. It would usually be fair, in Mashonaland, to think of 250 acres as providing about 20 to 25 acres of arable land, together with rough grazing for 20 to 25 beasts, a reasonable peasant holding. But this was the average for the whole country and in Matabeleland 250 acres might mean 10 acres of cultivation and a dozen beasts or less; few in Mashonaland can have had the equivalent of 250 acres. Further, communal land tenure is wasteful and these were not holdings but averages. Again, there were those not in the reserves to consider; many of them were away temporarily and would come back to claim a share in the reserve as an old age pension. Lastly, as the Commission rightly perceived, what is enough today may not be enough tomorrow. Everything depends on whether ability to produce food from the soil improves as fast as the population increases.

To this kind of improvement, the tribal tenure of land is a great obstacle; a man cultivates where the chief—on the tribe's behalf—says he may and though he has customary rights in such land it is not really 'his'; he cannot sell it, because it belongs to the tribe. And he is therefore unlikely to improve it much. The Commission recommended various improvements, notably the provision of surface water for drinking, and they visualized more intensive farming by both Africans and Europeans instead of the wasteful extensive methods of the past. But this could hardly happen without individual tenure of land and for that, they felt, very few of the inhabitants of the reserves were ready yet. So far as they looked ahead, the Commission were far-sighted; a class of landless labourer was bound to emerge, because there could not be holdings for everyone; the reserve in their view was precisely and exactly a reserve, not the lively developing part of the community, not the African's sole means of support, not his

only home, but a temporary refuge—until he should be sufficiently assimilated to the new economy to need protection no
longer. And from this important consequences followed:

The Commission has taken the view that it would not be justified
in considering only the interest of the native population of the territory. [And here, surely, they intend the immediate, short-term interests
of the native.] Those interests are closely bound up with European
developments; white and black must live together side by side for
many generations. Moreover the interests are often not capable of
being sharply divided. . . . The interests of black and white in certain
directions and a few areas have grown so close together and in some
cases are so interlocked that it was not possible to effect a division
without inflicting inconvenience . . . or loss and hardship on one or
the other . . . there is no clearly defined policy or principle which can
be applied to this question of existing interests except the policy that
the interests of black and white must be dealt with as having some
reasonably close relationship with one another and the principle that
if you deal honestly by the one you will be dealing honestly by the
other.

This was the corollary to the idea that reserves were temporary
and would disappear. As Africans became more and more used
to the new economy, the rigid separation that at first had seemed
essential would disappear, they would gradually come to be
integrated into an economic structure based in class instead of
race. The same view was taken by Mr. Wilson Fox, who was
employed by the Company as a research worker to make recommendations as to policy in the widest sense. He wrote:

How best to elevate and utilize its indigenous inhabitants is the most
pressing problem with which Rhodesia is confronted today. . . . Can
a system of social policy possibly be right or successful that bases itself
upon the principle of complete segregation from one another of the
European and native constituents of the body politic . . . ? . . . the ideal
condition on the contrary is that all industry should be co-operative
and that every European and every native throughout the country
should be jointly engaged in making the most of its resources to their
mutual benefit. . . .[5]

And from this general position he goes on to condemn the reserves as a hindrance to co-operation and to state that 'the reserves system has quite broken down' and 'is wholly unsuited to the circumstances . . .'.

Section 3: The Squatters

This then was the Doctrine, one in which most detached and thoughtful observers were agreed, and it can hardly be questioned that if one looked well ahead, integration and joint effort were in the interests of the country as a whole and of each race considered by itself. Yet, while the editor of *The Rhodesia Herald*, the Members of the Legislative Council, and the Directors of the Company preached this Doctrine, day by day, in scores of trivial decisions reached without thought, it was assumed unconsciously that the races must always be kept apart, that the African's true home must always be in the reserves, that all Africans would always be hewers of wood and drawers of water, above all that the interests of the two races were opposed.

Even the missionaries and the Aborigines Protection Society, protesting as they did against the loss from the Sabi Reserve of a broad strip along the railway, assumed that what was lost to the reserve was lost to the African, that integration was not taking place and never would. If they were right and this was so, the reserve was the African's sole refuge. But if the open land was truly open, surely the apostles of the Doctrine were in the long run right? Surely in that case the reserves were the enemies of African advancement? The true education of the African, said the apostles—the Directors, the Members of Commissions—lay in working for Europeans, in learning their methods of agriculture; this was their true road to advancement.

Perhaps subconsciously this was perceived by many who already began to dislike the thought of African rivalry. At any rate, in the newspapers, letters were constantly to be read which enumerated immediate reasons for a policy directly opposed to the Doctrine. They were to the effect that natives made bad neighbours and should be kept to the reserves, whence their cattle could not stray on to European land and infect, or even breed with valuable stock; where they would harm only themselves if they set the grass on fire; where they would not for ever be breaking down European fences. Nor must their farming be improved so that they might become rivals. 'There was the matter of selling breeding stock to natives. Many farmers considered it bad policy and were strongly against it, but it was no violation of the law.' This was at a farmers' meeting. 'The chairman admitted that he had sold heifers to natives but disapproved of the practice in principle.'[6] And the Rhodesian Landowners' and Farmers' Association told the Company in 1909 that in their view every unemployed native should be moved back into the reserves, 'every facility being given to natives to move with their families from the reserves on to private farms, provided they do so as bona fide servants of the farmer'.

This last protest was directed partly against natives still living on land not included in the reserves nor as yet given to European farmers—what was known as 'unalienated' land—but more specifically to unlicensed 'squatters' on European farms and indirectly to the practice known as 'Kaffir farming'. The term 'squatters' is misleading to English ears; there need be no implication that they are in possession without the consent of the owner, and to some forms of squatting no one had any objection. Sometimes a family, found in occupation on a farm granted by the Company to a European, were allowed to stay where they were on condition of providing so many months' work for the farmer; sometimes a labourer was engaged on a contract which permitted him to bring his family, graze a fixed number of animals, and cultivate one or two acres, these privileges forming part of his wages. There is, for example, an agreement reached a few months after the death of Rhodes between John Basil Michell acting on behalf of the Rhodes' estate at Inyanga and certain 'indunas', on behalf of 250 heads of families who live on the farms of the estate. Michell undertakes not to call out more than one-sixth of the adult males at any one time for work on behalf of the estate and no one man shall be called out for more than two months in one year; for such requisitioned work or *corvée* the estate will pay 10s. a month to a grown man and 5s. to a boy. Any labour beyond this will be voluntary and paid at market rates; those living on the land may continue to use the land they at present cultivate, but an annual rent of £1 a year will be paid.[7] The effect of this agreement on the 'adult male native' is that he can pay his rent to the landlord by the two months' *corvée*, but will still have to find his Government tax, and so will presumably work a little longer at market rates. After three months' work, if very abstemious and if meanwhile fed by his wife, he might begin to earn money he could spend. Such agreements as this were regulated by a series of ordinances.

What was objected to at the farmer's meetings was not licensed squatting but the unlicensed variety and also what was known as 'Kaffir farming', that is letting out the whole farm, or a considerable part of it, to Africans who cultivated it their own way and paid rent to the farmer. The objection was that the Africans were bad neighbours and that the grant was not being used as was intended; much the same, incidentally, was said by the Elizabethan English of a lord granted land in Ireland who preferred rather to 'inhabit his land with the Irish of whom he may exact than with the English by whom he may be strengthened'.[8] 'Kaffir-farming' was never a very wide-spread practice in Rhodesia and though farmers' meetings might pass resolutions about it, they were up in arms when it was proposed to legislate against it, because legislation was almost inevitably bound to modify their right to let land to labourers in return for work.[9] This had been legal since 1896; there had been provision for not more than seven families to live on a farm in a 'private location' and work in lieu of rent. The Private Locations Ordinance of 1908 laid down the conditions on which a licence for a private location would be granted; the agreement as to labour must be explained to the natives concerned by an official and recorded.

This was licensed squatting, of the kind outlined in Michell's agreement, and of this the farmers approved. But the Ordinance of 1908 specifically provides that so long as no agreement for labour is taken from them it shall be legal to let natives live on the farm without registration or a licence; it was to this that the farmers as a body objected, and to meet this part of their views it was further provided that a neighbour who was a genuine farmer might claim that 'the proximity of natives was undesirable' and the owner of the land on which the natives lived might be compelled to withdraw his permission. Even this did not meet the whole of some farmers' objection to unlicensed squatting; to a man short of labour, it might, one can see, be an irritation that on the next farm there should be natives wasting time on their own affairs.

Sometimes, no doubt, licensed squatting made one of the happiest relationships there could be between employer and employed; there was a permanence about it and often the employer would look after his people, physic them, sometimes provide an elementary school, lend them money, settle their disputes. But sometimes—and particularly if they had been there before the farm was granted—there was bitterness that now they should have to work for the privilege of living where they had always lived. This granting of land over the heads of occupants happened less and less frequently after the first years; it became the Company's policy to give land only where there was no native occupation or where compensation had been agreed and paid.

Still, it had happened often enough in the first years. And there was another feature of the situation anomalous from the point of view of the African who happened to be living with his family on unalienated land; he had to pay rent, while a mile away in the reserve his brother did not. The Company was of course partly a commercial body, but here a slight revenue was obtained at the expense of their official doctrine and true policy. The effect, as the Commission on Reserves noted, was to force the native to leave empty the 'unalienated' land and make for the reserves; the true policy, surely, was to make the unalienated land truly open and encourage farmers there, even small ones, even African farmers, if they were prepared to work and farm well. There was here a conflict of interest between the Company as a commercial body and as trustee for the future of the territory. From a purely commercial point of view it was to their interest to take up large areas of unalienated land themselves as ranches and sell them when the value of land appreciated. On the other hand, the success of this transaction depended on the successful development of the country, in which they were also interested as trustees, and for that purpose the policy of integration was seen to be best. No doubt this policy could hardly have been carried far at the time, because there were then very few Africans ready to learn better farming, but a cautious beginning might have been made with the training of candidates for some holdings in the 'open areas'. There might then have been a gradual and healthy development; as it was the Native Purchase Areas were begun when ideas had hardened into greater rigidity—and were begun with little training or enquiry. But hindsight is always easier than foresight.

Section 4: The Locations

At every point there arose, then, the clash between the Doctrine, the official view that the integration of the native into this new world was the right policy, and the assumption, short-sighted from the point of view of the territory as a whole, that the native was out of his place unless working for a white man or in the reserves, where it was best that he should develop as little as possible. The official Doctrine was, surely, repudiated by the setting up of a new kind of reserve, the municipal location, near the towns. These were based on the assumption that every African had a permanent home in the reserve, where his wife and children could support themselves while he was away; he came temporarily to the town to work, or might for a short time bring his wife on a visit, but this could never be his home, he would never be a permanent town-dweller. It was on this theory—which of course in these early days was based on undoubted facts— that the first locations had been set aside for Africans; sometimes the local body—the municipal authority—built huts, which at first were round huts of mud and thatch, and let them out for a rent of from 2*s*. 6*d*. to 10*s*. a month; sometimes the man built his own and paid a lower rent. But there is little home life (said the Native Affairs Committee of Enquiry of 1910) in any location and therefore disorder and immorality are prevalent. There is no recreation but gambling and drinking. All this should be changed —a European of good character should be in charge, there should be better huts or different kinds for 'the better class of native', there should be refreshment rooms and so on. But the principle of the location remained; it was to be the reserve for those temporarily away from the reserve, a place where the tribesman was segregated and kept away from Europeans.

Of course it was true that he was usually a bad neighbour, here even worse than near a farm. His ideas of sanitation were primitive because he had been used to living in a small group, all closely related, perhaps thirty or forty souls, with ample space all round him. Hunting was out of the question here and so were most of his tribal ceremonies, there were no village disputes to be settled by long-drawn timeless arguments; what recreations remained to him were noisy or, as the Committee put it, immoral. He was a bad neighbour; because he was a bad neighbour, he and his like must be herded together where they would give least offence. There they could be as noisy and dirty and immoral as they wished. And precisely because they were there, it became increasingly difficult for them to be anything else but noisy, dirty, and immoral.

Thus land more clearly than anything else showed the division between reason and practice. Reason, and the considered intention of that part of the body politic that corresponds to the conscience —or, if a more recent word is preferred, the super-ego—reason and intention stood on one side; they wished for integration between the races and a joint effort to develop the country. But, in practice, reason was often less successful than forces in the body politic which are based on impatient selfishness and immediate advantage—forces which correspond to what in the individual was once called original sin, more recently the *id* or the shadow. Contrast with the words of Wilson Fox or of the Commission on the Reserves the lucid and detached analysis of what he saw by the Belgian Henri Rolin:[10]

The white man will not take his meals at the same table as the black; he will not meet him on the footpath of the streets; he travels by rail in separate wagons; he forbids him, in principle though with certain exceptions, access to private property; he relegates him, at night, to 'locations' outside the urban centres. The farmer sees him as a *pilferer** and cattle-thief and fears his neighbourhood. Those who know the natives add besides that the antipathy of black for white is not less, and that is easily to be understood in view of the brusqueness, the complete lack of consideration, with which the European often treats the native.

Yet both sides must be seen; his good intentions are as much part of a man as his evil deeds. The farmers did not have it all their own way and almost every Ordinance passed by the Government shows signs of conflict between the Doctrine and the short-sighted interests of individuals.

* *Déprédateur*—perhaps marauder rather than pilferer, but if so an over-statement.

IV. The Inevitable Yoke

Section 1: The Native Commissioner

Very soon after the Company set up its administration a most important decision was made. In the first two or three years it had been natural—indeed almost inevitable—that they should rely on amateurs for the administration of justice. But where there are very clear class differences, amateur rulers tend to confuse the interests of their class with the ends of justice; it is hard to believe that a poacher in England would have been sentenced to transportation for life for netting a hare if the Justices, a century and a half ago, had not usually been preservers of game. The field-cornets of the early Dutch system at the Cape had been more interested in obtaining labour than in preserving game, but they were no more likely than English country justices had been to be impartial between their own class and landless labourers. They disappeared very early from the Rhodesian scene.

The officials who replaced them, Native Commissioners and Magistrates, were appointed with the same kind of duties as in other British colonial territories. They were meant to provide an impartial authority; they were to be accessible, to receive petitions, to take steps to right any injustice or wrong. They were to enquire into disputes regarding succession to a chieftainship, tribal boundaries and the like, to hear and settle water disputes. They might have the civil powers of a magistrate, they were not to receive presents, they were to register the inhabitants of their districts and collect taxes.[1]

This sounds familiar enough and is in accordance with the ideal of the British district officer in other parts of Africa, and for that matter of other parts of the world. And at first there was not much difference in practice either between the Rhodesian sub-species and his colleagues. The first Native Commissioners were picked whenever a man who seemed suitable became available. In Nyasaland Johnston met Sharpe over a buck which the one had shot and the other was sketching and made him his right-hand man; in the same way, Jameson chose a man he liked from the counter in a store or the desk in a telegraph office. They were sent out with a few instructions and a wide opportunity to create a tradition. In their diaries and letters, one can savour a life that was varied and as a rule leisurely, unhampered by too much correspondence, or by too much formality in what little there was. If one takes sample entries at random, a picture emerges.

A lion came into Mr. Gaynor's kitchen and killed a houseboy named Mombe while the family were at dinner, writes W. E. Scott from Hartley in 1897; locusts are bad across the river and the remedies suggested by the Agricultural Department are of no avail; a meeting has been held to appoint Banqira chief of the Mashiangombi. All the headmen of the tribe were present and many others. 'After asking whether they all still wanted Banqira, I told them you had approved their choice. And Banqira was appointed amid apparent satisfaction from those present. I impressed upon Banqira that he was a servant of the Government, that we looked on him as such, and that if he did wrong he would be punished as one of the Government servants; he was also to understand that he was to render all the assistance in his power to the authorities. . . .'

And so the diary continues. In September, the natives were troubling Mr. Scott a good deal for seed and he was letting them have what he could on a promise to return as much when they reaped; the Mashonas 'strongly object to build on account of the clayey nature of the soil, unsuitable for their favourite crop, ropoko' (Kaffir corn or millet; *Eleusine coracana*.) 'All the ground of the red clayey kind is not liked by the Mashonas . . . it is the white sandy soil covered with *Msasa* trees which the Mashona is so fond of.' On 6 September, he writes his report hurriedly at six-thirty in the morning, 'after a night-out at an open-air smoker—you know what that means . . .'. He was just back from a seven-day patrol on which he had 'seen very few natives'; no doubt he had come in to his headquarters from the bush, lonely for the sound of English voices and eager for the tinkle of the banjo and had hurried off at once to the concert. The scene is easy to picture: a fire had been lighted, perhaps to keep off the mosquitoes, and a hurricane-lamp or two slung from a tree to light the singer's face as he gave his rendering of the music-hall favourites he remembered from his last visit to the Empire or the Alhambra. There were not many amusements in Rhodesia in the early days.

On 5 October, Mr. Scott went out on a longer patrol. This was soon after the rebellion and indeed the rebellion was hardly done with; still, it is surprising to find that it was not till the 19th that he 'first came across any natives in the Hartley District; they are Makorekore, very black, well built people, speaking a dialect of Mashona'. For two days he lost the rest of the party and as he did not pick up the one buck he shot was reduced to eating locusts; on the third day without food he came to a Kaffir kraal and had a 'welcome feed of Kaffir corn porridge'. He reached Hartley on 2 November, 'with very little shoe leather left to his feet', but knowing a good deal more about his district. The Natives, he reports, are few in number and quiet, but 'very wild, running like buck when you come across them in the veld'.[2] It is a digression, but 'wildness' is not really surprising in the light of a notice published on 7 July 1897[3] requesting transport-riders and travellers not to fire at friendly natives on the assumption that they are rebels.

It was an odd double life that the Native Commissioner lived, alternating between the lonely patrol and the small circle of well-known faces in the station. Those transport-riders and travellers who fired at friendly natives were the people he met at the smoker; there too perhaps he would meet the farmer whose complaint that his boys ran away he must investigate. And he might find that there was another side to the farmer's story, a tale of harshness into the truth of which he would have to enquire;

it might be that the genial features he had seen through the cigar-smoke would then take on another look. In the same district of Hartley, for instance, two years earlier, Mr. Mooney briefly records a farmer's complaint that eight boys had run away before their month was up and that on enquiry two said they had been thrashed and two that their wages had not been paid. Mooney proudly notes that he has 'discovered' fourteen small kraals, with a total of 125 huts; he has given them a chief and created a paramountcy. In another area he found 102 huts scattered in the bush; 'if I can't get any tax from them next time I go', he wrote, 'I suggest moving them to a spot on the Sarue River . . . where they are at present they are not the slightest use for labour'. He found 448 more huts than his predecessor, and had supplied 800 natives for labour, but complained that 'the daily demand for labour makes it impracticable for me to absent myself from Hartley for long'.

'The natives of this district', he reported, 'are unwilling to work. If they hear I am in want of labour, they desert their kraals for weeks and stay in hiding till they hear I have got what I wanted. . . .' 'A man comes in wanting boys and generally wants them at a day's notice or less and thinks himself badly treated if I tell him he must wait five or six days. . . .' 'When I go out for a few days I find half a dozen men wanting boys when I get back.' Mooney's letters indeed are full of comment; the natives for instance—this was in 1895—are peaceful and civil towards Europeans yet distrustful. 'They would like them very well if they had not to work for them.' There is no serious crime; 'the Mashona are a very moral race'. Again, there is 'no such thing as a chief in my area. Their subjects will in no case go to those called chiefs; all bring their grievances to me'.

He adds that 10s. a month is a 'ridiculously low wage' and he is 'not at all surprised they are unwilling to work; after working 30 days they only earn 10s. for which they can buy 24 lb. of meal—just enough food for one adult for twelve days. A family of two would starve on such earnings. They all say they can feed better by collecting roots, fruits, and herbs than by earning; I should be very glad were I to receive orders to supply no labour under 20s. a month.'

Mooney's report on 24 May 1896 mentions the rumour of a plot by Matabele and Mahole to rise and kill Europeans; he attaches no importance to it, the natives being very quiet and civil. The next entry is dated 19 February 1897, Scott being then in charge and still enquiring into Mooney's murder.

Again, in December 1896, Mr. Drew, Native Commissioner at Victoria, writes for general guidance on his policy towards the Chiefs. He felt in the first place that his assistant should have greater powers and be in every way his deputy, so that he can be released from routine and do more patrolling. The power and influence of paramount chiefs, freed from the danger of the Matabele, are, he thinks, increasing and he would like to back them up in all they do. So far, however, he has only 'encouraged them to exercise their power over such of their people as want it and so far as the law permits'. But 'if the more common disputes could be dealt with by the Paramount, we should be saved a considerable amount of trouble. . . . Of course he would need watching . . . white police would be needed to patrol the country and arrest other offenders [by which he presumably means European offenders] and there would be Native Police under the Native Commissioner for the natives.'[5]

He had put his finger on a point of importance. There are contradictions in the first regulations for the Rhodesian Native Commissioners which are partly the result of South African tradition and partly of local circumstances. 'The Native Commissioner shall control the natives through their tribal chiefs and headmen' ran the regulations, but, in the very next paragraph, the Native Commissioner usurps some of the Chief's main functions. The Native Commissioner 'shall have the sole power of appointing lands for huts, gardens, and grazing grounds for each kraal on vacant land or reserves in his district and no new huts shall be built or gardens cultivated without his consent and approval of the position selected'. 'He shall from time to time . . . fix the number of houses which shall compose a kraal. . . .' These were the tasks a Chief performed, and if these were taken from him his whole authority was assailed; to give these duties to the Native Commissioner was to contradict the idea of control through the Chief.

Here in Drew's question was the germ of a theory of indirect rule, but Mr. Taberer, the Chief Native Commissioner, was against it;[6] he argued, and Mr. Tredgold, the Attorney-General agreed, that to let Chiefs try cases would be to invite corruption. The Chiefs' judgement was, he believed, 'frequently (not invariably) influenced by the present given . . . further if the Chief is a powerful one, he will help himself liberally to a portion of the judgement'. Even arbitration by Chiefs should be discouraged; but 'since natives know that they can appeal against the decision of the Chief to the Native Commissioner, the practice is a dying one'. And the whole idea of using the Chiefs was contrary to the official Doctrine; tribalism, like the reserves, was retrograde and it was the duty and the interest of the Government to assimilate the native into the new world, not preserve indigenous institutions.

Certainly in many parts of Mashonaland it would have been an uphill task to have built up sufficient authority for chiefs, many of whom were no more than the creation of the Government. In other African territories (for example Kikuyu and parts of Nigeria) where chiefships have virtually been created, the results have not been satisfactory. It is however in the earliest days of rule by a colonial power that indirect rule is of most value, when the ways of the foreigner are still strange; it is an irony that the theory of indirect rule did not develop until a stage had been reached in most territories when it was time to turn to assimilation. Mr. Drew, after retirement, wrote a series of articles on native affairs which were published in *The Rhodesia Herald* in 1920, all of which show a man with a practical mind and a sense of what can be done, yet not prepared to take for granted everything he found; there is clearly at the back of his mind a certain scepticism about the working out in practice of direct European rule, a feeling that for instance in matters of native custom, an alien court, however well informed and well intentioned, may go wrong. Other Native Commissioners, who never wrote to Headquarters about it, perhaps barely conscious of the same scepticism, practised at first a kind of indirect rule because it worked; but the decision had gone against them and the tendency, year by year, was to close more firmly the grip of the central administration.

Everywhere in the world, in the half-century from 1900 onwards, the web of administration grew more complex; the demand for statistics made more returns necessary; questions in Parliament made Ministers more anxious to know what was going on; judicial procedure became more formal. A public increasingly dependent on newspapers constantly demanded information from the headquarters of every territory and state, and headquarters increasingly demanded that every outlying centre of authority should not merely supply information but ask permission before acting. Swifter communications made it more and more difficult to rely on the old excuse that action could not be delayed till sanction had been sought; paper bred paper; clerks bred clerks.

All this reduced the initiative of the district officer even in administrations where everyone was concerned to keep it alive, where tradition was entirely on the side of the lonely man deep in the bush. But this was not so in Southern Rhodesia, where the official must always take account of a non-official opinion often hostile to himself and steadily growing in power. Officials had taken the place of amateurs, partly because there was too much for amateurs to do, partly so that they might be impartial between farmers and their source of labour. The farmers, in these early days, regarded the Native Commissioners as hopelessly biased in favour of the natives; even the Native Reserves Commission of 1915 classed them with missionaries, as partial to the natives.[7] To the natives whom they must persuade to work, the Native Commissioners no doubt seemed just as clearly biased in favour of the farmers.

But the point here to be stressed is that between 1900 and 1923 the farmers and miners were acquiring more and more influence and their attitude to the Native Commissioner was mixed; he was their man and they were on his side when he was suspected by the Colonial Office of recruiting forced labour, but the Native Commissioner was in their view seldom quite sound on the native question. Wilson Fox expressed a slightly different feeling when he wrote: 'He is an expert in natives. He speaks of them as "my natives" . . . he consciously or sub-consciously realizes that when there is no native district there will be no Native Commissioner.' The Native Commissioner then was suspect, alike to the officials who upheld the doctrine of assimilation and progress, and to the non-officials whose new and growing influence now began to be felt. To the upholders of the doctrine, he was heretical because he wished to preserve the tribal system; to the non-official, he was the champion of deserters and idle labourers, an enquirer into the truth of stories about wages withheld. This suspicion reinforced the world-wide tendency to rigidity and centralization.

And this reinforced tendency to centralize was once more reinforced by something else, a local feeling clearly displayed in a debate on Civil Service Appointments which took place in the Legislative Council in May 1912. Sir Charles Coghlan moved that in filling vacancies in the civil service preference should be given to residents of Southern Rhodesia. Rhodesian youths who had passed matriculation found it difficult to get employment; there was an impression that the Government preferred university candidates from England. This created a feeling of injustice; 'the gentlemen in the Universities had the whole Empire at their disposal'. The Government replied that their policy was a happy medium between the course Sir Charles recommended and that he feared; to recruit only Rhodesians straight from school—and there was of course no university—would produce a service with a narrow outlook; they must have a certain proportion of men with wider views who had been to a University.

But in spite of their reply, the Government were under continual pressure to appoint Rhodesians, which meant boys straight from school. And there arose a vicious circle; a young man from a University can very quickly be given responsibility, which nourishes a responsible outlook and builds a readiness for more responsibility. A boy from school cannot be given so much; no one has time to train him and so he is given what Lord Wellesley a hundred years earlier had described as 'the menial, laborious, unwholesome, and unprofitable duty of mere copying clerks'. And by such training he becomes progressively less fitted to take a broader view. The Government then becomes still more reluctant to trust and consult him and he to trust or consult either his subordinates or his Chiefs.

This was the danger. Of course there were men who triumphed over the system and there were always men who came in from other walks of life or from the Universities; but broadly it was true that men were taken younger than in the Colonial Service and that it took them much longer to reach a position of responsibility. Nor was the official body on the Native Commissioner's side so whole-heartedly as would have been the case in a Crown Colony. In such a colony, there would be as a rule one body of officials, a graduated hierarchy, in which those at the top had in their time served as district officers and district commissioners and still used their basic assumptions. But this was not so here, where 'Native Affairs' was not the groundwork of all administration but a separate *mystique*. The highest to which its practitioners could aspire was not Chief Secretary or Governor but Chief Native Commissioner. And the Chief Native Commissioner, who had not yet become also the Secretary for Native Affairs, was one departmental head among others, liable to be asked questions, through the Secretary, by his superior the Administrator or by the watch-dog of the Colonial Office, the Resident Commissioner; this position did not encourage the confidence that enables a central authority to devolve power. Thus headquarters dared not devolve power to the district and as less and less was left to the Native Commissioner he clung more closely to all he had and devolved less to the Chiefs; the whole spirit of the administration turned further and further from the idea of ruling through the Chiefs, more and more to a system of strict and direct control.

Thus instead of being the father of his people throughout the district, the Native Commissioner became the warden of a reserve—a national park where those curious creatures, the natives, could live their lives undisturbed. He and his charges together were an aspect of Rhodesia in which the average Rhodesian elector was not much interested except as a source of labour; 'the country is run on the pretence that the native is not here', a Native Commissioner said to me with a certain bitterness even as late as 1956. And more and more it became an unconscious assumption that the reserves were the place where the natives should be; their irruption into the world of cities was something to be covered up decently. But on the conscious level, when thoughtful people discussed a problem, fatherly care was the key note.

Section 2: Kaffir Beer and Native Schools

The metaphor of father and child was constantly used in relation, for instance, to liquor. It had been a concern of Parliament's, next in importance only to the slave trade, that the people of Central Africa should not be demoralized and degraded by the sale of spirits. To this altruism from afar had soon been added the practical concern of the settler that his dairyman should not every night drink himself either riotous or insensible and leave the cattle unmilked. Thus it was an offence to sell or give spirits, or indeed any European form of liquor, to an African anywhere, and the motives for the prohibition were as usual mixed, one being selfish and one not. But native beer brewed from *rapoko* was not forbidden in the reserves, nor was its consumption forbidden anywhere. Everyone agreed that used in moderation it was of value to health and most Europeans were aware, perhaps vaguely, that it was used in religious ceremonies and social gatherings. It was not therefore forbidden but the newspapers often contained complaints about its excessive use in 'locations' near the cities or 'private locations' on farms; not only were beer parties noisy and a nuisance in themselves, not only were the boys next day either absent or even more stupid than usual, but 'if it were not for Kaffir beer, there would be no crimes of violence in these territories'.[8] And already, by 1910, the Native Affairs Committee recorded that wherever reserves lay close to mines or urban locations, far too many natives were concerned in the trade in beer—'lucrative, illicit, and highly objectionable'— while two more serious evils had arisen, the adulteration of beer by noxious drugs, and the prostitution of women who brought beer from the reserves to the mines. The Committee therefore recommended control in mining and urban areas; as far as possible the mining company or the local authority should brew their own beer and sell it by licensed dealers in approved places, while private brewing should be forbidden.

It is difficult to see what alternative recommendation was possible in 1910; the Committee was unanimous and its recommendations were accepted. The evils were there; the facts were undisputed; action was needed. Yet here was another step in the disintegration of the old way of life; beer played a part in every gathering that marked the way through life of the Bantu tribesman; at birth, initiation, betrothal, marriage, death, beer was drunk with appropriate ritual. And the whole proceedings would take on a different look if the beer poured for the spirit of an ancestor had been brewed, not by the wife of his son, the mother of his grandson, but by a municipal brewery under the remote supervision of a European ex-sergeant of police. And the prohibition of private brewing opened the way to police interference in private life; no one might be in possession of an unreasonable quantity; it must not contain more than 3 per cent. alcohol; no one must leave a beer party after sunset; this kind of regulation set the police at constant variance with a people whom it had become their duty to detect in an offence regarded by the offenders as neither a crime nor a sin.

In another recommendation of this Committee, a kindly paternalism was unmixed with any other motive. At certain stores in the mine areas, it had become a custom for an African labourer to choose something which he would like to take home when, perhaps six months from now, his time at the mines or in the city should be ended. He would agree to pay for it so much a month and put it in a box where it was kept for him till he went. It was a kind of hire-purchase system, but with possession deferred till the last payment had been made. And since he might fancy something every time he went into the store, the mine boy sometimes found himself paying more than he could afford and so he would default on a payment and when at last he left for his home he would be unable to redeem all that was in the box. And then, it was said, he would often in despair forfeit all he had already paid and leave for his home with nothing. And the storekeeper would sell the goods to someone else. This, said the Committee, should be forbidden, and debts from a native should be made irrecoverable by law, so that he would not be allowed credit; to this recommendation there was general agreement in principle in the Council;[9] the box system was regulated and box-keepers had to be registered; but legislation did not go so far as the Committee had wished. Here was an admirable illustration of a conflict between immediate and ultimate good. To deny the African credit might protect him for the moment but helped to perpetuate the idea that he was an irresponsible child; it did more, it helped to keep him irresponsible.

If credit for Africans illustrates clearly the dangers in the most disinterested paternal protection, it is in the voter's attitudes to education for Africans that the inner conflict of motives is shown most clearly. And here, too, is starkly displayed a contrast between intention and achievement. In Southern Rhodesia, it seemed from the start natural that the state should help parents who came from Europe and South Africa to give their children an education at least as good as they would have had in the countries they came from. Education had been compulsory in England since 1870. And the new arrivals needed more help than they would have had at home, because distances were so great and the community so scattered: 'The main efforts of the Administration', said His Honour the Administrator, opening the Third Session of the Third Council on 6 May 1907, 'are directed to ensuring that at least the means of obtaining elementary education shall be brought within reach of every child of school age in the country.' This, of course, means every European child. He went on to promise 'liberal assistance towards the maintenance of boarding establishments' for children from outlying parts.

The Education Ordinance of 1899 dealt solely with Europeans; the education of Africans was still a matter for missionaries. In 1903, a grant was made by the state to the first industrial schools for Africans; by 1907 there were 30 schools for Africans receiving a grant; by 1908 there were 40, and the figure rose steadily to 150 in 1911. The total of the grant for all these schools was £1,192 in 1908, and by 1911 £3,470.[10] There had been 4,319 pupils in 1908; by 1911 there were 14,916. The scale was thus still tiny when the Committee of 1910-11 on Native Affairs made its report.

The Committee represented the employing class among white Rhodesians; it discussed the question of education at length and its report displays the considerations at work nicely balanced. The Committee had no doubt of 'the keen desire of all sections of the more advanced natives for education', nor of the increasing appreciation of this fact among 'the thinking public' (which means, of course, the thinking Europeans) 'who are commencing to realize the benefits accruing to all parties'. The ambition, the Committee believed, of most aspirants for education so far was 'to be able to read and write and thereby carry on a correspondence with their own people. Trivial and unimportant as this may seem, the Committee nevertheless recognize in it many influences for good'. News from home 'may well induce a longer and more contented period of employment', while 'it is a definite and important stage on the road of civilization and progress'.

That anyone should think it trivial and unimportant for a man to want news of his home may strike an English reader of today as inhuman, but in the England of Miss Austen, Cobbett, and Peacock, there are plenty of parallels among the sayings recorded of the rich about the poor. The Rhodesian Committee set side by side the two motives of duty and business, one perhaps a tribute to the conscience and the other to the constituency, both undoubtedly present in most Europeans. And the members of the Committee were clear for their own part that in this respect duty and business were on the same side. 'Our own development is so closely interwoven with that of the native that it is vital for our interests as well as for his own that he should be mentally raised . . .' they wrote, and again: 'there can be little doubt that the educated native desires something higher than his old standard of living and by the very desire to satisfy those growing needs is urged to more frequent and continuous labour.'

On the other hand, they do take note of a second set of business motives. Many Europeans, they believed, felt that a literary education was not desirable for natives and that religion and handicrafts alone should be taught; this of course grew from the fear that Africans if educated would compete with Europeans. Here the committee is referring mainly to the artisans, the Europeans who were themselves less educated; the Committee, whose members belonged to another social class, discounted these fears, coming down uncompromisingly for the view that the white man will always hold his own. And as to literary education, 'apart from the responsibilities of a dominant race, we should accept the inevitable . . .' though they add the rider that 'we should . . . retain control of this kind of education'.

From this consideration of arguments felt to be respectable together with those less presentable emerged cautious recommendations; literary and religious education should continue to be given by the missionaries, and grants in aid should continue, but should be increased wherever there was an approved teacher; a beginning should be made with a Central Training Institute for teachers who would be taught on secular lines. There must always be European supervision of any school; there must be no independent teachers starting schools of their own. Agricultural instruction should be given in the reserves; there should be central institutions for teaching agriculture and there should be demonstration plots. Handicrafts and trades—bricklaying, carpentry, blacksmithing, even printing and bookbinding—'should be taught with the conviction that the work performed, when not done for their fellow natives, will be mainly that of assistants to Europeans. . . .' And the views of the Committee with regard to higher education are important and should be quoted. The Committee were impressed with the danger of letting a young man go outside South Africa. 'When he returns, he is filled with a spirit of unrest and dissatisfaction with his surroundings and is imbued with ideas which, if communicated to the people among whom he settles, may become a source of danger to their peace and quiet.' A native who qualifies for higher education should therefore be encouraged to go to the Union and discouraged from going to England.

There was general agreement with these recommendations in the Legislative Council, though Colonel Grey would have gone further in the matter of controlling teachers and made it necessary for every teacher to hold a certificate and to be removable at pleasure.[11] And in the wider debate in the country, not only on the occasion when this Committee reported, but throughout these years, there was never any lack of voices to express the two sets of views which the Committee had noted. There were those who held it a mistake to educate natives at all, and particularly through missionaries; on the other side, a correspondent of *The Rhodesia Herald* pleaded for a much more vigorous and progressive policy on education:[12] 'What we make of the native now will affect for good or ill the prospects of those of our children who make Rhodesia their home. To a large extent, the local native is still in a mouldable stage and it is up to us as the dominant race, presumably representing all those fine and noble qualities attributed to the white man, to put our impress on him.' That note was struck by others too, while the official view was put by Rochfort Maguire in 1911 to a general meeting of the British South Africa Company in London: 'We believe that the true interest of the white inhabitants as well of the natives themselves lies in making the native as efficient as possible and so enabling him to contribute his maximum. . . .' But it was to be clearly if tacitly understood that his progress would be guided and that his ideas must not be allowed to get out of hand and endanger the Rhodesian way of life. To see the subject in scale, one should consider the figures: in 1911 there were 2,127 European pupils, who cost the state £39,041 or £19 7s. 1d. per child. Of the Africans, 14,916 children went to school, of whom 7,614 received some financial help from the Government. The cost was £3,469 15s. 0d. or about 9s. per child helped. And of course many African children did not get to school at all.

Section 3: Passes and Witch-doctors

We have been looking at the reports of committees and at letters to the papers; it is all we have that is certain. But what, behind all this, has become of the African, the man who has to marry a wife, bring up children, die and go to his fathers? How does he look on what has happened? It is hard to know, because he is still illiterate and inarticulate. But one can perceive certain points.

He has, in the first place, lost his freedom. There are 'vivid memories of complete freedom under tribal conditions', writes the Commission of 1915. 'An old native from the Magondi Reserve', writes Mr. R. M. Archdale, 'once said to me: The Matabele when they came killed us outright when they could but they didn't kill us all. You white men, you tax us and our wives, you tax our dogs and you tax our cattle and none escape. We preferred the Matabele.'[13]

Freedom is an abstract idea; the Mashona, many a farmer would say, were not interested in abstract ideas. What did the loss of freedom mean? Taxes, which meant work to earn the money and long absence from home in a new bewildering world; passes, to be carried whenever a man moved; interference with custom; punishment for what had once seemed natural. 'Gobo, a native chieftain reputed to be over eighty years of age . . . was charged . . . in that he delivered a gun to a native not entitled to bear arms. Accused pleaded not guilty and produced a permit entitling him to hold firearms. . . . Accused objected to having been subjected to the indignity of arrest . . . he had committed no offence and had been placed in gaol. . . . Accused presented an upright and imposing appearance in the dock. Evidence was led that a son of the accused was arrested for having killed a duiker and for having a gun in his possession. This son stated that he had obtained the weapon from the accused.' That is one thing that loss of freedom means.

Passes had existed since 1895. The law had been changed several times; by 1910, 'every adult male native' was required to carry a registration certificate. Outside his own district he must have a visiting pass, which would last twenty-one days, and in an urban area he would need a pass to look for work; the Government decided to simplify the system and in 1913 introduced a Native Passes Consolidation Ordinance, yet in 1920 a retired Native Commissioner wrote: 'A serious hardship is the fact that, owing to the numerous pass and trespass laws in force in this country, the native who comes to our towns finds it impossible to avoid the many pitfalls made for him and becomes an offender over and over again. . . .'[14] No doubt passes were 'absolutely necessary for police and administrative purposes'; no doubt by limiting the numbers who came to the towns they prevented some of the worst horrors in the growth of slums; it is hard to see how a responsible person could have voted against their continuance. But free men do not carry passes.

There was much argument about passes; the Attorney-General, moving the second reading of the Native Passes Consolidation Ordinance,[15] said that everyone accepted the principle that all natives must be registered: it was the object of the administration to make registration as little burdensome as possible. But there were members on the non-official benches, speaking undoubtedly for many of their fellows, who asked that the certificate of registration should be handed over to the employer when a man accepted employment; he would get it back, properly endorsed, when he ended his contract. The Attorney-General thought this was putting too great power in the hands of the employer; 'in the history of the labour problem in this country,' he said, 'there have been many complaints by the servants against the masters as well as by the masters against the servants.' A year later,[16] moving the second reading of the Native Labour Contracts Registration Ordinance, he elaborated the attitude: the Government had to look at the matter from two points of view: they wanted an effective contract but the labourer was not to be put too much in the hands of the employer; when a contract was registered—having been properly explained—the employer would hold the registration certificate but the native would get a 'working pass' in the meantime, which he could show as a substitute. He would thus be able to leave his employer's premises, but hardly his employ. To register in this way was permissible, not compulsory; still, once it was done, the employee was tied effectively.

That is the kind of controversy that took place; it was controversy between on the one hand private employers who thought first of their interest as employers, and on the other a more detached class of employer, the Government, who were conscious of the employer's interest but also of an ethical duty and a responsibility to Parliament. The Attorney-General was Clarkson Tredgold, married to a Moffat, and the son of a Cape lawyer, a man deeply conscious of his trusteeship for the Africans of Rhodesia, but in the Council subject to pressure from one side only, not an arbiter between two points of view equally represented. It was what a debate on poaching might have been in the House of Commons before 1832: there were a few members who did not preserve pheasants themselves, though their friends did, but the poaching classes were not there.

The poaching classes were not there. And as to this, the Committee on Native Affairs reported that opinion—which of course always means 'white' opinion—was practically unanimous. The natives were quite unfit for the exercise of any legislative franchise; they should be represented by the Secretary for Native Affairs. There were fifty-one on the electoral roll, all colonials (that is, from the Union), and they should be left on, but the present electoral law should be repealed and no more natives admitted. This was in fact never done; the common electoral roll for all races remained, a vestigial relic of Cape liberalism and Rhodes' famous saying about equal rights for all civilized men. The number of African voters had risen from fifty-one to about 500 by the time of Federation. There were no African members; laws were made for them by Europeans.

Free men live according to the customs they know. And it was clearly laid down that under the new dispensation native law and custom should continue to govern the lives of natives as between themselves, except where repugnant to natural justice or morality. But in the first place, this assumes an absolute standard of what is morally right, that of Europeans in the nineteenth century, and there may be injustice in this; secondly, there was taking place all the time an insidious and usually sinister impingement of new custom on the whole complex system of the old.

As to morality, the assumption that there are absolute authoritarian standards is today widely challenged; but surely there is a wide field on which most men can agree, a marginal area which can surely be distinguished. And we need not for the moment consider whether this implies any absolute standard or whether it is merely that certain kinds of behaviour constitute a highest common factor in the business of living together as human beings. Marriage customs, in particular, come into the marginal field and the circumstances of one people may dictate a practice which the philosophy of another rejects; some people, for instance, have thought it a duty and others a sin to marry a deceased wife's sister. Manslaughter has been approved in war, feud or duel; but no one, surely, has felt pride in the treacherous murder of a guest. An isolated tribe or sect may in special circumstances hold in esteem, and a whole nation may condone, a practice which most of mankind repudiate, but from an outlook with a wider horizon it will seldom be defended. There have been tribes to whom sodomy has had a ritual importance, peoples of high artistic achievement to whom it has seemed a trivial peccadillo; but it has not surely been defended as being on the credit side of a moral balance-sheet.

Whatever may be thought of this generalization, there was, as Livingstone had found, a wide area of agreement between Europeans and the Bantu peoples as to what practices were defensible. And over much of the area in which they had differed, the Bantu were quick to be persuaded. To a European, there could be no question that it was wrong to kill twins; it seemed particularly horrible that the mother should kill them herself, stuffing earth down the small throats with a stick till they died. This was common among the Mashona;[17] that it was wrong, they were soon brought to agree—just as in India no high-born Rajput would today defend the practice of killing an infant daughter, a custom which 100 years ago could often be prevented only by the use of force.

Witchcraft was quite another thing. Few Africans could bring themselves to believe, at European bidding, that there were no witches; indeed, they read of witches in the Bible and knew the injunction, 'Thou shalt not suffer a witch to live'. And clearly Europeans understood nothing at all about witches or the proper means of defence against them; they thought, for instance, of 'a witch-doctor' as a power for evil, a conscious impostor, whereas to an African the *nganga* or doctor was a power for good, a protector against the *muroi* or witch. It is hardly possible to over-emphasize here; even today, a Native Commissioner in Central Mashonaland has said to me: 'There is no such thing as natural death in my district.' Death, illness, a minor ailment, failure in an examination—any of these is likely to be the result of some action in the world of spirits—of witches, or of ancestors (the *mudzima*), of the guiding spirits of tribe or family (the *mhondoro*) or of one of the unattached spirits that are apt to possess human beings (the *shave*). Against all these evils, the *nganga* or doctor is the refuge and adviser. 'He is able to communicate with the spirits and find out what is necessary to propitiate them. He is the medium for the healing spirits of his forefathers who were doctors in this life . . .' writes Michael Gelfand,[18] himself a doctor of medicine who has spent many years in a sympathetic study of Mashona medicine. And he quotes Fr. Burbridge, S.J., his predecessor in this field, also writing of the *nganga*: 'He can tap the occult energy. He is the power for good as well as evil. . . .' Diagnosis may be by the throwing of bones or dice, interpreted in the light of observation and accompanying circumstance; treatment may be by herbs or essentially by faith, faith being often not only the patient's but the doctor's, not only in the methods used but in each other.

Gelfan considers that the *nganga* believes in his methods, as doctors in Europe believed in theirs in the Middle Ages; he considers that, with a few dishonest exceptions, the *nganga* believes himself to be the medium of a healing spirit, that he is often a skilled herbalist, a keen judge of human behaviour, a botanist of high calibre, and one anxious to help others. 'His is a noble profession in his society, giving the individual not only the opportunity to devote himself to the art of healing but also to act in the capacity of a priest who contacts the ancestral spirits' and thus one who is 'assured of high social status'. There is a case-study of a *nganga* by a Johannesburg psychiatrist[19] which confirms these opinions.

Of course there were dishonest *ngangas*, and no doubt even the best used elementary sleight-of-hand to create the faith on which their hope of a cure depended, extracting, for instance, fragments of bone and other foreign bodies from ailing parts. No doubt by their divinations many quite innocent people were accused of witchcraft and tortured or killed. But 'witchcraft' is a term used to cover a wide variety of beliefs and conditions of mind. An African might hold witchcraft responsible for many illnesses that an up-to-date physician might diagnose as the physical result of psychic stress, and others that he would regard as unquestionably a neurosis or psychosis, often but not always due to the patient's belief in witchcraft. There is good evidence from several parts of Africa that the results of witchcraft are thought to be worse since the coming of Europeans; this may be because the law now forbids the proper punishment of a witch, it may be because the whole situation provides a favourable breeding-ground for psychic stress and neurosis. In either case, there can be no doubt that belief in witchcraft is a living reality and not easily exorcized. Nor can it seriously be maintained that the belief is caused by the *nganga*; he is one manifestation of the belief and no doubt helps to keep it alive, but he is surely as much result as cause.

Little of this was known to the rulers of Rhodesia, or indeed to anyone else in the European world before 1914. They saw certain results, as every white Rhodesian did, and they looked for a cause, and the simpler the cause the better. Witch-doctors were thought of as conscious impostors, who were largely responsible for the beliefs by which they obtained a living. Hear Mr. H. H. Castens, speaking of a change in the Witchcraft Suppression Ordinance: 'Witchcraft was still very rife . . . and resulted in many brutal assaults consequent upon the opinion of witch-doctors consulted. It was hoped by this Ordinance to put an end to superstition and sorcery also to bone-throwing [divination by bones or dice] and boiling water tests . . . it would be possible if the Ordinance were passed to punish the witch-doctors, who were the real causes of the mischief, by imposing a sentence of seven years as well as lashes.'

Mr. Castens spoke for almost every white Rhodesian; the Ordinance became law, and thus was assailed an institution close to the centre of Mashona religion and the family life which centred round the worship of the ancestors. It was a major interference with custom, inevitable no doubt, no doubt productive of good, productive also of much doubt, uncertainty and suspicion, much secrecy about acts believed to be good in themselves but forbidden by the Government. Witchcraft was interfered with consciously and deliberately because it was repugnant to natural justice and morality. In the field of native custom that remained for the administration of the Native Commissioner, there was still in 1910 a great diversity of practice from one district to another and also a great diversity of opinion as to whether these customs should be codified. In the field of divorce, for instance, one Native Commissioner would grant divorce for adultery or for a long term of imprisonment but not for incompatibility of temper; another would regard incompatibility as a valid ground; a third might think the wife must wait till her husband came out of prison.[20] Some Native Commissioners feared that to codify custom on these matters would give permanence to a system in a state of flux and hinder the process of assimilation. In fact, of course, practice did become steadily more uniform and, for that reason, and because it was administered by people who used writing, it became more rigid than it would have been.

As for the insidious impingement of an alien culture on every branch of the African's life, a whole book might be written on that alone, and many have. Consider the life of a man with his wife or wives and children as it had been. It was constantly on the lips of most settlers that this was a life of idleness, where the males 'spend most of their time lying on their stomachs basking in the sun', but the Southern Rhodesia Committee on Native Affairs followed their predecessors in South Africa in finding that this was emphatically not so. There was an elaborate division of labour between the sexes; each man and woman had a task. Neighbours came in to help with certain operations and of course gathered for many ritual occasions, birth, initiation, betrothal, marriage, death; the wife brewed on these occasions beer which the husband poured in libation to his ancestors, between whom, and the children who would one day pay the same respect to him, he stood, poised in time, the middle rung in a ladder. But now he must go away for months at a time to earn money for the tax and the whole structure crumbled. From each of these essential ceremonies, the central figure is missing and the wife is left alone with responsibilities far beyond her training.

But the point need not be laboured. It was clear enough at the time to any who thought about the African at all and the newspapers are full of letters noting the result. 'None who has had the opportunity of observing the difference between the native in his more or less natural state . . . and the native who has spent a year or two in towns . . . can honestly deny that in the majority of cases and from nearly every point of view, except perhaps in the matter of some . . . technical skill, there is a very perceptible deterioration.'[21] 'We have destroyed the power of the native chiefs and in its stead have substituted nothing but the authority of the tax-collector. . . .'[22] 'It is not chiefly in schools or churches that the native is at present being educated. We are teaching him in our stores, homesteads, compounds, gaols, bars, canteens, and brothels.'[23] And the Committee on Native Affairs spoke for all when they found that the natives had degenerated, especially sexually, that, 'the superstitions which for them represent religion having been suppressed too suddenly', they had lost respect for parental or tribal authority and that from this many evils had resulted.

The years had brought the inevitable yoke and to shoulders unaccustomed to such discipline; they had brought for the African tribesman an end of the old simple static life, they had brought freedom from tribal authority, from the restraints of custom, from the fear of raids; they had also destroyed freedom, the freedom of living by the discipline of customs felt to be one's own.

V. Trial by Jury

Once the first pioneering days were done, and very soon after the rebellions, the Rhodesians began to feel it as a reproach that they should be without one of the most treasured of British institutions, trial by jury. Perhaps only a few attempted to analyse the advantages; they simply felt that a British community must have trial by jury, just as they must observe Christmas and play cricket. But it is an institution that may have real advantages; it tempers the idea of an authoritarian absolute code of justice with the very different concept of justice as the people's will; if public opinion changes, a point may be reached where juries will find excuses for not convicting. Further, it is to some extent an insurance not only against tyranny but against that pedantry—a concern for technicalities of procedure at the expense of truth and equity—which is always a danger to men trained in the law. That at least is the theory, and it is broadly true where society is not sharply divided into classes or where the jury can be drawn at random in such a way as to provide a fair sample of the whole community. But where this is not so there are corresponding dangers.

It was not so in Rhodesia, where there were two societies; with what degree of justice the jury system worked here is a question of opinion. Statistics—even if easily available, which for this period they are not—can provide only a limited kind of information; the full impact on flesh and blood is hardly to be known even by those who have sat through the whole of a trial, and since there is often room for the most widely varying opinions on even a single trial, how can generalizations be possible? What is proposed in this chapter is to recount the changes made in the jury system in this period, describing in outline certain cases which seem to have been partly responsible for changes in opinion and in the law. The cases are not 'typical' or representative; if they were not unusual they would not have caused a stir. The emphasis is intended to fall rather on public reaction to the cases than on the cases themselves, but the cases themselves insist on being re-counted because of the light they throw on assumptions and habits which are taken for granted in Rhodesia and would be surprising elsewhere.

And since this is a matter of opinion and no one is free from bias, it is as well to state the writer's own bias. I have spent some years as a magistrate in India, sitting daily; the service to which I belonged was responsible for peace and good order as well as for trying cases and we were generally supposed (except by the police) to look with too favourable eyes on the prosecution; I admit to a personal sympathy for swift justice dealt out under a tree, provided always that it *is* just, to an impatience of results known to be contrary to the facts but necessitated by technicalities or procedure. But I believe that justice depends on exact procedure in some respects, notably in connexion with identification. I am concerned that justice should be seen to be done and am more interested in the results of a system of justice on human beings than in exact conformity with law. I do not expect an illiterate witness—or any witness who looks on the court as alien—to tell the truth without exaggeration or even without an element of pure fiction; I do not expect doctors or senior policemen to en-danger their professional prospects by lying without cause; in any case in which many of the witnesses are ill-educated or feel the system of law to be strange and hostile, I expect the most telling points for the prosecution to lie in the admissions of the defence and in material evidence.

Until 1899, Rhodesian trials were heard by a judge sitting with three assessors. Of this system, the Attorney-General, Mr. Clarkson Tredgold, said in 1912 that it provided 'absolutely the best Court he had ever practised before . . . expeditious and sound and justice was rapidly and fairly meted out'.[1] But, said the voters of Rhodesia, 'we have always been accustomed to trial by jury' and so trial by jury it had to be, for everyone, black or white. But the jurymen were drawn from the list of voters and so the jury was white. This was in criminal cases; civil disputes between Africans were tried by Native Commissioners and are for the moment not to be considered. In a criminal case which was serious enough to go before the judge and jury, as in a civil dispute between European and African, the same legal machinery applied to both races.

There was occasional bewilderment on either side. The rigidity of procedure was sometimes baffling to the African; one case is reported, an extreme example of something not infrequent, when a supposed witch had been murdered on the bank of a river by two Africans. They were observed to go through the ritual purification proper after taking life; someone had disappeared; there was talk, a police enquiry, an accomplice confessed, they confessed themselves. But there was no corpse; apart from surmise, there was nothing against them but their own admission, the evidence of an accomplice, and the purification ceremony. In accordance with a very clear direction from the judge, the jury found them not guilty; they were told they were lucky and left the court 'with an expression of jubilation'.[2]

This was bewildering to Africans. To the jury, and often to the judge and counsel, it was native custom that was puzzling. There is for example a long account by Mr. A. Drew, in one of his articles on Native Affairs in 1920, of a case he had studied in detail in which six men were convicted and executed; he believed that no murder had in fact taken place, that the court had been misled by evidence of a native custom that was incorrect in the first place and irrelevant in the second, and that the accused would not have been convicted if they had been properly defended from the start. Mr. Drew may have been mistaken about this case, though his arguments sound sensible, but there was really no dispute about his main point, that courts were often, as he says, 'fogged' by native custom. The Native Affairs Committee, speakers in Council, and letters to the newspapers are in general agreement on this point by 1911. But it did not excite much attention among voters and it was not till 1927 that a change was made. Today Africans accused are tried by a judge with experienced Native Commissioners as assessors; even now, questions put by the assessors are (I have been told by counsel) often baffling to judge and counsel, though they may prove vital to the case.

In spite of these perplexities, the jury system was not itself put on trial until 1908. In that year, two cases occurred which involved Africans and Europeans and which caused much feeling. The first was the trial in May of William Hopkirk Laidlaw, who was indicted for the murder of one Neti. There are a few facts not in dispute. Laidlaw was a farmer and one afternoon was at work with his men (or, in Rhodesian terms, boys) when he saw the deceased Neti 'on the road' and called him to show his pass. He was unwilling to come; the 'boys' were sent to fetch him; the pass proved to have been altered. Laidlaw decided that Neti was a deserter from a neighbouring farm, to which he sent a note; meanwhile he tied him to a tree and left him for the night. In the morning he was dead.

Prosecution and defence were agreed on these points. When the police arrived, they were told, both by Laidlaw and his boys, that the deceased had had a wound on the back of the neck when he arrived, that he tried to escape, was recaptured and resisted being tied up, was dragged to the tree and his buttocks injured in the process; he was tethered to the tree rather than tied, so that he could sit up or lie down—though how this was possible without his being able to untie himself is not clear. The police investigator did not believe this story and said so. Later in the day, the 'boys' deserted from Laidlaw's farm and came to the police; they now said that Laidlaw had thrashed Neti on the bare buttocks and struck him across the stomach, kicked him three times on the back of the neck with heavy boots, and tied him to the tree in a standing position with his arms stretched out. This became the prosecution case.

The case was made confusing by various minor discrepancies in the evidence, which at this distance of time appear quite irrelevant in that neither party seem to have any rational motive for lying about them. But even if these were set aside as unimportant, there remained an excuse for perplexity in the evidence as to wounds on the body, which ought to have been conclusive. Sub-Inspector Myburgh, who investigated the case, said the injuries looked to him as though caused in the way described by the 'boys'; the doctor said that the wounds on the buttocks were circular, not as though due to thrashing, and might have been caused by dragging, with the trousers on; the wound on the neck was older and might have been caused by a fall; death was due to failure of the heart, with injury to the head as secondary cause; if the deceased had been tied with arms outstretched as described, all chance of recovery would have been removed. The trousers, which might have provided important and even conclusive evidence, are not mentioned in the reports.

The doctor changed his opinion as to the cause of death between writing his post-mortem report and giving his evidence and he did not see marks which Myburgh did see; it is hard to resist the conclusion that he stretched his evidence in favour of the accused. In his summing up, the judge told the jury that this was the most serious case ever to come before a Salisbury jury, the only apparent motive being callous disregard of human suffering. If correctly reported, he can have left them in little doubt that he believed Laidlaw guilty, but not necessarily of murder. If he had not meant to cause death, the verdict should, the judge explained, be one of culpable homicide. The jury, no doubt confused by the medical evidence, could not agree; the accused was tried again, this time at Bulawayo, found guilty of assault only, and sentenced to six months' imprisonment. The impression the whole case leaves is that both the judge and the police endeavoured to secure justice irrespective of any considerations of race or class; that the doctor did all he could to help the accused, that both juries may have been genuinely puzzled by the conflict of evidence and therefore anxious to give the benefit of the doubt; finally that Laidlaw was very lucky.

There are aspects incidental to the case. The native seen on the road and summoned from a distance to explain himself; the assumption that he is a 'deserter' and should be detained—all this is revealing though not of much importance judicially. Any white employer can take the law into his hands and arrest an African he sees wandering about on his own affairs. From the point of view of justice the importance of the case lay in the effect it produced on the views of the judge (Watermeyer) and the Attorney-General. But the case did not attract so much public interest as a case that followed, tried in November 1911, which confirmed and amplified an uneasy feeling that Laidlaw had not had justice. This, the Battlefields case, was a very different matter because there really could be only one honest opinion as to the facts, hardly any of which were in dispute.

A visitor at the Battlefields Mine reported that some money had been stolen; the manager said he would find out who had done it. There had been other thefts in the district and, he said, an attempt at rape; he was determined to get to the bottom of the thefts. Three 'boys' in the compound were suspected; they would not confess so were tied up and flogged till they fainted. They were tied up for the night and were flogged again, making in all three successive days; two of them, Mangesi and Sixpence, died, one of them on the day after the third flogging. The immediate cause of death was pneumonia in one case, pleurisy and pneumonia in the other; exposure and chill following severe shock were said in the medical evidence to be likely to cause pneumonia. The accused—Macaulay, Fraser, Murray, and McBryde—were charged with culpable homicide, not murder, as it was not alleged that they had intended to cause death—though they might well have been expected to know that death was likely to result. Their plea that they were all under the influence of one Mac-Arthur can hardly be taken seriously; still less another plea that the three natives had flogged each other. No verbatim report of the summing-up is in existence, and *The Rhodesia Herald*'s report must obviously contain gaps; in this report, the judge leaves it open to the jury to decide whether the accused were so much under MacArthur's influence as not to be responsible for their actions but he must surely be assumed to have told them something of the law. Even orders given to a person under military discipline do not constitute a defence for an act in itself illegal. He did, even in the report, make it clear that 'provocation' applies only to an act done 'in hot blood', and with ironic understatement he left it to them to decide whether such unbearable provocation could be supposed to last three days. The only plea the accused can really have had any belief in was that, since there were no police in the area, it was their duty to keep order. But they could hardly have pleaded that as self-appointed police they were entitled to use torture to extract confessions. It took the jury only ten minutes to reach a verdict of not guilty on all counts.

This verdict was editorially condemned by *The Rhodesia Herald* and by a number of letters to the editor. The principle that an individual might take the law into his own hands was wrong; the confidence of Africans in the Government was undermined; 'a few cases like this will effectually destroy any lingering respect in the mind of the native for the justice of the white man', wrote one. 'No proper control will be maintained by the dominant race if such injustice is condoned by the white community', said another. One letter on the other side—which was answered by *The Herald* in a disapproving leader—argued that the Government was to blame for law-breaking, that the Government forced every man to be his own policeman, and that a jury was right to exercise its discretion; this letter has a grim interest of its own because it is signed 'Sam Lewis, Bulawayo', and it was a case against a Sam Lewis of Bulawayo that three years later made some Rhodesians change their minds about the jury system.★ Apart from this contribution, the general tone of letters was strongly disapproving of the verdict.

It may all the same be surmised that nearly all Rhodesians would feel some sympathy with a farmer who would punish a

★ There is a Sam Lewis well known in Rhodesia today, whose signboard may often be seen by a plantation of blue gums that are being cut. He is not the man whose trial is here referred to.

'boy' himself on the spot rather than go through all the formalities of the law, wearisome to both parties in any case, and doubly so when the court was 100 miles away. But the articulate part of society felt overwhelmingly that the behaviour of the Battle-fields accused was a betrayal of paternalism, that the verdict was worse, a betrayal of all that was best in their scheme of life. They had after all come to bring British justice instead of the tyranny of Lobengula. The community felt as an individual feels when he is rightly charged with an act that he suddenly perceives to be shameful by his own standards. They became aware of base instincts in the community which they had thought decently buried. But even after the Battlefields case only the most detached were prepared to go a stage further, repent publicly, and abandon the jury system altogether. It is against this background that the official sequence of events is to be seen. After the Laidlaw case, the Administrator reported to the High Commissioner that the Judges, the Attorney-General, and a Conference of Superintend-ents of Natives agreed that the jury system had failed generally throughout South Africa. The Judges, however, but not the Attorney-General and the Superintendents of Natives, thought the system should be given another chance. An ordinance was put before the Council; introducing it, the Attorney-General dwelt first on the practical inconveniences of the jury system in a country where there were so few voters; except in Bulawayo, it was seldom possible to get through the year without making someone serve on a jury more than once, and since jurors might have to be brought forty miles, it became a serious hardship. Further, he went on, there had been cases lately in which 'verdicts had been based on nothing but racial prejudice'; he 'did not predict rebellion but they must expect some sort of retaliation'. He was himself in favour of a return to the old system—a judge with assessors—but failing that must ask for a jury which might convict by a majority of seven to two.

The Attorney-General's pleading was perhaps too vehement. Everyone agreed with him about the inconvenience and if he had been a shade less honest, a shade more of a tactician, had stressed the inconvenience and touched on the failure of justice almost as incidental, he might perhaps have got his way; but, as it was, there was a rally to the defence of Rhodesian juries. 'The average of intelligence and honesty of juries in Rhodesia was as high as in any part of South Africa', said Mr. Coghlan, and the point was generally taken up by other unofficial members. There was too much government by officials in any case; the jury system had stood the test of ages. There was an inherent right in all British countries of being tried by jury; in hundreds of cases juries had behaved properly and it was making a mountain out of a molehill to change the system because of one or two cases of injustice—and so on. One obstinate man at present could spoil a whole case; if a majority verdict was made possible, there would be no more such miscarriages. The Government accepted this view and a majority verdict became legal, though the Attorney-General continued to regard this solution as a second-best and referred to the fact that he had never yet succeeded in convicting a white man for causing death by negligence as a result of shortcomings under the Mining Law.

This debate was in the summer of 1908 and before the Battle-fields case.[3] After the Battlefields case, Lord Selborne, the High Commissioner at Cape Town, wrote: 'These two miscarriages of justice* are a stain on the British name; they also constitute a public danger. Not only is it a matter of national honour that justice should be administered fairly between man and man of every colour throughout the British dominions but I am profoundly convinced that it is only possible for a mere handful of my fellow countrymen to fulfil their task of governing vast bodies of natives if they rule them with scrupulous justice as well as with absolute firmness.' So far Rhodesians were with him, but they were still not prepared to say, on the basis of two cases, that trial by jury had failed; the suggestion was, they felt, a slur on Rhodesia and put them at once on the defensive. Conservatism was an element in their resistance; the jury was something known and tried. Stronger perhaps was the feeling that change was a

* Laidlaw and Battlefields.

blow to prestige; progress was towards British institutions in their entirety. To go back to assessors was retrograde, a return to the nursery. Deeper, and probably unconscious, was uneasiness at a first breach in the idea that Rhodesia was to be in every respect a little England across the seas, at a first indication that she might develop into something quite unfamiliar.

A Committee of Council was appointed to enquire and report, and the whole question was debated again. The Attorney-General was still far from satisfied that justice was likely to be done, but it was the general view that the present jury system—under which a jury could find a verdict by majority vote—'had been in force for so short a period that a miscarriage of justice in an isolated instance could not be regarded as having proved it wanting'. One outspoken speech, by Mr. Brown, representing the Western Division, expressed a view that was certainly strong in the country. It was not long, he said, since Lobengula had gouged out the eyes of his subjects for the most trivial offence and only ten years since natives were dashing out the brains of babies. It was a marvel there had been so few miscarriages of justice; Laidlaw, he believed, was innocent, but the Battlefields case could only be regarded as a disgrace. But that did not justify intervention from outside; 'people at Home were not competent to give a fair judgement between black and white'. And anyhow, the native was not concerned with justice; he preferred the old system of robbery and murder.

So trial by jury continued for another three years. On 19 December 1911, it was Sir Charles Coghlan, the leader of the elected members, who moved that 'the present system of trial by jury has proved unsuited to cases where Europeans are charged with the commission of serious crimes against natives'. He had changed his mind since three years ago; 'a certain class of case imposed too great a strain upon jurymen' and it was better they should be relieved of responsibility. He was thinking of cases where crimes of violence had been committed by white men upon natives in consequence of grave crimes of violence committed by natives upon white women, 'a class of case which happened in this country to be bound up quite incidentally with the colour question'.

Here was the voice of the upper-class Rhodesian, who perceives that antagonism between races in Rhodesia repeats some features of antagonism between classes in England; that however is for the moment a digression. The elected members supported the motion, with the exception of Colonel Grey who ranged himself rather doubtfully on the other side. It is worth repeating a passage from the speech of Mr. Eyles: 'No person who studied in a sympathetic and broad spirit the conditions of South Africa could blind himself to the fact that race prejudice did exist. The existence of race prejudice must have the effect that, whenever a case of that description came for trial . . . they took it that the feeling of the white race had been injured . . . an injury had been done to the race and they put a native upon his trial, before a jury of white men, who in a secondary sense . . . were injured parties.'

Thus the decision of three years earlier was reversed; the jury system must be modified. This must surely have been due largely to the case of Sam Lewis at Bulawayo, who was tried for murder earlier in the same year. Here too the facts are not in dispute. The deceased, Titus, was a newspaper delivery boy (a phrase which need not mean that he was juvenile), who had for some time been making indecent advances to May Lewis, the daughter of the accused, a girl of fifteen. He made suggestions on several occasions; he offered her money; he exposed himself; he had not attacked her but the suggestions had been going on for about three months. May had told her mother, who at first kept it from her husband because she did not want a court case in which her daughter would have to give evidence. But at last, hearing her father speak of some similar case in the Union, the girl told him how the newspaper boy had behaved. Lewis went that afternoon to the office of *The Bulawayo Chronicle*, where the delivery boys were lined up for identification. But Titus was not there, nor was he there next morning, when the parade was repeated. Later that day, however, May saw him and pointed him out to her father, who took him by the collar, led him behind a building, put a revolver to his ear and shot him, took his daughter home and then started for the police-station in a cab to give himself up. The pleading at the trial was that in defence of the chastity of his daughter the accused was driven beyond human endurance.

It appears, from the newspaper report of the summing-up, which may easily be inadequate, that the judge felt the case was so clear that he need merely indicate the law; provocation, he said, might unhinge a man's mind to such an extent that he could not be held responsible for what he did. Were the circumstances such in this case? The jury could not decide, even by a majority of seven to two; the accused was tried again, evidence being led this time to show that he did not ordinarily carry a revolver but had apparently been carrying one for two days in case he met the deceased. And this time the judge seems to have given a much more direct exposition of the law. The right of self-defence arose only when there was *immediate* need to preserve life, liberty, person or honour; 'the only thing that could excuse the accused was his ignorance that he was doing a wrongful act'. In the face of this direction, the jury took only ten minutes to return a verdict of 'Not Guilty'.

In the public reaction to this case, there are distinctions to be made. Everyone felt sympathy for Lewis's anger, many for his impatience of the law's delays, some for his suspicion that the law would not punish severely enough, fewer for his action. This case took place in Bulawayo and the argument that the police were far away did not apply; nor can it be argued that the course Lewis took saved his daughter any publicity. Suspicion that the law might be too mild is the only rational motive for Lewis's obviously deliberate action; this suspicion—and perhaps also and to a lesser extent some irrational motives such as repressed hatred and fear of Africans in general—was shared by many, some of whom found Lewis's bail and organized a fund for his defence. Until the verdict, sympathy with Lewis was the note struck most often in the comment; the verdict, however, produced general condemnation. The South African papers joined in the chorus; the case was a blot on the name of British justice (said *The Rand*

Daily Mail) and *The Pretoria News*, with a hint of smugness, added that 'the privilege of trial by jury should be removed in Rhodesia'. *The Rhodesia Herald* repudiated absolutely the idea that 'every white man has the right to be judge, jury, and executioner' in his own case. The *Chronicle* made the same point, but destroyed the force of its arguments by wondering whether every father would not have done the same as Lewis.

Two other notes were sounded which deserve to be put side by side and need no comment. One anonymous correspondent of the *Chronicle*, arguing for every man's right to be his own executioner, asserted that the natives respected Lewis for what he had done. A labour agent a few days later reported that in a recruiting speech he had said that the law gave the same protection to blacks as to whites. 'You have not told the truth', said one of his audience. 'There was no law for Sam Lewis of Rhodesia.'

This trial, surely, was the main reason for Sir Charles Coghlan's change of view; he and most Rhodesians who thought with any detachment felt that there must be no more cases like this. To many Rhodesians it had perhaps come as a shock to perceive the inconsistency between that twinge of sympathy for Sam Lewis which they had felt for a moment and their disgust at a verdict so plainly perverse. But there remained a feeling that it was a backward step, derogatory to Rhodesia, to entrust the right of decision to a judge, sitting with assessors who expressed an opinion but had no voice in the finding of the court. 'It was weak to go back,' said Sir Charles. Doubtfully and rather against his judgement, the Attorney-General put forward an alternative proposal for a 'special jury', of five persons specially selected, in cases where Africans and Europeans were involved. It was not a very happy solution; from the African point of view, the Court was still white; from the European, the idea of a jury 'specially selected' was unattractive; it sounded very like a 'packed jury'.

There has been no case since that I have heard of which has aroused so much attention and in which the verdict has been so startling as in that of Lewis. It does not follow that this is because of the special juries. Opinion changes and is much less tolerant than it was forty years ago of a man taking the law into his own hands; in a trial reminiscent of the Laidlaw and Battlefields cases, which took place while I was in Rhodesia in 1955, the verdict was irreproachable but the lightness of the sentence was almost universally criticized; it may be argued that even ordinary juries would not again have sunk to such depths as in 1911. I have been told by members of the legal profession that they have not found the special juries to differ in any marked degree from ordinary juries in respect of impartiality.

Here, in this matter of the jury system, lies exposed the corporate conscience of Rhodesia at work. Here is an intention to be fair and provide British justice, something infinitely superior to Lobengula's; there are, however, regrettable lapses because, as Mr. Eyles had said, in certain cases the whole white community felt itself attacked and injured and it was hard for members of a jury to be impartial in a case to which they were themselves virtually a party. There is warfare between two contradictory sets of values—on the one hand, justice as between man and man, fair play and a fair trial, ideals felt with pride to be part of the English heritage; on the other, the purity and prestige of the dominant race and the preservation of its dominance. It is a fluctuating warfare, in which a battle is won now by ideals of justice, now by the stark impulse of self-preservation. But opinion has shown itself ready to change and ready to be outraged by a gross injustice.

This is interpretation, comment on the facts set out; one can form no more than an impression, and it is based on imperfect records.[4] Nor, it need hardly be said, has every case been studied, even in the imperfect state in which it is preserved. But in the course of considering the jury system and the operation of the courts, a number of cases have been read and the cases have been supplemented by conversations with members of the bench and of the bar; impressions have inevitably been formed.

First, Rhodesia has on the whole been fortunate in her judges, of whom little more need be said than that they have maintained the standards of their profession. Sentences of imprisonment were usually more severe in the case of Africans than Europeans, but not more so than would be justifiable on the theory, by no means confined to Rhodesia, that prison is a more serious punishment for a rich man than a poor; on the other hand, for trifling offences the complementary maxim, that a fine is less of a punishment for a rich man, was not always borne in mind by magistrates. Next Rhodesia has been fortunate in her police. Allegations against them one does, of course, hear, but seldom supported with chapter and verse, and often in forms highly improbable; there are allegations against the police in every country in the world, but the British South Africa Police seem on the whole to have been much more like the English constabulary than like, say, the Indian or the American. There was competition for vacancies; troopers were often men of good family and education or non-commissioned officers from the Army or Navy with good records. There is good evidence that in rural areas, and even recently, African peasants would come to a British South Africa trooper on patrol for advice and ask him to settle a dispute with no police or criminal element in it; in the towns, the relationship was bound to be more rigid and less personal.

And from the start justice has been thought of in formal terms, as a matter in which an organized administration would play its part, in which 'the law' could be ascertained and applied. There have been lapses, as when a man was lassoed in the dock and only saved by the energy of the British South Africa Police from instant lynching; there have been dissident voices, proclaiming the doctrine of the white man's right to be his own executioner; there have occasionally been juries which appear to have accepted that doctrine. But such lapses have been unhesitatingly condemned by *The Rhodesia Herald*; condemned with an occasional afterthought by *The Bulawayo Chronicle*; condemned, but with condonation and indeed commendation for paternal punishment that falls short of manslaughter, by *The Livingstone Mail*. The rule of law has been asserted without question in Salisbury, with more hesitation nearer the frontier of an Africa almost exclusively black.

But there is a marked contrast with the frontier states of

America, where settlement seems to have pushed into the prairie ahead of either administration or justice, where in vast areas the only representative of the law might be an amateur sheriff whose standards of justice were sometimes behind those of the people he represented. In Rhodesia, there was not only never a lynching but there were no mail robberies, no bush-rangers, no professed killers, bad men, outlaws, as in the pioneer days of Australia as well as the Middle West. The pioneers of Mashonaland moved in as a disciplined force, and that was perhaps part of the reason why though rough and vigorous they were a law-abiding people. But it was not the sole or even the main reason; in the four provinces of South Africa too, there was a respect for the law. Among Afrikaners, this was due perhaps in part to reverence for the written word of the Bible, a reverence extended to the idea of 'law' in the abstract, perhaps in part to the patriarchal organization of their treks into the wilderness and the habit of discipline enforced by encounter with Bantu tribes. And surely the lesson cannot have been missed that it was the disciplined tribes that were formidable. Among the British there were always many men with experience of service discipline. All this, however, is speculation of a kind on which only a fool would be positive.

Rhodesia then, whatever the reason, was concerned that justice should be done to an extent that hardly occurred to the pioneers of Australia and America. That is not to say that procedure was not rough, and particularly (it seems to an observer from outside) in the matter of identification. One dubious identification has already been mentioned in Rex v. Sinanga,* the Umtali case in which the accused eventually obtained his liberty by the alleged intervention of a baboon. Another case is as surprising; in this too the accused was charged with attempted rape, but the offence, one suspects, would have been entered as simple assault in a country where there were no legal distinctions between classes of citizens. The complainant went out for a walk between four and five in the afternoon; she passed a native as she walked; a

* See above, Part III, Chapter II, pp. 248 ff.

little later she was attacked, she believed by the same native; she struggled with him 'for twenty minutes' and eventually gave him a blow in the face, at which he ran away bleeding profusely from the nose. She later identified a man, changed her mind, identified another, changed her mind again, picked the accused (Dumba alias Sixpence) from a parade of nine. This was shaky enough; in most courts, identification would be vitiated by the two previous mistakes. But to add to the uncertainty, Dumba's employer, whose word as a white man was unimpeachable, said that at five o'clock Dumba was milking peacefully and showed no signs of bleeding or anything else unusual. Dumba was found guilty by a majority of seven to two and sentenced to six years' hard labour and twenty-five lashes.[5] Did he get the benefit of any reasonable doubt? As Laidlaw did?

The Rhodesians wished to do justice. But in their approach to justice they were necessarily governed by their basic assumptions, high among which came a fixed mental picture of 'the African' as lustful and violent, only to be kept in place with a stern hand. And to that picture went an unspoken, unformulated, perhaps unconscious, feeling that when a native has committed a crime, a native ought to be punished; one should try of course to punish the right man, but if by any chance it should be the wrong man, well, punishment would still serve to discourage the others. Perhaps no one would have put that feeling into words; perhaps it did not exist; if not, it must at least have seemed as though it existed to Dumba and his friends.[6]

The Dilemma in Being

The conqueror faces a dilemma as soon as the last battle is won. He cannot for ever maintain the high mood of the paean and the feast; he will wake, with victory sour in the mouth, to a colder light in which he must make peace. And if he is a realist, the kind of peace open to him is never wholly to his liking. This is true of any conqueror; the dilemma is the more poignant if the victor proposes to live in the country of the vanquished.

There are two kinds of peace open to him. Of this he is seldom aware; he does not, as a rule, sit down to think them over, deliberately choose one and reject the other; indeed, historical decisions are taken in that way far less often than most historians appear to suppose. No, to the conqueror, as a rule, one kind of peace alone presents itself as possible; he endeavours to impose it; gradually it is borne in upon him that the nature of the peace is changing, that it is turning into the other kind of peace; he may on reflection welcome the change, he may accept it with resignation, he may resist it, but it will come, and he will in the end find himself living side by side with the vanquished on new terms, that will largely depend on his attitude to this change.

Rhodesia was the geographical meeting-place of two peoples who had been separated by immense distances in culture and achievement, by immense possibilities of misunderstanding; one conquered the other and was faced with the problem of what kind of peace they wanted. The conquest was not complete until after the rebellions; it took place in three stages—the march of the Pioneers in 1890, the Matabele War in 1893, the rebellions in 1896. And the peace too, was made by driblets; a beginning of an accommodation, a way of living together, was made before 1893, another after; only after the rebellions did the form of the peace begin to settle and harden into shape; it was still far from rigid by 1918.

And there can be no question which kind of peace it was originally meant to be. It was to be one in which victors and vanquished should remain separate from each other and all power should be in the hands of the conquerors. It was imposed by a people who set a high value on kindliness; those on the spot were themselves professing Christians and were directed from afar by statesmen officially Christian and responsible to a public opinion which admired Christian virtues and found them much easier to exercise at a distance than at home. It was a settlement which was intended in the end to bring both enlightenment and material progress to the vanquished. But it was not such a settlement as was made with the French Canadians, nor again with the Afrikaners in 1910, both deliberately designed to enable two peoples to live together in unity and equality; it was not such a settlement as Sebituane and his Makololo had made with the Barotse;[1] nor such as Warren Hastings had dreamed of in India, by which the influence and teaching of the military victors would have pervaded a nexus of self-governing states; nor such as Lugard made with the Emirs in Nigeria. It could not be expected to be like any of these, because historical circumstances are never exactly repeated; indeed, a settlement envisaging a future of equality would not at the time have seemed possible, could hardly have occurred even as a flight of fancy to the most imaginative.

Yet very soon a trend displayed itself to which such an outcome was the logical development. It was not possible to think in terms of equality, but as soon as Wilson Fox set himself to the consideration of broad problems of development and policy, he saw at once that the aims must be unity and integration rather than separation and permanent domination. 'The native population of Rhodesia', he wrote 'under good government will certainly increase. It must be dealt with as a permanent element of the body politic and neither its existence nor its welfare can be ignored in any schemes for future development. It would be both wrong and short-sighted to ignore them and the real problem for the statesman is to make the native play his part in that development under conditions that will best conduce to his welfare and advancement. . . .'

Thus the official Doctrine was born, that the right course for Rhodesia lay along the road of assimilation. That is a word and an idea which may mask an intolerable arrogance, the assumption that one culture, one religion or one system of national standards alone is valid. But it need not be so; it is possible for a people to be assimilated into a new economic system and a new tradition in art, education, and religion, yet mould all these into shapes of their own, as is happening in the West Indies and in Brazil. Such possibilities were however still far from the minds of Wilson Fox and the Directors of the British South Africa Company in the period before 1914; to them the problem was 'how best to elevate and utilize the indigenous inhabitants' and the Doctrine at this stage confined itself to economic integration. The object should be to increase the natives' wants; 'only contact with civilization will do this and the branch of civilization most needed is commerce, in the shape of the trader, farmer and pioneer'.[2]

The Doctrine then involved taxes, meant not so much to bring in revenue as to force the native out to work, and make him meet the trader and the farmer, make him learn new wants and decide to work longer in order to satisfy them; taxes would provide not only labour but a market for goods. But the Doctrine implied much more than taxes; it meant a new kind of peace and a slightly different approach to every point of contact between the races. It involved for instance the idea that reserves of land were a temporary expedient, to last only while the native needed protection; they would gradually give way to open areas in which anyone might own land. Tribalism was a decaying force and its decay should be encouraged; chieftainship as an institution would wither away; superstition would melt; the Africans of Rhodesia would gradually become a working class, and would grow more and more like the British working class—and perhaps, though this was not stated in so many words, there would be men in Rhodesia as in Britain who would rise from the ranks of the working class to positions of wealth and power.

This was the detached upper-class form of the doctrine, which was acceptable to the directors of the Company, in which the Attorney-General, the Judges, and the Chief Native Commissioners would have concurred. It appears in a form basically the same but subtly and slightly transmuted in the report of the Native Affairs Committee, which included members responsible to electors in Southern Rhodesia; here the progress and well-being of the native is still the aim but there is also a readiness to perceive the value of native institutions and an inclination to preserve the best of them, a touch of the Museum Attitude. This is an attitude which may arise from concern for the native, but also from a concern that he shall stay as he is and not be a rival to anyone else. The Commission on Reserves preached in general the sincere milk of the Doctrine, but they showed also that it might be used to support what was contrary to its basic intention; that reserves would one day be merged in open areas could for instance become an argument for driving through the Sabi reserve a ten mile strip which would carry the railway, an act justifiable if this strip was really to be an open area, not if it was to be used for white farmers and if it meant moving Africans back into tribal reserves.

The Doctrine of assimilation was accepted, then, by the reasoning and directing party of the community, though even in their hands it might be distorted or modified, and particularly by those whose upper-class detachment was shaken by responsibility to voters with a sectional interest. It was by no means accepted by every Rhodesian. One may guess that in most conquests it has been easier to show a tolerance for the vanquished from the top; a Norman baron, secure in possession of half a county, could see that the interest of the countryside lay in Norman and Saxon working together; he could afford to dispense impartial justice. The man-at-arms who had come with him, with not much but his Normanness to show his superiority, would be the one who was reluctant to give up privilege. So even today the barrister and the doctor do not fear African competition; they are a trained aristocracy of the intellect used to sharp competition, and from any quarter; not so the manual worker who knows African muscles are no weaker than his and that his own skill can be learnt. He begins very soon to feel uneasy about the dangers of rivalry; his voice begins to be heard in the first decade of the century; he has little but his whiteness to rely on for a position much better than he would enjoy in England. He therefore stays faithful to the original idea of a settlement after conquest, of which it is the essence that dominion by one race over the other shall be maintained indefinitely. This applies not only to the artisan but to the clerk and the lower grades of civil servant. They will be the first to be displaced when there is a flow of Africans from the secondary schools; to them the policy of 'elevating the native' may be for the good of the territory as a whole but is likely to be a personal disaster.

This is the first basic dilemma that confronts every conqueror; maintain the position by force and make certain of hatred in the end, or aim from the start at an equality which involves an immediate sacrifice of power. From that first dilemma another develops. That part of the community which is in power—and likely to be more intelligent and more detached in outlook— soon perceives that the second of these choices is in the long run the lesser evil; how are they to convince their followers, to whom that second choice is likely to mean an immediate personal loss? Are they to sacrifice the support of their own people in order to win the co-operation of the vanquished? Or must they abandon the policy they believe to be morally right and from their own point of view in the highest degree prudent? If they abandon it, they do so for the sake of the least intelligent and the least ener- getic of their own community, and at the expense of the most intelligent and the most energetic of the vanquished. That is the second pair of horns.

And there is a third, as sharp as the other two if more delicate, a pair which present themselves with particular menace to conquerors nursed in the tradition of English freedom. Their history rings with the cries of men determined to be free; it has been a long struggle against despotism, against the irresponsible rule of kings, barons, and borough-mongers within, against absolute monarchy and the dictatorial empires of Spain, France, and Germany without; their songs, plays, poetry, the speeches of their great leaders—all they are taught at school tells the same tale. They come of a stock that has refused to be humbled, mainly perhaps from a fierce awareness of their own selfhood, but partly from a belief that freedom is something good in itself. They are proud of their stock and of its tradition, even though they may express its basic ideals incoherently in terms of cricket and fair play. They may spend most of their working hours in pursuit of gold but the fact of their own freedom is important to them, and among themselves they display the methods of freedom—consultation and persuasion, compromise, willing co-operation. Are they to belie all they stand for by denying freedom to others? Or must they forfeit their heritage by losing their identity among an alien and defeated people? Shall they teach freedom and provoke revolt? Or shall they suppress the lesson of their own history and themselves become as miserable and as leaden-eyed as is usually the fate of conquerors who are slaves to their own fears?

This last choice of evils has been expressed in national terms as particularly poignant for those nursed in English traditions. It should be at least as sharp for any people who profess to be Christian; the essentially Christian view on this dilemma of self-preservation was put in South Africa by Jan Hofmeyr, who applied to it the words: 'Whosoever shall seek to save his life shall lose it, and whosoever shall lose his life shall preserve it.'[3] This aspect too was present obscurely to many a Rhodesian mind, to a few clearly.

The Rhodesian appears then to be faced with no simple choice between two evils, but with a bristling entanglement, a *chevaux-de-frise* of unpleasing lines of conduct. Yet in a sense the dilemma is one and he has one broad choice to make. Few however commit themselves finally and any historian who suggested that they did would distort the truth. It is more usual to flinch from one horn and fail to drive home the second. There are those who in theory accept the doctrine of assimilation but in practice do nothing to forward it, and sometimes act on principles completely opposed; having settled a problem in accordance with one body of principles, they make up for it by dealing with the next on assumptions quite contradictory. And a shift in emphasis is taking place the whole time. Take for instance the reserves. One distortion of the doctrine has already been mentioned; on the grounds that Africans would not always need protection, some of their land was taken away and given to Europeans. And something more far-reaching was on the way. The reserves were a temporary arrangement to protect the African from the full onslaught of modern life, but it came gradually to be felt that because the African had protection from the European, the European too should be protected against the African and the whole country divided into reserves for one or the other; this did not happen till 1923 but the beginnings of the change were to be felt before the war. This was a defeat for the Doctrine; in other fields, the issue hung wavering in the balance.

Take again two contradictory attitudes towards the African by Europeans, alike only in that both are benevolent. For these the missionary and the game-warden may stand as symbols. There is no sign of the game-warden to begin with; native customs are heathen and beastly and there are only two white attitudes towards them; the missionary—a term used for the moment in a sense not narrowly religious—wants to reform them altogether, others are hostile or indifferent. But very soon the game-warden appears as a sub-species of missionary. His attitude first arises from realistic observation and the growth of a tolerant understanding. Daniel Lindley's change of attitude to *lobola* has already been quoted;[4] he came to see the practical advantages of an institution that helped to stabilize marriage. Many others saw a real deterioration in the African when he was first exposed to town life—a loss of self-respect, of balance, of accommodation to life; a loss of old moral standards and nothing to take their place. And it was a natural reaction to suggest that in future he should be shielded from the influences that had brought this about, that his original institutions should be preserved. To this might easily be added the proprietary touch Wilson Fox had noticed in the Native Affairs Department; 'these are my natives and I am an expert in natives'—once a man begins to think in such terms as these he has a vested interest in keeping things as they are. There was also a touch now and then of the romantic, anxious to preserve the virtues of the noble savage, of whom his own idea may be largely fiction.

The game-warden is benevolent. His intention is to preserve. But intentions are sometimes reinforced by allies less respectable than themselves. To an Englishman of average skill and intelligence, enjoying a position that in his own country he could have attained only if his skill and intelligence had been outstanding—a man of kindly impulse and as yet unaware of his own fear of a coming rival—to such a man it would be shocking to hear himself say: 'I mean to keep the African poor and ignorant for as long as I can because it is to my interest.' But he need feel neither surprise nor disapproval if the remark he overhears from himself is couched in the form: 'The Zulu or the Matabele as he used to be—he was at least a man. But I can't stand these educated natives.' Or perhaps: 'Well, in his proper place, I like the native. You wouldn't find a better man than my old head messenger'—or cook or sergeant—'but then he was the old-fashioned sort. . . .' The Committee on Native Affairs could note the deterioration in the morals and bearing of some Africans, yet point to real gains in other respects. In common speech, in the assumptions of many of the white farmers and miners, the gains would be forgotten and the implication of the kind of remarks just quoted would often be that the new ways had led only to deterioration, that it was certain to get worse, that the remedy was to slow up the pace of progress, provide no education but the simplest, segregate the African in his own culture and preserve it. Such an implication would mean in practice to keep him poor and ignorant, yet the words that carry the implication can be said with a feeling of benevolence and understanding.

Thus what had been born of sympathy became the servant of fear and repression It was surely a sign of grace in Daniel Lindley when he perceived that *lobola* was not the crude purchase of a woman that he had supposed; it was surely with deeper if unconscious motives of a very different kind that it came to be argued by the 1920s that 'the native has the right to develop on his own lines'. The sad thing is that it is long years after the arrival of the first European before Daniel Lindley's second stage is reached, while it would have been at the beginning that such an understanding would have been most valuable. There are more years to wait before Rider Haggard begins to write of that grand old savage Umslopogaas; even after that there are still more years to wait during which administration and debates proceed on the basis that native customs are to be changed as quickly as possible. By the time the man in the bar is saying that the native has good qualities of his own when he is in the kraals and the reserves, the African has himself begun to wish for assimilation and it should now be the intention of a wise Government to speed up the process. But it is precisely now that the value of native custom begins to be appreciated, that governments appoint anthropologists, that the theory of indirect rule is produced, that there is talk of separate development for the native on his own lines.

By the twenties, the attitude of the game-warden had become so wide-spread that it infected even so ardent a champion of the African as the Reverend Arthur Shearly Cripps, who had many times spoken and written fiercely against what he believed to be injustice.[5] Even he could now write of the policy of dividing the land and segregating the races that under it the Native tribes 'may be granted a fairer chance than ever before to bring their peculiar and unique contributions, their Racial Glory and Tribal Honour, into the Treasury of the City of God', and argue that 'every Native Area in colonized Africa should be safeguarded as an inviolable sanctuary which may shelter African tribal life and foster its self-development'. This is entirely the language of the game-warden and a long way from Livingstone's belief in progress and legitimate commerce; if such a view could be sincerely held by a man so devoted to Africans, it is little wonder that the farmers and miners could feel that to segregate in national parks all Africans not needed as labour was a policy not only convenient but humane.

This book has been an attempt to marshal certain evidence about the meeting of people in Africa and the growth of a situation which presents the victors with a dilemma as yet unresolved. We have seen tribes who before the European came had made progress in personal and family relationships, had sometimes achieved political structures of some complexity, had sometimes an advanced concept of law, but had taken few steps towards control of their physical surroundings, and no more solved the problem of how political units can live together in peace than the city states of Greece or the nations of modern Europe. To them came the Victorian English, the young light-hearted masters of the world, confident that their own achievement in every sphere of life was the best—the highest point so far reached in a process of continual improvement. In the situation that arose, once the period of conquest from 1890 to 1896 was over, there are many complex factors, and as a metaphor to help the organization of thought—like all metaphors inexact if pushed too far—one may think of those factors as arranged like a pedigree.

The sire is the official Doctrine of assimilation, the dam is the simple unofficial reaction, that conquest means rule by one race over the other indefinitely, and that such rule implies keeping the races separate in every sphere of life. On the sire's side, there is a long and complicated pedigree which need not be considered generation by generation, but the Doctrine is bred by enlightened self-interest out of the generous concern of the United Kingdom for all sufferers at a sufficient distance; among the remoter ancestors are, from England, dislike of the slave trade and forced labour, an uneasy conscience about slums and class inequalities, a general dislike of absolutism and an affection for the idea of liberty, and the Treasury's anxiety that every dependency should be financially self-supporting. A distinct strain in the breeding of enlightened self-interest is the Company's desire for dividends and the teaching of the classical economists as to the true nature of wealth; this new country, it is perceived, will be rich much more quickly if it is developed by the labour, skill, and industry of all its inhabitants, not of a few.

On the mother's side of the chart, the side of white domination, of segregation, and separation, one may trace such immediate forebears as the influence of South Africa, greed for a quick profit, a fear of rivals; more remotely, there is local pride and dislike of control from Whitehall, a conviction that this is a problem which no one else understands, that the man on the spot will be father to the native in every sense; sometimes there is an irritated certainty that people so hopeless as labourers must really be profoundly and permanently different from Europeans. Broadly speaking, the influences marshalled on the side of the sire are remote, those of the dam are local. And as the progeny grows to maturity, the characteristics inherited from the sire remain but are increasingly overlaid by the continuing influence of general environment and particularly of the mother.

From these ingredients have slowly developed a convention of behaviour between white and black, something like that which once existed in the Southern States, but with a different philosophy behind it. As in the States, a white man must be spoken to cap in hand and with some term of respect; in reply the white man will use Tom or Jack, a made-up name being as likely as the real one. There can be no behaviour that implies equality, particularly social or sexual equality. But there is no Southern philosophy behind this; in Virginia, the old Southern white families were a nation of aristocrats, looking back to the eighteenth century; they were gentlemen, who duelled, carried on feuds for generations, treasured the family lace, silver, and portraits. The lawlessness and the gentility were alike strange to the Rhodesian; his origin was from a less aristocratic age and usually from a layer nearer the middle of the parent society. He had also less need than the American to insist on differences between himself and the black man; the meeting was so recent, the differences of language, culture, and religion were so sharp and obvious, that they went without saying. There were no memories of slavery, nor had the Rhodesian been constrained by civil war to give up an institution that he prized.

On the other hand, the white Rhodesian was outnumbered in racial terms far more completely than the Southern American and it was hard to forget the rebellions. His problem ultimately was not to preserve his position as an aristocrat but to stay alive, to keep his job, to bring up his family; but of this on the conscious level he was as yet hardly aware. He faced the same clash as the Southerner between his social practice in regard to race and his avowed religious and political creed, but the pulls on him were stronger; for the Rhodesian, there was no expressly worded declaration of human rights in the constitution, while the fellow countrymen who embodied his traditional political beliefs were separated from him by many thousands of miles of land and sea; he never disliked them so heartily as the Southerner disliked the Yankee, nor need he pay so much attention to their fads. He did not shrink from making a difference in law between himself and the African which the American after Gettysburg could not do. For the moment, that is till the 1920s, he felt his position to be more secure than the Southerner could his, though he had more at stake; his antagonism to outside mentors had the less need to be overt.

A convention had grown up, but it was still far from rigid and practice was changing year by year, while express theory changed in step with practice. A conflict was in progress, within society, to a varying extent within every Rhodesian; it was basically a conflict between what reason perceived to be the best solution in the end and for the country and immediate desires for the individual which could only be met at the expense of the wider solution. The conflict was as yet—that is, until 1914—staged in Southern Rhodesia, affected from without by a limited number of factors only—English liberalism, the results of a similar conflict in South Africa, and, very faintly, the rivalries of European powers. Hardly any African from the territory had been to Europe; the speed at which thought was transferred was still leisurely. The War of 1914-18 shook the world's ideas, began a process by which 'world opinion' came to have a meaning, shadowy at first, but something quite distinct from the more limited and usually more selfish views of the Great Powers or of any combination of powers who could previously be said to have a common opinion. That new force, world opinion, was later to have an importance for Rhodesia; for the moment, one cannot feel that the Rhodesia of 1920 differed in racial matters from the Rhodesia of 1914 except by the continuation of processes then already in being. It was still a country out of the current of world events and not for four or five years would even the beginnings of that stupendous change in world affairs become apparent in Central Africa.

One aspect of the liberalism in Britain that affected Rhodesia runs back to the American Revolution; here England had failed through refusing to delegate power. After the Durham Report, she had delegated power to Canada and the result was brilliantly successful; she was set on the road of granting political independence to those of her colonies where there were people of European stock, but it had hardly occurred to anyone yet that this might involve all dependencies, and all their inhabitants. Southern Rhodesia was thought of as a white dependency that would soon be ready for self-government, which meant the delegation of power to white voters; by 1913 debate on this subject was already fierce; by 1923, the grant of virtual independence was made. Northern Rhodesia and Nyasaland on the other hand were tropical dependencies whose autonomy could safely be postponed to an indefinite future.

Indeed, so far were these two from independence in the shape of parliamentary democracy that the late twenties saw the adoption of indirect rule as a principle of policy, the deliberate building up of the chief as a local authority, a sharp swing away from the missionary towards the game-warden. If only—one is bound to feel—someone had been far-sighted enough and powerful enough to start indirect rule thirty years earlier! If that had been done, this would have been just the moment to abandon it for a more progressive policy. But in those early days, with so tiny a force at his disposal, Johnston had had no choice; he had to reduce the power of the chiefs in order to establish his own and could not at once begin to build up theirs. Order and unity were what he had to impose.

Northern Rhodesia and Nyasaland then developed from the start on lines quite different from Southern Rhodesia's. They were not—as has been said—regarded officially as white man's country but as tropical dependencies; very few Europeans came to make their homes there for life; those who came were missionaries or civil servants as often as planters or traders. The raids of the Angoni, the Bemba, and the Barotse seem seldom to have been so devastating as those of the Matabele, but the Arab slavers regarded Nyasaland as one of their best hunting-grounds and the Yao were their hunting-dogs. Remembering the pedigree sketched for Southern Rhodesia, one perceives that the strains drawn from the father's side are all present in Nyasaland, but the mother is different, though related; in her breeding—that is, the network of local influences—there are different lines and her influence is not so strong. A situation arose with a different set of ingredients; to understand what these were and how they fused together involves considering in some detail the exciting story of the first missionaries and the dilemma in which they found themselves, a dilemma distinctly different from the Rhodesian.

It is a story which must be reserved for another book. Here there is only room to outline the initial dilemma; the missionary arrives, with a gospel of peace, love, and poverty, a retinue of porters and servants from the coast, a few rifles and guns for protection and securing game. With permission of a chief, he sets up house and begins to cultivate; he builds a church and a school; a cluster of huts surrounds them. And then the Yao raid his village for slaves, or capture a woman from the village;

or fugitives from a Yao raid come to him for sanctuary; or a crime is committed in his village. And he suddenly becomes aware that he is alone in a strange land where there are no policemen; he must either acquiesce in intolerable evil or himself become the avenger of blood and the protector of the innocent. If he chooses action—as in Nyasaland he usually did—he becomes at a stroke a Nyasaland chief, one secular power among many. To maintain his position, he must assert it; he cannot stand still. The pure spiritual ministry he had dreamed of is almost lost to sight in a jungle of administration, diplomacy, trade, and armed force.

That briefly is how Nyasaland began; it is a tale that gains by being told at length and there is no room for it here. Nor would it be wise at this point to attempt any comparison between the two mixtures which resulted from the two sets of ingredients in Southern Rhodesia and Nyasaland; Northern Rhodesia may for the moment be thought of as being in its north-eastern part an overflow from Nyasaland, in its North-Western an overflow from Southern Rhodesia. That was how it began; it developed increasingly a distinguishable life of its own, but that too must be described in another book.

This book must end by turning a final regard to the African inhabitant of Southern Rhodesia. The third part of the book has been an attempt to describe some aspects of the settlement between white man and brown in this territory; it has been occupied in the main with the action, thoughts, and sayings of the Europeans, and that of necessity, first because they unquestionably held the initiative and secondly because they are so much more articulate. As to African reactions to what was happening, one can hardly dogmatize; there are no newspapers, books or debates to tell what Africans thought or felt. And in a matter of this kind, the evidence of other people as to what Africans believed must be treated with caution. There had been a rebellion which had been firmly suppressed. It had taken the Europeans of Rhodesia by surprise; that in itself is enough to prove the point that they did not know what the 'natives' were thinking. It is hardly likely that the natives would be more truthfully communicative after the rebellion than before.

It is not easy, even with the best will in the world, to communicate ideas across the barriers raised by language and by habits of thought so remote from each other as these were. All men protect themselves to some extent from the contemplation of what they dislike or fear by thrusting it firmly into a cupboard of the mind; they hide their thoughts even from themselves. Africans, whether by temperament or by long necessity, seem to have developed more highly than most men the art of banishing the disagreeable and living happily in the moment. There are fewer scowling faces in this continent than in most, yet laughter, a superficial politeness, even a genuine enjoyment of the greater part of life, do not mean content. A traveller in East, Central, and South Africa today who makes a determined attempt to meet Africans and talk to them will hear many tales of humiliation and injustice. He will be limited to those who speak English; the tales will, no doubt, be made dramatic by added touches; they will lose nothing in the telling, but he will see for himself enough of bad manners to confirm much of what he hears. These tales will usually be told with good humour and even with laughter. Should the traveller let fall a word of wonder at the patience with which such things are endured, he will be told that life must be taken as it is, that these slights have to be borne and are best borne with a laugh. This is the reaction of the educated who have consciously made up their minds to this apparently light-hearted fortitude; countless illiterates for 300 years have followed the same advice without perhaps putting it in words.

It is not only Africans who behave like this. Soldiers in constant danger of death do not as a rule talk or even think much of what may happen to them; they make themselves as comfortable as they can and joke about their discomfort. This does not mean they do not fear death nor that they like discomfort. So it had been with those Mashona who had seemed so peaceful just before the rebellion. Most of the time, no doubt, they were thinking about the next meal or the last; they were enjoying the physical flow of life as it passed over them. They thought perhaps of the presence of Europeans in general as seldom as they could and as reluctantly as the soldier thinks of death. That did not mean they would not rise when the Mlimo sent them orders. There is a level of consciousness at which men go about their work, eat their meals; laugh, dance, and drink; tell the boss they have no complaints—and mean it. There may in the same men be another level, of which they are most of the time unaware, at which there is a deep, perpetual, and bitter resentment. But at an emotional summons of a particular kind this may leap into view.

There was a rising in Nyasaland in 1915, of which more in another place. The reports from districts the previous year, the report on the colony for the year, all stress the peaceful and law-abiding character of the native of Nyasaland. No one had known, yet a bitterness was beneath the surface that would drive men to take life and face death. The truth is that white men have no monopoly of wearing two faces without conscious insincerity. If the European farmer genuinely believes in such abstract ideals as fair play, justice, the equality of all before the law and before God, yet in practice will sometimes behave as though his African dairyman was a being to whom such concepts do not apply, the dairyman too may appear contented and today may say with truth that he takes no interest in politics, yet tomorrow will vote if he gets the chance for the most extreme nationalist he can find—and with no more hesitation than his grandfather displayed when he followed the Mlimo.

And on both sides there is an inner conflict, an inner clash of interests, short-term against long, reason against emotion. For the European, reason and the long-term interests of the community—and of himself if he has capital, initiative, education, and energy—join to recommend bringing the African closer and closer into his own economy. On the other hand, emotion and immediate greed fight to prolong domination. To this the African counterpart is a more complex struggle; emotion may counsel some hasty act of insubordination, while reason and immediate interest reply that this will be disastrous. The ultimate interest is freedom—whatever that may mean—but whether that is more likely to come by co-operation or opposition is a matter which in African eyes is usually open to argument. Reason will often seem to advise first one and then the other; in the United States, Booker Washington chose the road the white man would prefer the Negro to choose, the way of gradualness and self-improvement; he was soon repudiated by the majority of American Negroes; those who followed his advice came to be known contemptuously as Uncle Toms. Some degree of compromise between the extremes of complete co-operation and active and continuous revolt is probably made by every African in South African or British colonial territory, by every American Negro in the South. For the professor, the struggle is continuous and conscious; the farm-labourer is most of the time hardly aware of it. But he does, none the less, compromise all the time; the urge to revolt may show itself in unpunctuality, in bad work, in drunkenness, not planned or willed, just happening because the whole man is not emotionally committed to his work or his way of life. But a prophet may at any moment startle to the surface all that lay below.

There are white Rhodesians today who will tell you that since the rebellions the Mashona and the Matabele have settled down into the most contented peasantry in the world. One who knows them well, and has worked for them and with them, not as an official but as an act of grace, a white South African by birth, told me that the simple folk in the Mashona reserves are today concerned only with their family affairs and with making ends meet. Looking after his cattle and his bit of land, educating his children, this takes up the life of the peasant; indeed all his energy seems to have gone into his family life and building up a happy family relationship. He is not much interested in politics and likes to have a master; now he has a white master instead of black and in many ways it is better; he would rather the British South Africa Police investigated a murder than his tribal chief; he has great faith in the police and the Native Commissioner.

That is a description sincerely believed and based on evidence sincerely given. It will bring pleasure to the eye of any white Rhodesian; 'Do these people look miserable?' he will ask. 'Have you heard them singing and seen them laughing?' Yet hardly any educated African would confirm it; his picture will be of a people struggling against handicaps at every turn, bitter because they have so little land and see European farms only partly developed, bitter because their cattle are limited in number and ruthlessly culled by the Government, bitter because they must spend so much of their money on education. That too is sincerely believed and based on statements believed sincerely by those who made them. The conflict is continuous and two faces are presented to the world; both are genuine, because hardly anyone can be bitter all the time, least of all an African. Yet there can be little doubt which of the two levels of feeling is the deeper.

To the European, this is very convenient. He can assuage the strife within himself by choosing the picture he prefers; any sign of that deeper bitterness he rejects as not in accordance with what he has been told. The educated African, he will say, is not representative; he does not know his own people, nor do they trust him. And these beliefs, too, are held sincerely.

This double strife within each individual of each community is going on today; it had already begun in the period before the First World War. The Mashona and the Matabele had learned from the rebellions that they could not rid themselves of the Europeans by force; they had learned to accommodate themselves to a world in which they must stand in a queue to get their passes, take their laughter when they could, and be content with such simple pleasures as remained. They must fit themselves into a new world, which presented to them, as it did to their masters, a dilemma, a choice between two courses of which both were distasteful. And for the moment they must take neither; they must wait. They are a people in waiting. It is with their masters that the initiative rests as yet, and for some time to come. It is on their masters' reaction to their own dilemma that the world will fix its eyes.

NOTES

Part One. Chapter I

(Place of publication is London unless otherwise stated)

1 David Livingstone: *Narrative of an Expedition to the Zambesi and its Tributaries, and of the discovery of the Lakes Shirwa and Nyassa, 1858–1864* (John Murray, 1865), p. 223.

2 David Livingstone: *Missionary Travels and Researches in South Africa* (John Murray, 1857).

3 Frederick Courteney Selous: *A Hunter's Wanderings in Africa* (1881; 4th ed., Richard Bentley, 1895).

4 Livingstone: *Missionary Travels.*

5 Livingstone: *Narrative.*

6 François Coillard: *On the Threshold of Central Africa: Twenty Years among the Barotsi.* Trans. C. W. Mackintosh (Hodder & Stoughton, 1897), p. 22.

7 Livingstone: *Missionary Travels.*

8 Coillard: *On the Threshold.*

9 Edwin W. Smith: *The Life and Times of Daniel Lindley (1801–80), Missionary to the Zulus, Pastor of the Voortrekkers, Ubebe Omhlope* (Epworth Press, 1949).

10 Livingstone: *Narrative*

11 ibid.

12 ibid.

13 ibid.

14 John Smith Moffat: *The Lives of Robert and Mary Moffat* (T. Fisher Unwin, 1885).

15 ibid.

16 Livingstone: *Missionary Travels.*

17 Livingstone: *Narrative.*

18 ibid.

19 ibid.

20 C. W. Mackintosh: *Coillard of the Zambesi: The Lives of François and Christina Coillard* (T. Fisher Unwin, 1907).

21 Coillard: *On the Threshold.*

Notes

Part One. Chapter II

1   Selous: *A Hunter's Wanderings.*

2   Smith: *Daniel Lindley.*

3   Smith: *Daniel Lindley.* This view of *lobola* is arguable and has been argued:
    that marriages among the Zulu, where Lindley worked, were as a rule
    stable seems to be generally agreed and, though *lobola* among them was
    high, it does not follow nor seem likely that the stability of the marriages
    was solely due to a high *lobola.* Surely it would be simple-minded to look
    on any one cause as responsible for so far-reaching an effect; surely it would
    be as misleading to state in general terms either that the *lobola* was high
    simply because the marriage was likely to last and therefore the husband was
    getting good value, or that the marriage was likely to last simply because
    a good price had been paid and because of the economic interests involved.
    There can really be no question of putting the cart before the horse; there
    is neither cart nor horse, no simple causal relationship involved. For a
    whole series of complicated reasons, the outlook of the Zulus on father-
    hood and the upbringing of children and the position of women tended to
    make for a stable marriage. The prospect of a stable marriage made
    possible a high *lobola*; this again was a prop to stable marriage, and Lindley
    and his Zulus were surely right in seeing *lobola* as a symbol of stable
    marriage and one of its props. See Dr. Max Gluckman: 'Kinship and
    Marriage among the Lozi of Northern Rhodesia and the Zulu of Natal',
    in A. R. Radcliffe-Brown and Daryll Forde, eds.: *African Systems of
    Kinship and Marriage* (Oxford University Press for the International
    African Institute, 3rd imp., 1956). Here Dr. Gluckman argues that stable
    marriages usually go with a strong development of the rights of the
    father.

4   See O. Mannoni: *Prospero and Caliban: The Psychology of Colonisation.*
    Trans. by Pamela Powesland (Methuen, 1956); also Elenore Smith Bowen:
    Return to Laughter (Gollancz, 1954).

5   J. A. Barnes: *Politics in a Changing Society: A Political History of the Fort
    Jameson Ngoni* (Oxford University Press for the Rhodes-Livingstone
    Institute, 1954).

6   Selous: *A Hunter's Wanderings.*

7   Livingstone: *Missionary Travels.*

8   See M. Fortes and E. E. Evans-Pritchard, eds.: *African Political Systems*
    (Oxford University Press for the International Institute of African
    Languages and Culture, 1940).

9   See J. C. Mitchell: 'The Yao of Southern Nyasaland', in Elizabeth Colson
    and Max Gluckman, eds.: *Seven Tribes of British Central Africa* (Oxford
    University Press for the Rhodes-Livingstone Institute, 1951).

10 Audrey I. Richards: 'Some Types of Family Structure amongst the
    Central Bantu' in Radcliffe-Brown and Forde: *African Systems of Kinship
    and Marriage,* and 'The Bemba of North-Eastern Rhodesia' in Colson and
    Gluckman: *Seven Tribes.*

Notes

Part One. Chapter III

1 John Smith Moffat: *Robert and Mary Moffat.*
2 See Max Gluckman: 'The Lozi of Barotseland in North-Western Rhodesia', in Colson and Gluckman: *Seven Tribes.*
3 Coillard: *On the Threshold.*
4 In the Introduction ·to Max Gluckman: *The Judicial Process among the Barotse of Northern Rhodesia* (Manchester University Press, 1955).
5 See Paul Bohannan: *Justice and Judgment among the Tiv* (International African Institute, 1957). The Tiv are a semi-Bantu people in Nigeria.
6 Coillard: *On the Threshold.* All the quotations that follow in this chapter are from this source unless otherwise marked.
7 Colin Harding: *Far Bugles* (Simpkin, Marshall, Hamilton, Kent, 1933).
8 Journal, quoted by Mackintosh: *Coillard of the Zambesi.*

Part One. Chapter IV

1 Frederick Courteney Selous: *Travel and Adventure in South-East Africa* (Rowland Ward, 1893).
2 Richards: 'The Bemba', in Colson and Gluckman: *Seven Tribes.*
3 ibid. Also in Audrey I. Richards: 'The Political System of the Bemba Tribe—North-Eastern Rhodesia' in Fortes and Evans-Pritchard: *African Political Systems.*
4 *Transvaal Argus*, 1867. Quoted in Hugh Marshall Hole: *The Making of Rhodesia* (Macmillan, 1926).
5 See Eric Axelson: *South-East Africa, 1488–1530* (Longmans, Green, 1940) and particularly Hugh Tracy's map of Fernandez' journeys.
6 Damiao de Goes: 'Chronicle of the Most Fortunate King Dom Emanuel' in G. McC. Theal: *Records of South-Eastern Africa, collected in Libraries and Archive Departments in Europe* (Government of the Cape Colony, 1898–1909), vol. iii, p. 129.
7 Joao de Barros: 'Da Asia', in Theal: *Records*, vol. vi, p. 257.
8 Mtasa of the Manica, Makoni of the Wa-ungwe: see the Decade of A. Bocarro, in Theal: *Records*, vol. iii, pp. 354-6, and F. W. T. Posselt: *Fact and Fiction: A Short Account of the Natives of Southern Rhodesia* (Bulawayo, Rhodesia Printing & Publishing Co., 1935).
9 Francisco de Souza: 1710.
10 This word used in this sense is the property of J. A. Barnes: *Politics in a Changing Society.*

Notes

11 C. Bullock: *The Mashona: The Indigenous Natives of Southern Rhodesia* (Cape Town, Juta, 1927).

12 J. D. Krige and E. J. Krige: 'The Lovedu of the Transvaal', in Daryll Forde, ed.: *African Worlds: Studies in the Cosmological Ideas and Social Values of African Peoples* (London, Oxford University Press for the International African Institute, 1954).

13 See Posselt: *Fact and Fiction*, and Bullock: *The Mashona*.

14 Bullock: *The Mashona*.

15 Selous: *Travel and Adventure*, p. 339.

16 Theal: *Records*, vol. iii, pp. 489-90.

17 All these quotations are culled from a rich store in A. L. Rowse: *Expansion of Elizabethan England* (vol. 2 of *Elizabethan Age*, Macmillan, 1955).

18 In all this chapter I have helped myself liberally from Gertrude Caton-Thompson: *The Zimbabwe Culture: Ruins and Reactions* (Oxford University Press, 1931), which supersedes everything before it; I am grateful to Miss Caton-Thompson for the information regarding the dating of beads and the piece of tambootie which has been tested by the C-14 process.

Part One. Chapter V

1 Max Gluckman: 'The Kingdom of the Zulu of South Africa' in Fortes and Evans-Pritchard: *African Political Systems*.

2 Audrey I. Richards: 'The Political System of the Bemba Tribe', in Fortes and Evans-Pritchard: *African Political Systems*.

3 Bullock: *The Mashona*.

4 Gluckman: 'The Lozi of Barotseland' in Colson and Gluckman: *Seven Tribes*.

5 Krige: 'The Lovedu', in Forde: *African Worlds*.

6 Gluckman: 'The Lozi of Barotseland', in Colson and Gluckman: *Seven Tribes*.

7 Gluckman: 'The Kingdom of the Zulu', in Fortes and Evans-Pritchard: *African Political Systems*.

8 Richards: 'The Bemba', in Fortes and Evans-Pritchard: *African Political Systems*.

9 J. F. Hollemann: 'Some "Shona" Tribes of Southern Rhodesia', in Colson and Gluckman: *Seven Tribes*.

10 Bullock; Hollemann: verbal information to the writer. See also Krige and Krige on the Lovedu, who may be the best clue to what happened in the time of the Monomotapa.

11 Livingstone: *Narrative*.

Notes

12 E. Colson: 'The Plateau Tonga of Northern Rhodesia' in Colson and Gluckman: *Seven Tribes.*

13 See Harding: *Far Bugles.*

14 E. E. Evans-Pritchard: *Witchcraft, Oracles, and Magic among the Azande* (Oxford University Press, 1937).

15 Godfrey Wilson: 'The Nyakyusa of South-Western Tanganyika', in Colson and Gluckman: *Seven Tribes.*

16 Arnold J. Toynbee: *A Study of History* (Oxford University Press for The Royal Institute of International Affairs, 1934-54).

17 See J. F. Ritchie: *The African as Suckling and as Adult (a psychological study)* (Livingstone, Rhodes-Livingstone Institute, 1943); also J. C. Carothers: *The African Mind in Health and Disease: A Study in Ethnopsychiatry* (Geneva, World Health Organization, 1953).

18 Verbal information: diagnosis by Dr. Gelfand of Salisbury from clinical evidence in Livingstone's writings.

19 J. J. Maquet: 'The Kingdom of Ruanda', in Forde: *African Worlds.*

20 Mary Douglas: 'The Lele of Kasai', in Forde: *African Worlds.*

21 Laura Bohannan and Paul Bohannan: *The Tiv of Central Nigeria* (International African Institute, 1953).

22 Krige: 'The Lovedu', in Forde: *African Worlds.*

23 Gunter Wagner: 'The Abaluyia of Kavirondo (Kenya)', in Forde: *African Worlds.*

24 Krige: 'The Lovedu', in Forde: *African Worlds.*

Part Two. Chapter I

1 Reported by Sir Sidney Shippard to Sir Hercules Robinson, 24639/65: March 1889. *Africa* (South), No. 369.

2 Adrian Darter: *The Pioneers of Mashonaland: Men who Made Rhodesia* (Simpkin, Marshall, Hamilton, Kent, 1914).

3 Nancy Rouillard, ed.: *Matabele Thompson: an autobiography; edited by his daughter* (Faber, 1936).

4 Shippard to High Commissioner, 18 October 1888. *Africa* (South), No. 369.

5 Lionel Décle: *Three Years in Savage Africa* (Methuen, 1898).

6 C. C. Thomas: *Thomas Morgan Thomas, Pioneer Missionary* (MS. in Central African Archives).

7 Rouillard: *Matabele Thompson*; J. Cooper-Chadwick: *Three Years with Lobengula* (1894).

8 Coillard: *On the Threshold.*

9   *Africa* (South), No. 369. This series is printed for the use of the Colonial Office and can be seen in the Colonial Office library.

10 Robert U. Moffat: *John Smith Moffat, Missionary, a memoir* (John Murray, 1921).

11 Lord Randolph Churchill: *Men, Mines, and Animals in South Africa* (Sampson, Low, Marston, 1892).

12 C. 5237 (H.M.S.O.).

13 Basil Williams: *Cecil Rhodes* (Constable, new ed., 1938).

14 ibid.

15 Eric Walker: *Lord de Villiers and his Times: South Africa, 1848-1914* (Constable, 1925).

16 See William Plomer: *Cecil Rhodes* (Peter Davies, 1933).

17 Rose Blennerhassett and Lucy Sleeman: *Adventures in Mashonaland, by two hospital nurses* (Macmillan, 1893).

18 See Selous's letter to *The Times* of 4 January 1890, with detailed evidence of this.

19 Hole: *Making of Rhodesia.*

20 *Africa* (South), No. 369.

21 *Africa* (South), No. 358: 5633, No. 5.

22 *Africa* (South), No. 358 (p. 88), 1144/81.

23 *Africa* (South), No. 369.

24 *Africa* (South), No. 369; Encl. to No. 64.

25 The Rudd Concession is printed in full in Hole: *Making of Rhodesia*, also in H. Wilson Fox: 'Memorandum on the Position, Policy, and Prospects of the B.S.A. Company' (Waterlow & Sons Ltd., 1907).

26 *Africa* (South), No. 369: 22432/42.

27 John Moffat to R. U. Moffat.

28 ibid.

29 There is a list on p. 103 of Hole: *Making of Rhodesia.*

30 Hole: *Making of Rhodesia.*

31 *Africa* (South), No. 372: 12074/95.

Part Two. Chapter II

1   Robert U. Moffat: *John Smith Moffat.*

2   *Africa* (South), No. 392: 7473/132.

3   *Africa* (South), No. 358.

4   Hole: *Making of Rhodesia.*

5 Secretary, British South Africa Company to Imperial Secretary, 5 March 1890: *Africa* (South), No. 392: 6114/99.

6 *Africa* (South), No. 392.

7 H. Wilson Fox: *Constitutional, Political, Financial, and other questions concerning Rhodesia* (B.S.A. Co., 1912).

8 Hole: *Making of Rhodesia.*

9 Ian Duncan Colvin: *Life of Jameson* (Edward Arnold, 1922).

10 Moffat to Shippard, 17 April 1889: *Africa* (South), No. 372.

11 Lobengula to Loch for the Queen, 24 June 1890: *Africa* (South), No. 392: 17128/291, End. 3.

12 Tel. from Imperial Secretary Cape Town to Secretary, British South Africa Company, 6 June 1890: *Africa* (South), No. 392, p. 240.

13 *Africa* (South), No. 403, p. 62: 1292/59.

14 *Africa* (South), No. 403, p. 204: 7986/248.

15 *Africa* (South), No. 414: 24191/1.

Part Two. Chapter III

1 Arthur Glyn Leonard: *How We Made Rhodesia* (Kegan Paul, 1896). See also W. D. Gale: *One Man's Vision: The Story of Rhodesia* (Hutchinson, 1935); Hole: *Making of Rhodesia,* etc.

2 Selous: *Travel and Adventure in South-East Africa.*

3 ibid., p. 381.

4 Leonard: *How We Made Rhodesia.*

5 *Africa* (South), No. 454: 11396/3.

6 *Africa* (South), No. 441: 86/3.

7 ibid., 9805/117.

8 ibid.

9 *Africa* (South), No. 426. The story is scattered through pp. 178-256.

10 ibid.

11 Hole: *Making of Rhodesia.*

12 Archibald Ross Colquhoun: *Matabeleland: The War and our Position in South Africa* (Simpkin, Marshall, Hamilton, Kent, 1912).

Part Two. Chapter IV

1 *Africa* (South), No. 441.

2 *Africa* (South), No. 454.

3 *Africa* (South), No. 461, p. 129.
4 C. 7555 (H.M.S.O.).
5 ibid.
6 *Africa* (South), No. 454.
7 ibid., 26 August 1893.
8 *Africa* (South), No. 454.
9 *Africa* (South), No. 459.
10 *Africa* (South), No. 454.
11 *Africa* (South), No. 495.
12 Hole: *Making of Rhodesia.*

Part Two. Chapter V

1 *Africa* (South), No. 461.
2 *Africa* (South), No. 459.
3 ibid.
4 ibid.
5 *Africa* (South), No. 461.
6 M. Gelfand: *Medicine and Magic of the Mashona* (Cape Town, Juta for the Interracial Association of Southern Rhodesia, 1956); Bullock: *The Mashona*; verbal information.
7 Barnes: *Politics in a Changing Society*, pp. 133 f.; Gluckman: 'The Kingdom of the Zulu', in Fortes and Evans-Pritchard: *African Political Systems*, p. 45; A. T. Bryant: *The Zulu People: As They Were Before the White Man Came* (Pietermaritzburg, Shuter & Shooter, 1949); J. Y. Gibson: *The Story of the Zulus* (Longmans, Green, 1911); E. A. Ritter: *Shaka Zulu: The Rise of the Zulu Empire* (Longmans, Green, 1955).
8 *Africa* (South), No. 495.
9 *Africa* (South), No. 461.
10 F. C. Selous: *Sunshine and Storm in Rhodesia* (Rowland Ward, 1896), pp. ix-x.
11 *Weekly Cape Times*, 30 June 1897.
12 *Africa* (South), No. 552. See also Olive Schreiner: *Trooper Peter Halket of Mashonaland* (T. Fisher Unwin, 1897) as evidence not of what occurred but of what was believed to have occurred; also C. F. Andrews: *John White of Mashonaland* (Hodder & Stoughton, 1935); neither constitutes direct evidence.
13 Harding: *Far Bugles.*
14 See particularly Gelfand: *Medicine and Magic of the Mashona.*

Notes

15 Selous: *Sunshine and Storm.*
16 Hole: *Making of Rhodesia*; Selous: *Sunshine and Storm.*
17 Andrews: *John White.*
18 Sarah Gertrude Millin: *Rhodes* (Chatto & Windus, 1933).
19 Harding: *Far Bugles.*
20 *Africa* (South), No. 520.

Part Three. Chapter I

1   Letter to Mr. Chamberlain, 4 October 1901: *Africa* (South), No. 694.
2   *Africa* (South), No. 559.
3   Cd. 1200 (H.M.S.O.).
4   Circular No. 18 from Chief Native Commissioner's Office, 1897.
5   Cd. 1200.
6   *Africa* (South), No. 574.
7   *Africa* (South), No. 694.
8   ibid.
9   Cd. 1200.
10 *Africa* (South), No. 656.
11 *Africa* (South), No. 694.
12 *Africa* (South), No. 659.
13 Cd. 1200.
14 *The Rhodesia Herald*, Weekly Edition of 31 January 1903.
15 *Africa* (South), No. 659.
16 *Bulawayo Chronicle*, 24 January 1908.
17 Inspector of Native Compounds Report.
18 *Daily Telegraph*, 2 March 1908.
19 *Africa* (South), No. 574: Report of Civil Commissioner, Victoria, 1899.
20 *Africa* (South), No. 656.
21 *Rhodesia Herald*, 17 August 1910.
22 Hugh Marshall Hole: *Old Rhodesian Days* (Macmillan, 1928).
23 *Rhodesia Herald*, 12 March 1909.
24 Cd. 1200.
25 Legislative Council Debates, 1899-1907, p. 193.
26 Mashonaland Farmers Association, quoted by H. Wilson Fox: *Problems of Development and Policy* (1910), p. 23.

Notes

Part Three. Chapter II

1 See I. D. MacCrone: *Race Attitudes in South Africa: Historical, Experimental, and Psychological Studies* (reprinted by Witwatersrand University Press, 1957), for one of the most revealing accounts of this development.

2 *Melina Rorke, her Amazing Experiences in the Stormy Nineties of South Africa's Story* (Harrap, 1939).

3 Gertrude McLaren in the *Livingstone Mail*, 28 April 1921.

4 *Rhodesia Herald*, 20 June 1913.

5 *Africa* (South), No. 574.

6 See also J. E. Stephenson: *Chirapula's Tale: A Bye-way in African History* (Bles, 1937), a book of a higher literary standard than most reminiscences.

7 Alfred Bertrand: *The Kingdom of the Barotsi, Upper Zambesia.* Trans. by A. B. Miall (T. Fisher Unwin, 1899).

8 Henri Rolin: *Les Lois et l'Administration de la Rhodésie* (Bruxelles, Etablissement Emil Bruylant; Paris, Augustin Challamel, 1913).

9 Criminal Law Amendment Act, 1903.

10 Legislative Council Debates, 1899-1907, pp. 114-15.

11 Hole: *Old Rhodesian Days*; Percy M. Clark: *Autobiography of an Old Drifter: The Life Story of Percy M. Clark of Victoria Falls* (Harrap, 1936).

12 *Rhodesia Herald*, Weekly Edition of 31 January 1903.

13 ibid., 4 April 1903.

14 Debates, 1899-1907, p. 57.

15 *Livingstone Mail*, 9 July 1910.

Part Three. Chapter III

1 Chad Chipunza in *The Central African Examiner*, 14 September 1957.

2 See John Barklie: *The Title Tangle in Southern Rhodesia* (Bulawayo, 1913); also Wilson Fox, Hole, and others.

3 H. Wilson Fox: *Land Settlement in Rhodesia* (Memorandum in Central African Archives).

4 See Part II, Chapter V, p. 185.

5 Paper on 'Problems of Development and Policy' (1910).

6 *Livingstone Mail*, 12 April 1918.

7 8 December 1902: Central African Archives N.1/1/4.

8 Rowse: *Expansion of Elizabethan England*.

9 See *Bulawayo Chronicle*, 8 May 1908 and 15 May 1908.

10 *Les Lois et l'Administration de la Rhodésie*, p. 242. My translation.

Notes

Part Three. Chapter IV

1 *Africa* (South), No. 559.
2 Central African Archives N.1/1/3.
3 Supplement to *Rhodesia Herald* No. 145: Government Notice 100 of 1897.
4 Central African Archives N.1/1/3.
5 Central African Archives N.1/1/12.
6 Central African Archives N.3/1/3.
7 Report of the Southern Rhodesia Native Reserves Commission, para. 36.
8 A view expressed to the Native Affairs Committee of Enquiry, 1910-11.
9 5th Council: 2nd (Extraordinary) Session.
10 Wilson Fox: *Memorandum on Constitutional, Political, Financial and other questions concerning Rhodesia, op. cit.*
11 2nd (Extraordinary) Session, Fifth Council, 1911.
12 *Rhodesia Herald,* 17 May 1912.
13 *Rhodesia Herald,* 24 December 1926.
14 A. Drew (1920): Articles on Native Affairs in *Rhodesia Herald.*
15 Hansard (51 H.C. Deb. 5 s.), 16 April 1913.
16 7 May 1914.
17 Report of Native Commissioner: Central African Archives, N./1/1/3; and in any book on the Mashona.
18 *Medicine and Magic of the Mashona.*
19 Wulf Sachs: *Black Hamlet: The Mind of an African Negro Revealed by Psychoanalysis* (Bles, 1937).
20 Committee on Native Affairs.
21 *Livingstone Mail,* 27 April 1912.
22 *African Review,* 3 November 1900.
23 *Rhodesia Herald,* 17 May 1912.

Part Three. Chapter V

1 Debate on High Court Assessors Ordinance, 3rd Session, Fifth Council, 6 May 1912.
2 *Bulawayo Chronicle,* 23 February 1912.
3 The Ordinance passed its Third Reading 2 July; the Battlefields trial was in November and related to events in July.
4 In many early cases, no record is available, in others there is the preliminary enquiry before a magistrate but no record of the trial; sometimes there is a shorthand record of the evidence but not of the summing up.

Notes

5   R. *v*. Dumba alias Sixpence; 4 June 1909.
6   There is an article by Roger Howman in *The Rhodes-Livingstone Journal*, No. 7, 1949: 'Trial by Jury in Southern Rhodesia', to which I am much indebted. His conclusions are much the same as mine, though expressed in sociological language; it is a language that is designed for the purpose of generalization and to my mind, apart from its obscurity, leads to generalizations that become over-rigid. But today he repents of the language; the thought of his article has been most helpful. I have also been helped by an advocate of the Salisbury bar who has been through a number of cases and given me his opinions, which I have not always accepted. The material used in this chapter is where possible the judicial record of the case, supplemented by press reports.

Epilogue

1   See pp. 37–8, above.
2   Alexander Davis: *The Native Problem in South Africa* (Chapman & Hall, 1903). Quoted with approval by Wilson Fox.
3   Luke, Ch. 17, v. 33.
4   See p. 29, above.
5   See his poems, many articles in newspapers, and his novel *Bay-Tree Country: A story of Mashonaland* (B. H. Blackwell, Oxford, 1913).

INDEX

Index

Index

Labour—*cont.*
274; taxes meant to encourage, 153, 226, 314; Matabele and, 190–1, 196, 204; Native police and, 193, 204; in Rhodesia, 219–37; supply and demand, 225, 231, 234, 235; farms and, 225, 265–7, 277; increased wants encourage natives to work, 227, 284, 314; manual labour to keep natives in subjection, 252–3, 264–5, 284; Magistrates and recruitment of, 271, 274; creation of working-class, 315–16; segregation of non-labourers, 321

Labour Board, S. Rhodesia, 224
Labour Bureaux, Rhodesia, 224, 226
Laidlaw, William Hopkirk, 298–9, 302–3, 304, 308, 311
Lake Bangweulu, 56
Lake Mweru, 56
Lake Ngami, 112
Lake Nyasa, 21, 41, 56, 74, 85, 214; tribes of, 26
Lake Tanganyika, 56
Land, King owner of all, 46, 76, 77, 100, 165; grants by B.S.A. Co., 143, 150, 258–9, 265, 266, 267; Matabele and, 183, 185–6, 190, 193; cause of racial strife, 238, 255, 330; quality in Rhodesia, 256, 257–8, 259–60, 262; ownership in Rhodesia, 258
Land Commission, 185–6, 188–9
Latin America, 239
Law, among Lozi, 48–9, 79, 321; justice and equity, 49; customary, 49, 77, 152, 162; distinguished from morality, 49, 292; King subject to, 77, 80; impact of alien, 79, 296–7; among Lovedu, 95; among Barotse, 98; law and order, 113, 121, 144, 152, 154, 157, 158, 161, 167–8, 325; Rhodesia and, 295–311
Lawley, Captain, 223

Laziness of Africans, 60, 65, 84, 160, 293
Lead mines, 61
Lele tribes, 93
Legal difficulties in Rhodesia, 161 fictions, 136, 141, 142, 144, 154, 157; Europeans and, 148, 154
Legislative Council, S. Rhodesia, 217–18, 264, 278, 282, 288
Lekhotla, Lozi Assembly, 51, 52
Lendy, Captain, 155–7, 158, 163, 166–8, 170
Leonard, Arthur Glyn (quoted), 147, 148
Lepanto, Battle of, 2
Lewanika, Lozi King, 26, 45, 50, 51–4, 55, 79, 89, 98, 166
Lewis, May, 305
Lewis, Sam (I), trial of, 301, 305–7
Lewis, Sam (II), timber contractor, 301
Limpopo, River, 16, 17, 27, 36, 112, 119
Lindley, David, 22, 28–9, 36, 318–19; *Life of*, 22
Lippert Concession, 123, 161
Liquor Laws, 185, 218, 247, 280
Little Englanders, 126, 171
Living conditions, of Irish, 71; of Africans, 75, 269
Livingstone, David, and conversion of natives, 17, 24; on natives' behaviour with strangers, 19, 20, 21, 22, 151; journeys of, 17, 19, 20, 21, 27, 81, 112; on men's colour, 23; inconsistent views on natives, 24, 25; quarrelsome, 25; on Africans' ideas of morality, 26, 290; on Sebituane, 36, 38; mission destroyed by Boers, 37, 111; keen on 'progress', 43, 321; on Mashona, 75; on devastation of countryside, 81, 88; praises salt, 86; Mzilikazi and, 112; mentioned, 41, 86, 215
Lobengula (Lo Bengula), Matabele King, raiding by, 27, 158, 163, 166, 172; fear of annexation, 105,

Index

Index

Raids, slave, 22, 41, 53, 79, 325
tribal, 34, 36, 41, 48, 52, 79, 81,
145, 294, 325; effect of, 81; by
Matabele on Mashona, 36, 72,
75, 79, 81, 118, 163, 172, 231,
325; by Matabele on Rhodesia,
167, 168, 171, 174; military
action compared with, 229
Railways, 111, 113, 127, 130, 259,
260, 315
Rainmaking, 62, 76, 96, 100
Rajputana, 44; Rajputs, 63, 86, 290
Ranching, 259
Rand, The, 114, 225
Rand Daily Mail, The (quoted),
306
Rape, 246-9, 310
Read, Professor Margaret, 11
Registration certificates for Africans,
287-8
Religion, 95-6, 292, 294 (*see* Christianity)
Renaissance, 2, 32
Renaud, Major, 87
Resident, Dutch, 119, 120
Resident Commissioners, 153, 218,
221, 224, 228, 230, 278
Renny-Tailyour, Mr., 123, 137
Rent, for land, 266, 267; for 'location'
housing, 268-9;
Reserves, native, 185-6, 209, 258,
259-64, 267, 268-9, 276, 279,
281, 314, 315, 318, 329; agricultural training in, 284
Rhodes, Cecil John, Lobengula and,
9, 140, 171; occupation of
Mashonaland, 112, 116-18,
122, 138, 141, 143; character,
114-16, 125; Rudd Concession
and, 122-5, 134, 136; progress
and, 125, 145, 254; Chartered
Company and, 126-9; Pioneers
and, 147; idealist, 148; Ministry
of, 153; buys Lippert Concession,
161; foresees Matabele War, 164,
169-71, 174; grave of, 181;
negotiates on future of Rhodesia,

184-5; Matabele and, 192, 193-4;
Matabele surrender to, 193,
205; *Life of*, 205; and the imperial factor, 217; estate of, 265;
and equality, 289; mentioned,
2, 149
Rhodesia, future of, 6-7, 312-30;
important for race relations,
7-8; in Federation, 19, 289;
labourers in, 34; rumours of
gold in, 57; Zulus enter, 62;
huts in, 72; Mashona, 74-5;
climate of, 84; health in, 85;
administration of, 127, 271-80;
companies in, 129; legal fictions
and, 136, 141, 142, 154, 157;
boundary of, 151; law and order
in, 152, 154, 156-8, 161; cost of
living in, 159; beginnings of,
160, 181; England and, 162, 217;
Matabele and, 163-4; sentiment
over self-sacrifice, 181; British
Government and, 184-5; witchcraft in, 195, 290-2; Matabele
Rising, 199; British Press and,
201; Africans and Europeans in,
215-55; wages in, 235-7; miscegenation in, 240-51; rape and,
246-9; lynching and, 249, 309-10; social problems, 254; justice
in, 271, 295-311; amusements
in, 273; replica of England, 304,
305; contrasted with America,
322-3; mentioned, 16 (*see* North-Eastern Rhodesia, Northern Rhodesia, Southern Rhodesia, White
Rhodesians)
Rhodesia Herald, The (quoted), 219,
222, 232, 241, 242, 250, 252, 264,
276, 285, 300, 301, 309
Rhodesia Women's League, 240-1
Rhodesian Landowners and Farmers'
Association, 227, 265
Riley, Mr., 123
Rinderpest, 77, 194, 199
Ripon, Marquess of, 170, 172, 174,
184, 188

361

Index